More of the Internet Serv[ices] Covered in This Book

gopher

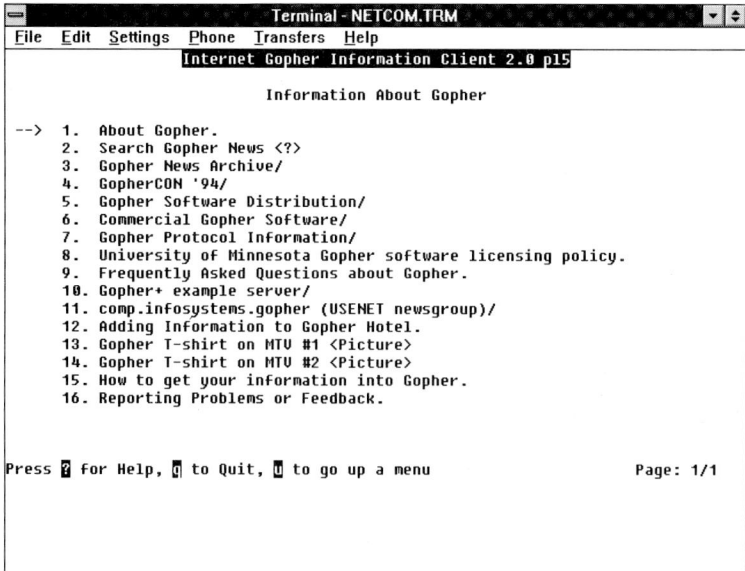

I'll show you gopherspace, where you can browse or search for information and programs by simply choosing items off menus. I'll tell you how to run different gopher clients and how to search indexes of gopher menus to find the topics you're interested in. (I'll also show you how to log in to other computers with telnet and transfer files directly with ftp.)

WorldWide Web

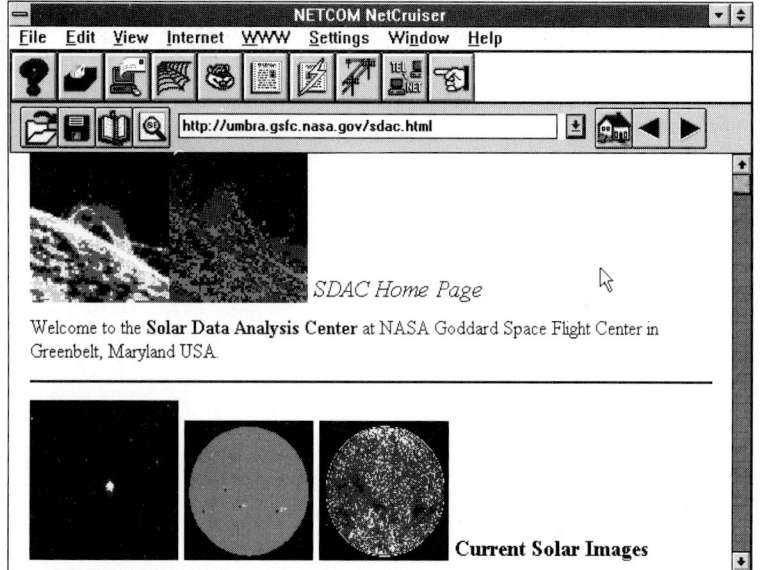

I'll show you the WorldWide Web, and tell you how to surf it, using a variety of Web browsers. I'll give you lots of possible starting points, and send you to some interesting destinations—some serious and informational, some humorous and entertaining.

For every kind of computer user, there is a SYBEX book.

All computer users learn in their own way. Some need straightforward and methodical explanations. Others are just too busy for this approach. But no matter what camp you fall into, SYBEX has a book that can help you get the most out of your computer and computer software while learning at your own pace.

Beginners generally want to start at the beginning. The **ABC's** series, with its step-by-step lessons in plain language, helps you build basic skills quickly. For a more personal approach, there's the **Murphy's Laws** and **Guided Tour** series. Or you might try our **Quick & Easy** series, the friendly, full-color guide, with **Quick & Easy References**, the companion pocket references to the **Quick & Easy** series. If you learn best by doing rather than reading, find out about the **Hands-On Live!** series, our new interactive multimedia training software. For hardware novices, there's the **Your First** series.

The **Mastering and Understanding** series will tell you everything you need to know about a subject. They're perfect for intermediate and advanced computer users, yet they don't make the mistake of leaving beginners behind. Add one of our **Instant References** and you'll have more than enough help when you have a question about your computer software. You may even want to check into our **Secrets & Solutions** series.

SYBEX even offers special titles on subjects that don't neatly fit a category—like our **Pushbutton Guides**, our books about the Internet, our books about the latest computer games, and a wide range of books for Macintosh computers and software.

SYBEX books are written by authors who are expert in their subjects. In fact, many make their living as professionals, consultants or teachers in the field of computer software. And their manuscripts are thoroughly reviewed by our technical and editorial staff for accuracy and ease-of-use.

So when you want answers about computers or any popular software package, just help yourself to SYBEX.

For a complete catalog of our publications, please write:

SYBEX Inc.
2021 Challenger Drive
Alameda, CA 94501
Tel: (510) 523-8233/(800) 227-2346 Telex: 336311
Fax: (510) 523-2373

SYBEX is committed to using natural resources wisely to preserve and improve our environment. As a leader in the computer book publishing industry, we are aware that over 40% of America's solid waste is paper. This is why we have been printing the text of books like this one on recycled paper since 1982.

This year our use of recycled paper will result in the saving of more than 15,300 trees. We will lower air pollution effluents by 54,000 pounds, save 6,300,000 gallons of water, and reduce landfill by 2,700 cubic yards.

In choosing a SYBEX book you are not only making a choice for the best in skills and information, you are also choosing to enhance the quality of life for all of us.

TALK TO SYBEX ONLINE.

JOIN THE SYBEX FORUM ON COMPUSERVE®

- Talk to SYBEX authors, editors and fellow forum members.
- Get tips, hints, and advice online.
- Download shareware and the source code from SYBEX books.

If you're already a CompuServe user, just enter GO SYBEX to join the SYBEX Forum. If you're not, try CompuServe free by calling 1-800-848-8199 and ask for Representative 560. You'll get one free month of basic service and a $15 credit for CompuServe extended services—a $23.95 value. Your personal ID number and password will be activated when you sign up.

Join us online today. Enter GO SYBEX on CompuServe. If you're not a CompuServe member, call Representative 560 at 1-800-848-8199

(outside U.S./Canada call 614-457-0802)

SYBEX
Shortcuts to Understanding

A Guided Tour of the Internet

Christian Crumlish

San Francisco • Paris • Düsseldorf • Soest

Guided Tour Book Concept: David Kolodney
Acquisitions Editor: Joanne Cuthbertson
Developmental Editors: David Peal, R.S. Langer
Editor: Guy Hart-Davis
Technical Editor: Samuel Falkner
Book Designer: Claudia Smelser
Page Layout and Typesetting: Len Gilbert
Production Assistants: Renée Avalos, Emily Smith
Indexer: Matthew Spence
Cover Designer: Joanna Kim Gladden
Cover Photographer: Michael Lamotte
Cover Illustrator: Steve Björkman

Screen reproductions produced with Collage Plus and Collage Complete. Collage Plus and Collage Complete are trademarks of Inner Media Inc.

SYBEX is a registered trademark of SYBEX Inc.

TRADEMARKS: SYBEX has attempted throughout this book to distinguish proprietary trademarks from descriptive terms by following the capitalization style used by the manufacturer.

Every effort has been made to supply complete and accurate information. However, SYBEX assumes no responsibility for its use, nor for any infringement of the intellectual property rights of third parties which would result from such use.

Copyright ©1995 SYBEX Inc., 2021 Challenger Drive, Alameda, CA 94501. World rights reserved. No part of this publication may be stored in a retrieval system, transmitted, or reproduced in any way, including but not limited to photocopy, photograph, magnetic or other record, without the prior agreement and written permission of the publisher.

Library of Congress Card Number: 94-68473
ISBN: 0-7821-1619-1

Manufactured in the United States of America
10 9 8 7 6 5 4 3 2 1

Acknowledgments

I'd like to thank the fine people at Netcom, my Internet service provider, for their support and for access to their Net-Cruiser for Windows product. Thanks especially to Glee Harrah Cady, who spent a frustrating day and a half helping me get a program configured.

Of the many wizards I've met or asked advice of through the Net or in the real world, I'd like to particularly thank Michael Brooks, Dallman Ross, and Richard Frankel. I found Paul Hoffman's Internet Instant Reference, also published by SYBEX, to be a great resource—an excellent, compact Internet reference. I'd like to thank Peter Kaminski and Ritesh Patel for allowing me to adapt information from their service provider listings; Joel Furr for sending me details on one of the soda machines on the Net; James "Kibo" Parry, for allowing me to reproduce a Usenet article; and David DeLaney and Dr. Memory for useful information. Lance Druger volunteered some UNIX tips. Thanks also to Mark Kraitchman for his work maintaining the gdead.berkeley.edu ftp archives and his other good works in the nethead community.

At SYBEX, I'd like to thank: David Kolodney for dreaming up the Guided Tour concept, and Claudia Smelser for implementing it in the design; David Peal and R.S. Langer for helping develop the plot; Guy "Text Butcher of Bakersfield" Hart-Davis for assorted editing beyond the call of the wild; Samuel Falkner for reviewing the manuscript; Len Gilbert, typesetter supreme, for helping shoehorn everything into the space available; Renée Avalos and Emily Smith for handling the production of the book; and Matthew Spence for putting together the fine index.

Thanks as always to Briggs, who has stood by me through insane deadline crunches, and to my whole family, who rarely complain when I don't call or write.

To the Bay Area Tapers Group

Contents at a Glance

		Introduction	xix
CHAPTER 1		Getting Started	1
CHAPTER 2		Getting Unstuck and Getting Help	9
CHAPTER 3		E-Mail—The Lifeblood of the Internet	15
CHAPTER 4		Reach Out and Touch Someone	45
CHAPTER 5		Composing Mail and Creating Files with Text Editors	55
CHAPTER 6		Getting on Mailing Lists	69
CHAPTER 7		Usenet News	77
CHAPTER 8		Newsreaders	91
CHAPTER 9		Managing Your Files and Directories	123
CHAPTER 10		Downloading Files back to Your Computer	133
CHAPTER 11		Fetching Files from Around the Net with ftp	139
CHAPTER 12		Finding Files for ftp with archie	151
CHAPTER 13		Remote Login with telnet and Other Programs	161
CHAPTER 14		Looking for Things with a gopher	167
CHAPTER 15		Surfing the WorldWide Web	181
APPENDIX A		Getting Connected	201
APPENDIX B		Quick Reference to All Them Nasty UNIX Commands	231
APPENDIX C		Glossary of Internet Jargon and Related Terms	237
		Index	255

Table of Contents

Introduction — xix

CHAPTER 1 Getting Started — 1

What Kind of Connection Do You Have? — 2
Dialing Up Your Provider — 4
Logging In — 5
The UNIX Prompt — 6
Change Your Password from Time to Time — 6
UNIX Commands and Programs — 7
You're on the Net — 7
Logging Out — 8
Hang Up—Exit the Terminal Program — 8
If You're Stuck — 8

CHAPTER 2 Getting Unstuck and Getting Help — 9

Stop This Crazy Thing! — 10
Erasing a Command — 11
Retyping a Command — 11
Error Messages — 12
Getting Help — 12
Just the FAQs, Ma'am — 14

CHAPTER 3 E-Mail—The Lifeblood of the Internet — 15

Your E-Mail Program Depends On Your Type of Service — 16
Things to Do with E-Mail — 17

TABLE OF CONTENTS

Handling E-Mail with elm	17
Sending Mail to People on Other Networks	*20*
Handling E-Mail with pine	29
Handling E-Mail with mail	35
Windowed Mail Programs	36
Offline Mail Readers	*37*
Recovering Lost Messages	40
Going on Vacation	40
Forwarding Your E-Mail	42
Don't Fly Off the Handle	43

CHAPTER 4 Reach Out and Touch Someone — 45

Say "Send Me E-Mail"	46
Finding People on the Net	46
Mailing Postmaster@	46
Finding People with finger	47
Finding People with Whois	48
Finding People with Netfind	49
finger the Pop Machine	*49*
Asking the Knowbot	52
Chatting in Realtime	52
"Talking" from Screen to Screen	*53*

CHAPTER 5 Composing Mail and Creating Files with Text Editors — 55

Composing Mail	56
Using a Word Processor	56
Changing Your Editor	58
General Text-Editor Stuff	58
vi Basics	59
pico Basics	63
Attaching Files to E-Mail	65

Table of Contents   **xiii**

Privacy and Security   67

CHAPTER 6   Getting On Mailing Lists   69

Mailing Lists versus Usenet Newsgroups   70
Finding Mailing Lists   71
Subscribing to Lists   72
Unsubscribing to Lists   74
Posting to Lists   75
Participation   75

CHAPTER 7   Usenet News   77

Where Everybody Knows Your .signature   78
Some Newsgroups Are Mailing Lists Too   78
What Is Usenet?   79
What Is a Newsgroup?   80
One Way Not to Look Like a Newbie   81
What Is an Article?   82
Usenet Puts the R in James R. Kirk   83
What Is a Newsreader?   84
Semi-Anonymity   84
Usenet as a Public Forum   85
Being a Good Netizen   85
Shooting Stars and net.spewers   86
IMHO Hep   86
What Kinds of Groups Are Out There?   88
The Quality of Usenet   88
Imminent Death of the Net Predicted—Film at 11   89
Getting Help   90

CHAPTER 8   Newsreaders   91

Net News by Mail—If You Don't Have Usenet Access   92
Newsreading Basics   94
The Other Way to Prep Your Newsreader   95

What Does "Ob" Mean?	98
Your Identity on Usenet	99
Some Advanced Stuff You Should Know	100
Types of Newsreaders	101
Reading News with trn	102
The WorldWide Web Might Be the Best Newsreader Someday	102
Reading News with tin	108
Reading News with nn	114
Reading News with rn	118
A Windowed Newsreader	119
Usenet Interfaces for Online Services	120

CHAPTER 9 Managing Your Files and Directories — 123

UNIX Directories	125
Comparing UNIX and DOS Directories	125
What's in the Directory?	127
UNIX Files	128
Including Wild Cards in File Names	128

CHAPTER 10 Downloading Files back to Your Computer — 133

Text Files and Binary Files	134
Potential Problems Uploading Text Files	134
Downloading Protocols	135
File Transfers	135
Straight Text Transfers	137

CHAPTER 11 Fetching Files from Around the Net with ftp — 139

ftp—Protocol or Program?	140

How to Find ftp Sites	140
How to Do ftp in General	141
Transferring Files with ftp	142
Recognizing Compressed Files by Their Extensions	*142*
Automating ftp Logins with a .netrc File	*143*
Other ftp Commands	146
ftp Directly to Your PC	146
ncftp—A Better UNIX ftp	148
ftp by E-Mail If You Don't Have "Real" ftp	149

CHAPTER 12 Finding Files for ftp with archie   151

General archie Procedures	152
Running an archie Client	152
–s and Other Switches	*153*
Telnetting to archie	154
Searching for Files When You Don't Know Their Names	*157*
archie by E-Mail	158
Combined archie and ftp with Anarchie for the Mac	158

CHAPTER 13 Remote Login with telnet and Other Programs   161

What Is telnet?	162
General telnet Procedure	162
Hytelnet—A Smart telnet Program	164
Logging In to Other UNIX Machines with rlogin	*164*
telnet Sites to Check Out	165

CHAPTER 14 Looking for Things with a gopher   167

Surfing the Net	168

How to Use the gopher	168
Running a UNIX gopher	169
telnet to a gopher Server If You Haven't Got a Client	170
Running a Windowed gopher Client	176
Sifting through gopherspace with veronica	178
Searching gopher Menus with jughead	180

CHAPTER 15 Surfing the Worldwide Web — 181

What Is Hypertext?	182
What's on the Web?	183
Different Types of Web Browsers	183
Using Web Browsers	184
Browse the Web with lynx	184
HTTP, HTML, and URLs	186
Change Your Home Page	190
Browse the Web with www	190
Browse the Web with Mosaic	192
Browse the Web with NetCruiser	194
Web Help and Info	195
Keep Up with What's New	196
Using Other Internet Resources via the Web	196
Get EFF's Internet Guide as Hypertext on the Web	196
Some Interesting URLs	199

APPENDIX A Getting Connected — 201

Different Types of Connections	202
Equipment You'll Need	203
Finding a Service Provider	205
Providers Available on Public Data Networks	206
The Chicken or the Egg	229

APPENDIX B Quick Reference to All Them Nasty Unix Commands — 231

Getting Started in UNIX — 232
Run a Mail Program — 232
Look for People on the Net — 232
Chat with People in Realtime — 233
Compose E-Mail — 233
Read Usenet News — 233
Manage Your Files and Directories — 233
Download and Upload Files — 234
ftp Commands — 235
Finding Files for ftp with archie — 236
Log In to Other Computers and Networks — 236
Look for Things with a gopher — 236
Browse the Web — 236

APPENDIX C Glossary of Internet Jargon and Related Terms — 237

Index — *255*

Introduction

In the margins you'll see this character filling you in with explanatory commentaries, helpful anecdotes, warnings, and directions to further information. (In real life, I'm much more handsome.)

I assume you're a regular person. You own a computer or have access to one, but it's not your favorite toy. You don't think like a geek and you don't want to know too much technical drivel, just enough to get going.

Will the Internet hype never end? It seems like there's a newspaper article or magazine cover story every day. You probably saw hundreds of other Internet books on the shelf where you picked this up. Most of those articles are full of breathless prose about an "information superhighway," or vague first impressions that betray not only a lack of understanding but also a deadline looming large.

Still, more and more people are connected to the Net everyday, and some businesses are beginning to rely on it for communication, for information, and even for the transportation of certain types of products, such as software or writing. Maybe you've already got access to the Internet through your work or school, or maybe you're considering getting a modem and trying it out for yourself.

This book is different from most of the other books out there. It's not a puff piece, full of generalities and futuristic hype. Neither is it a technical manual. I assume that you generally don't care *why* things work the way they do. Instead, this book tells exactly *how* to get things done on the Internet.

How This Book Works

For most people, the basic appeal of the Internet is e-mail. I devote a lot of this book to e-mail because I realize that that's all

I assume you want to know how things are, not how they'd be in some perfect world. So if I think a program's not worth using, I'll tell you straight. Some of the material out there on the Net is pretty crude, as are some of the people, but I'm not going to pretend that, say, the alt.sex newsgroups don't exist, or that people aren't badmouthing you when they are. I figure you need to know these things so that you can deal with them.

There are really two uses for the Internet. One is person-to-person communication. The other is finding information. I cover both, starting with the person-to-person stuff because it's easier to get into and it's what you hear about most.

some people are going to want to do. Eventually, though, you'll be tempted to look into some of the other resources available via the Net, and I cover the most interesting ones.

The Internet is a great resource and you're bound to learn more about it once you're connected. For now, I'm just going to tell you enough to get you over the threshold. That's all you really need.

The book contains fifteen chapters and three appendices.

First Things First

Chapter 1: *Getting Started*, and Chapter 2: *Getting Help*, are both quick and short, so you'll be through them in no time. They're just there to get you oriented.

Person-to-Person Communication

Next, Chapters 3 through 8 cover all the ways to communicate with other people over the Internet.

Chapter 3 covers the basics of e-mail. It tells you all you need to know to send and receive mail over the Internet. Then there are a couple of more advanced sections on how to forward your mail and what to do about your e-mail when you go on vacation.

Chapter 4 tells you how to find other people on the Net, and how to "chat" with people live, if that's what you want to do.

Chapter 5 covers the best ways to compose mail messages, either directly in your mail program while connected, or on your desktop computer ahead of time. It also touches on keeping your e-mail secure.

Chapter 6 tells you all about mailing lists—how to get on them, how to contribute to them, and how to find them. This will be your first taste of "virtual communities" of people united by common interests, no matter where they are geographically.

Chapter 7 explains the Usenet news network, a huge assortment of newsgroups devoted to interests and topics of every imaginable stripe. Chapter 8 tells you the practical details of running a newsreader program to read and contribute to newsgroups yourself.

Moving Files Around

Once you've explored the personal side of the Net, you might get interested in some of the other, practical uses. If you've got an Internet account that you log in to over a modem, you're going to have to know a little bit about keeping track of your files. That's all covered in Chapter 9.

You'll also want to know how to grab files and bring them back to your desktop computer. Chapter 10 covers the step of moving files from your account to your desktop computer. Chapter 11 explains the more interesting step of getting files from enormous archives all over the Net. Chapter 12 helps you figure out where the things you're interested in are located.

Finding Programs and Information

The final step in learning your way around the Internet is navigating the Net itself, moving around from place to place hunting things down. You'll never know what's there if you don't look. Chapter 13 tells you how to log into other computers and networks on the Internet. Chapter 14 explains gopher, a progam that lets you pick things off menus and makes it easy to zoom around the Internet without having to learn a lot of gibberish first. This chapter also explains veronica and jughead, two utilities that simplify the process further.

> In some ways the Net is like the phone system. It's another tool for contacting people, but it works only if the other people you want to reach are also on the system.

Chapter 15 covers the WorldWide Web, the exciting and fairly new Internet resource that allows you to surf from one hypertext document to another, simply by pointing and clicking (or pressing Tab and Enter), picking things up along the way.

Appendices

The three appendices could be a book in themselves. Appendix A tells you how to get an Internet connection, starting from scratch if necessary, and includes the largest, most comprehensive list anywhere of service providers. Appendix B gives you a quick reference to the annoying and cryptic UNIX commands that are hard to avoid on the Internet, especially if you have a dial-up account. Appendix C is an essential glossary of the Internet jargon you hear bandied about nowadays (and other things you'll hear about on the Net and want explained).

Conventions I Use in This Book

When I want you to type something, I'll put it in **boldface**. To show you things that appear on your screen or give you useful Internet addresses or references, I'll put the information `in this font` or even

> `on a line by itself.`

Sometimes, the specific text you need to type will vary from case to case. If so, I'll include some dummy text, in *italics* (in the sidebars and commentaries, the dummy text will be underlined). Don't type the italicized or underlined words! Instead, substitute the relevant file name, directory name, newsgroup name, etc. When the time comes, you'll know what to do.

Because there are so many different programs that perform similar functions on the Net, there's no way I could cover

---

Throughout the book, I suggest additional ways for you to find information if you want to pursue subjects further. Whenever possible, I point you toward relevant Usenet newsgroups, mailing lists, ftp sites, gopher servers, Web pages, and so on.

them all. Therefore, I always take you on a general run-through so you know how the type of program works and what to look for, no matter which one you're using. Fortunately, Macintosh and Windows programs are usually straightforward and easy to use, *once you know what you're trying to do*. Unfortunately, it's likely that you'll be using UNIX programs. Therefore, I cover pertinent UNIX programs in great detail, so you'll know exactly which arcane series of keys to hit to get the results you want.

No matter what kind of Internet connection you have or get, I've got you covered.

Getting Connected

Before you can get on the Net, you need a connection. If you've already got one through work, you're fine. If you need to find a service provider for a personal Internet account, look in Appendix A. It's got the largest, most up-to-date listing of service providers, organized by area code so you can find one that won't cost you an arm and a leg in phone bills.

Stay in Touch

If you find anything incorrect or misleading, if you'd like to point me toward something you think I've overlooked, or if you'd just like to give me some feedback (or even flame me), please write me at:

If you correct an error, I'll fix whatever's wrong in the next edition of the book, and even thank you in the acknowledgments.

>
> Christian Crumlish
> c/o SYBEX Inc.
> 2021 Challenger Drive
> Alameda, CA 94501

Or send me e-mail at xian@netcom.com and put the word Guide in the subject line of your message.

CHAPTER 1

Getting Started

Featuring

- Your Internet connection
- Dialing up your provider
- Logging into your account
- Just a little UNIX
- Logging out (or off)
- Hanging up the modem

This is the on-ramp. You are sitting in front of your desktop computer, in the office, at home, or at school, and you are not yet actually connected to a machine on the Internet. (If you work with a Mac or PC, or even a UNIX machine, that's directly on the Net, then you can skip most of this chapter.) This means you have to run a communications program to dial your modem, so it can connect you over the phone lines to a UNIX machine on the Net. (What's UNIX, you ask? Don't worry. We'll get to that in a few pages.)

I'll take you through these steps and you'll be ready to roll.

GETTING STARTED

What Kind of Connection Do You Have?

If you don't yet have your own connection to the Internet, see Appendix A, "Getting Connected."

There are many different ways to connect to the Internet, and there are different levels of connectedness itself. The minimal connection is an e-mail gateway that allows you to send e-mail via the Internet to other people who are themselves either directly connected to the Internet or connected to some other network with its own e-mail gateway to the Internet. (E-mail is explained starting in Chapter 3.)

Most of the fun and interesting things that can be done with the Internet can be done through e-mail, so even a minimal connection can be very powerful if used to its fullest.

For most of the Internet's existence, the vast majority of computers connected to it have been UNIX machines, so almost everything you can do on the Internet can be done with UNIX commands. If you are connected through a network at your work or school (or if you have a SLIP or PPP connection you can dial up with your modem—you'll know if you do have such a connection), then you might be able to access the Internet through the interface you are accustomed to on your computer, which might be a Macintosh, Windows/DOS, or UNIX machine.

Throughout this book, I will provide alternative approaches to the various Internet services that require only e-mail. Then, as long as you have e-mail access to the Internet, you'll be able to use even some of the services that your provider does not offer you directly.

Most likely, though, you have access to a UNIX machine and will have to cope with the UNIX environment, instead of being able to take advantage of your favorite features of your own computer. Your computer will function as a "dumb terminal," showing you the UNIX prompt and allowing you to send commands to the UNIX computer and receive results back from it. (On the other hand, you should still be able to cut and paste to and from the terminal window, as you can with other windows on your computer. This can come in handy for saving people's addresses and other useful information that you come across on the net.)

What Kind of Connection Do You Have?   3

Table 1.1 shows the most common types of Internet access currently available, with the degree of access, and the type of environment—GUI (Graphical User Interface) or shell.

TABLE 1.1

Internet Access Types and Environments

Type of Internet Access	Typical Available Services	Working Environment
Bulletin board (BBS)	E-mail, Usenet, ftp, usually	Menus or shell
Client-access provider	E-mail, Usenet	DOS or GUI offline software
Internet provider UNIX shell account	Full Internet access (e-mail, Usenet, ftp, gopher, Web, and so on)	UNIX shell
Internet provider SLIP or PPP account	Full Internet access	GUI
Employer's network	E-mail, sometimes Usenet	GUI or shell
University network	Full Internet access	GUI or shell
Online service (CompuServe, Prodigy, America Online, GEnie, and so on)	E-mail, possibly Usenet and ftp	Menus or GUI

If you get your Internet services through an on-line service provider such as Prodigy, CompuServe, America Online, Delphi, GEnie, the Well, etc., then you have special menus or interfaces supplied by your provider to access the Internet services. In that case, the general information I provide will help you understand what to do and how to do it, but the specifics will depend upon your provider.

Because the majority of users still have to operate within the UNIX environment, even if they call up from a PC running Windows or DOS, or from a Mac, most of the specific instructions I give you will cover UNIX commands and applications. Whenever possible, I will explain the alternatives that might be available, and I will always give you a general explanation of how to do what you're trying to do, so that you can figure out the details of your own system yourself, or at least know exactly what questions to ask your service provider.

4 GETTING STARTED

Fortunately, if you're lucky enough to have Internet access that allows you to simply run programs in your PC's normal environment (whether that's a Mac or IBM-compatible environment), then the programs you'll use will be much easier to learn and use than UNIX programs, and they'll function the way all your other programs do, with predictable results. If you understand the gist of the type of program I've described, you should be able to figure out the equivalent in your own environment without too much trouble.

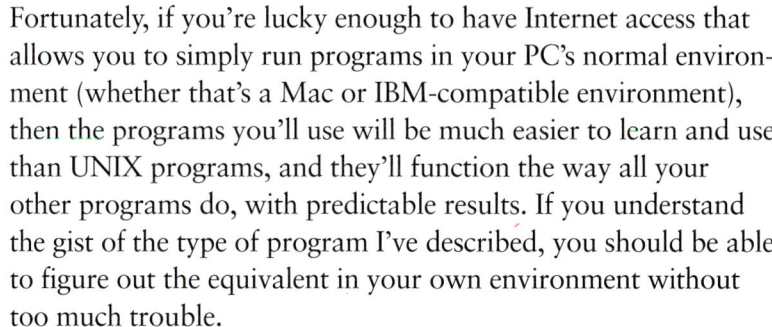

If you're thinking of buying a modem, plan for the future, as faster modems can always slow down to communicate with slower modems. For most purposes, 9600 bps is the minimum acceptable speed, and prices of 14,400-bps modems have dropped to around $100.

Dialing Up Your Provider

Begin by running a communications, or terminal, program that can have your modem dial up your provider. ProComm is a popular communications program—some people swear by it. Microsoft Works also includes a perfectly decent communications module. I have several comm (communications) programs installed on my computer, but I often just use Terminal, the accessory that comes with Windows.

You'll need to supply the following information in your program and save it all to a file, so you don't have to think about it again:

- the access phone number of your service provider (tell your program to redial automatically if it can)
- the baud rate (speed of the connection)—this should be the maximum that both your modem and your provider can handle
- the type of connection, in terms of "data bits," "stop bits," and "parity." Don't worry about what this all means. It's almost always **8, 1, n** or **7, 1, e**—your service provider will tell you which.

Depending upon your communications program, you might also be able to choose some terminal preferences, such as whether function, arrow, and Ctrl keys will work as they normally do

If the sound of the number dialing and modem whine bug you, type **ATM0** and press Enter in the Terminal window (before dialing) to turn off the modem's speaker.

in your operating environment (for example, Windows) or be passed through to the UNIX shell. You can change these options again at any time.

Save all this information to a file called "Internet" (or use the name of your provider, or whatever else makes sense to you).

Then tell the program to connect or to dial the number you entered.

The program will call up the host machine to which you plan to connect. When the connection is made, a message such as **CONNECT** will appear in the window. If the connection fails or the line is busy, you will get a message such as **NO CARRIER**. Use your program's redial feature to call repeatedly.

If your modem is not responding, cancel the dialing procedure and type **ATZ**. (This resets the modem to its initial factory settings.)

Logging In

When the connection is made successfully, you will need to log in to your Internet account. First type your *login*, your Internet "handle," and then type your password. (Your password will not appear on the screen.)

Your comm program might allow you to set up a script to complete the login automatically. When you've logged in successfully, you might see some initial messages from your provider.

If you use a login script, anyone can log in from your computer without having to know your password.

For some connections, you then have to specify the type of terminal that your program is pretending to be (or else things will look funny on the screen). This is usually a VT100 unless someone tells you different. If you don't want to have to do this each time, you can put the command **setenv TERM vt100** in your startup file. My startup file is called .cshrc, but yours might be something different (.login, or .profile, or something else) depending on the flavor of UNIX your provider runs.

You are now running a UNIX session. Do not be alarmed.

6 GETTING STARTED

> Your password should be at least 8 characters long, contain both letters and numbers, and be meaningless (not your birthdate, your partner's name, pet, driver's license number, or anything like that).

Change Your Password from Time to Time

If you have a dial-up account, then your desktop computer is not itself on the Internet, and is therefore not vulnerable to crackers (malevolent hackers), but your UNIX account itself can still be broken into. If this happens, whoever does it will have access to all your files and incoming mail, and can send mail under your name as well. The best thing you can do to prevent this from happening is to have a good password and change it from time to time.

For safety's sake, it's a good idea to change your password every now and then. To do this, type **passwd** at the UNIX prompt and press Enter. You'll see

> Changing NIS password for *your-login* on nfs-serv.
>
> Old password:

Type the old password. Then you'll see New password:. Type the new password that you want. Then you'll see Retype new password:. Type it again. Finally, you'll see NIS entry changed on nfs-serv. Your password is changed.

> There are many different kinds of UNIX shells that differ in subtle ways—namely, some of the commands are different, but it shouldn't matter much to you which type of shell you have. If there are variations on any of the commands I tell you about, I'll let you know.

The UNIX Prompt

With all this talk of UNIX, maybe I should explain what it is. UNIX is an operating system that runs mainly on workstations. Some parts of DOS were originally based on UNIX. Your connection to the Net can be called a "UNIX shell account." The UNIX shell is the program that interprets the commands you type and starts the programs you run. Your connection can also be called a "character-based" connection, because your modem sends the characters you type to the UNIX machine you're connected to and displays the characters that return in the terminal window.

You're on the Net

The other thing you need to know about UNIX is the UNIX prompt. Every UNIX shell presents you with a prompt, a character or string of characters on the screen that tell you that it's okay to type a command. The prompts differ from shell to shell and they can be customized, so I can't show you every possible prompt.

In the figures that show examples from my own Internet account, you will see a prompt like {netcomx:y}. The *x* stands for the particular computer at Netcom that I happen to be logged in to at the time, and the *y* stands for the number of commands I've sent so far (or actually the number of the next command I send).

Prompts are customizable, but that's too boring to get into.

UNIX Commands and Programs

To issue commands, just type them. At the UNIX prompt, you also need to press Enter. In some programs, you don't press Enter—instead the command takes effect as soon as you type it. I'll always tell you which programs do this. This is important because if you press Enter when it's not necessary, you might be accepting some default for the next step of your procedure, and if you fail to press Enter when you need to, you can sit there all day waiting for something to happen.

Most of the things that you do on the Internet through your shell account you do by running programs—mail programs, newsreading programs, file-transfer programs, and so on. Throughout this book I will be telling you the programs to run and how to get things done in those programs.

UNIX is case sensitive. This means that capital and lowercase letters are not equivalent. When I tell you to type a command, type it exactly the way it's shown.

You're on the Net

Now you're ready to do whatever you got on the Internet to do. Read on for specifics. When you are finished with an Internet session, you should log off to tell your provider's computer that you're done. (Eventually your modem would hang up for you if you walked away, but that's sloppy and wasteful of resources.)

Logging Out

When you're finished with a session, you log out (or off). At the UNIX prompt, type **logout** and press Enter. If that doesn't work, try **bye** or **exit**.

Hang Up—Exit the Terminal Program

Logging out is not hanging up. Even after you log out, your modem is still connected for a while, and charging time if that's how your phone system works. So after logging out, hang up. Then quit your terminal program.

If You're Stuck

Some things might go wrong and confuse you. Sometimes it seems like nothing's happening in the middle of a process. Other times you've gotten yourself into something you don't understand. Chapter 2 will explain how to escape from confusing situations as well as how to find out more information about the programs you're running.

CHAPTER 2

Getting Unstuck and Getting Help

Featuring

- Getting out of trouble
- Killing a process in UNIX
- Closing the connection
- Getting help in UNIX
- Getting help from InterNIC
- A free guide to the Net

As I mentioned in Chapter 1, sometimes things will just freeze up on you. This may mean there's a problem with the command that you issued, a problem with an Internet server such as the mail server or the newsfeed, or a problem with your provider's network. This chapter gives you a list of things to try when you're hung up.

10 GETTING UNSTUCK AND GETTING HELP

There could also be a problem with your PC, your modem, or the phone lines. If any of these seems to be suffering to have conked out, try basic resuscitation procedures—reset the PC or modem, check the phone line, and try dialing again.

Kill commands vary from one UNIX system to another. If the commands I suggest here don't work for you, ask your system administrator for your equivalents.

See Chapter 9 for more on files and file management.

For general problems, UNIX systems have a certain amount of built-in help information, usually in the form of online manuals. Yes, I know manuals are sometimes impossible to deal with, but you should at least know how to look at that information.

Stop This Crazy Thing!

When things start going wrong or nothing is happening at all, you sometimes have to interrupt the process. This might mean canceling it entirely or just stopping it temporarily.

Killing a Process

If you want UNIX to stop whatever it's doing (because it's going crazy and you don't understand what's going on or because it's hung up and apparently nothing is happening), you have to issue a kill command. On most UNIX systems, this means pressing **Ctrl-C** (hold down the Ctrl key and type **C**, you might have to hold down Shift as well). On some systems, the equivalent command is the Delete key. So if **Ctrl-C** does nothing, try pressing Del.

If the normal kill command doesn't seem to work, you can try pressing **Ctrl-**. This should kill any process and create something called a *core dump*, which mainly means there will be a new garbage file in your directory called **core**. To delete this file, type **rm core** at the UNIX prompt and press Enter.

Stopping a Job

It is also possible in UNIX to interrupt a process (also called a "job") without canceling it completely. To do so, press **Ctrl-Z**. If the job is stopped successfully, the word **Stopped** will appear on the screen. If so, the job still exists and can be resumed at any time. Although this is not as complete a way to end a wayward process, it will work in a pinch.

To restart a stopped job, type %1 and press Enter. If you have more than one stopped job, you have to use the specific number of the job, not necessarily 1.

To kill (cancel) a stopped job, type kill %1 and press Enter. If you try to log out with stopped jobs that you haven't killed, you will get the message There are stopped jobs.

Go ahead and kill the stopped jobs.

> You could just type **logout** again and leave the stopped jobs, but this is irresponsible—the orphaned processes might waste a lot of resources before being killed.

Bailing Out Completely

Ultimately, if you can't get the attention of your UNIX shell, you can always just hang up your modem through your terminal (communications) program. This will (eventually) sever the connection to your provider, though it is always better to log out when you can.

> For more help with UNIX, consult the UNIX FAQ, which is posted to the Usenet newsgroup comp.answers regularly. Also, check out the newsgroups comp.unix.shell and comp.unix questions. Both of them have "Welcome" articles that are also posted regularly to comp.answers. For more on Usenet newsgroups, see Chapters 7 and 8.

Erasing a Command

Usually, you press Delete to erase the character you just typed. On some systems you can use Backspace, just as you can on a PC, but watch out! Often it only appears that you have erased what you typed. Instead, the old text is still there, followed by a "backspace" character. When most other people see what you've typed, the error and the correction will appear, separated by any number of ^H symbols.

If you want to erase a command that you're in the middle of typing, press Ctrl-U.

Retyping a Command

Sometimes you get ahead of the screen printout and not all the characters you type appear on the screen. If you're unsure of what you've typed so far, press Ctrl-R. This will repeat what

> Make sure you are really deleting something when you think you are. It can be embarrassing when your mail or post contains something like "Thanks a lot, you are an idiot^H^H^H^H^H^H^H true friend."

GETTING UNSTUCK AND GETTING HELP

you've typed on a new line. Or you can just press Enter, ignore whatever error message appears, and start over.

Error Messages

If you get an error message such as Command not found, check your spelling and spacing very carefully. UNIX is very picky and will not tolerate even mistakes of capitalization.

Getting Help

Throughout this book I will try to anticipate the types of problems you might run into and how to deal with them as they arise. Whenever you run into trouble in a UNIX program, try typing **h** or **?** at the command prompt—these are the two most common help commands.

All UNIX systems have manual-type information about the various commands and programs available. These are called the "man pages." They're better than nothing. Some UNIX systems also have specific help systems with better written, easier to understand help. Some UNIX systems also have a faq command. The word faq stands for *frequently asked questions*, and you will see it again many times. Others have a help command. Try faq and help as well as man.

The man Command

To see if there are man (manual) pages for a command you are interested in, type **man** *command* (and press Enter) at the command prompt, substituting the name of the command or program you are interested in for *command*. Figure 2.1 shows the first screen that appears when I type **man cp** at my prompt.

> Whenever you are trying to do something that someone else on that Net has recommended, try to cut the exact wording from the screen and then paste it in at the command prompt.

Getting Help | 13

FIGURE 2.1

The first screenful for the man pages for the cp command.

When you type **man cp** and press Enter, Unix cleans the screen and starts spitting out manual pages for the cp command

```
                Terminal - NETCOM.TRM
 File  Edit  Settings  Phone | Transfers  Help
Reformatting page. Wait... done

CP(1)                   USER COMMANDS                    CP(1)

NAME
     cp - copy files

SYNOPSIS
     cp [ -ip ] filename1 filename2
     cp -rR [ -ip ] directory1 directory2
     cp [ -iprR ] filename ... directory

DESCRIPTION
     cp copies the contents of filename1 onto filename2. The
     mode and owner of filename2 are preserved if it already
     existed; the mode of the source file is used otherwise. If
     filename1 is a symbolic link, or a duplicate hard link, the
     contents of the file that the link refers to are copied;
     links are not preserved.

     In the second form, cp recursively copies directory1, along
     with its contents and subdirectories, to directory2. If
     directory2 does not exist, cp creates it and duplicates the
--More--(26%)
```

This line shows that there's more to come, and that you've already seen 26% of the infromation. Press the spacebar to see the next screenful.

> You can send **man** pages to a file and then download them to your home computer and print them so you can read them at your leisure. To send **man** pages to a file, type **man command > file-name** and press Enter. See Chapter 10 for instructions on how to **download** a file.

If there is more information available than will fit on one screen, you will have to press the spacebar (or any key, really) to see each successive screenful. At the end of the man pages there might be references to other related commands that you could also look up.

For the man pages on the man command itself, type **man man** and then press Enter.

The Nice People at InterNIC

Another way to get help or answers to your questions is to contact InterNIC. InterNIC is a National Science Foundation–funded center founded to help Internet users and people interested in the Net. (NIC stands for Network Information Center.)

> See Chapter 3 for how to send e-mail. See Chapter 14 for how to use gophers.

14 GETTING UNSTUCK AND GETTING HELP

The Electronic Frontier Foundation, a lobbying group devoted to the preservation of freedom on the "electronic frontier," electronically publishes a fantastic guide to the net, now called EFF's Guide to the Internet, v.2.21. (previous versions were called The Big Dummy's Guide to the Internet.) This book is available via ftp, gopher, and the WorldWide Web. As I explain how to use these various Internet services, I will give EFF's guide as an example, so that you can get this priceless source of information and advice.

Just the FAQs, Ma'am

Sorry, I couldn't resist that pun.

Whether or not your UNIX shell account has a faq command, you will encounter this term on Usenet and elsewhere. The various FAQs secreted around the Net are treasure troves of accumulated information and answers. Volunteers in mailing lists and newsgroups compile these FAQ lists or documents in response the questions that come up over and over. There are several newsgroups devoted solely to the republishing of FAQs on a regular basis. These groups have names such as news.answers, rec.answers, alt.answers, and so on. For more information on mailing lists, newsgroups, and FAQs, see Chapters 6, 7, and 8.

There is also a series of documents, called RFCs (Requests for Comments) that contain much useful information about the Internet. To get them, ftp to ftp.internic.net, go to the /rfc directory, and transfer the files. ftp is explained in Chapter 11.

There are many ways to reach InterNIC with your questions. You can call their hotline at (800) 444-4345 or their regular number at (619) 455-4600. You can fax them at (619) 455-4640. Or you can send them email at Info@is.internic.net. In addition, they have a Gopher server also at is.internic.net.

Finally, you can send them regular mail (what people on the net call "snail mail") at the following address:

P.O. Box #85608
San Diego, CA 92186-9784

CHAPTER 3

E-Mail—The Lifeblood of the Internet

Featuring

- Sending, reading, and replying to e-mail
- Making signature files
- Working with elm and pine
- Working with Eudora and other mail programs

Okay, we made it. This is the real stuff. The reason why you're on the Net. E-mail! Instant (more or less) communication with people all over the globe.

As usual, there are many different e-mail programs, and I can't hope to cover each one. Fortunately, there are several very popular programs and you are likely to have at least one of them (if not all) available on your system. Nonetheless, I will start off by spelling out the most common activities associated with e-mail.

Your E-Mail Program Depends On Your Type of Service

If you've got a UNIX shell account, then you'll handle your mail either by running one of the common UNIX e-mail programs (most likely elm or pine) or by setting up an offline mail program, such as Eudora, that will run on your normal operating system and connect with your shell account only to receive and send mail.

If you have a SLIP or PPP account, or if you connect to the Internet through a network at your work or school, then you'll run a mail program in your normal operating environment. If you get your Internet access through a commercial network, such as America Online or CompuServe, then you'll use their built-in mail programs, and sending mail over the Internet will require only that you use the proper sort of Internet mailing address.

In general, windowed mail programs, such as the types that run under Windows or on Macintoshes and the types provided by commercial services, are the easiest to learn and use. But the UNIX programs elm and pine are reasonably well designed and featured full-screen programs, and they're not too hard to pick up either.

When you get used to sending e-mail, you'll find that it's as useful a form of communication as the telephone, and it doesn't require the other person to drop whatever they're doing to answer your call. You can include a huge amount of specific information and the person you mail to can reply in full in their own good time.

In the unlikely circumstance that you have none of the specific programs that I cover, you'll have a list of actions to look for in the help portion of your e-mail program or to run by your system administrator for advice.

Things to Do with E-Mail

These are the things that you will do most often with e-mail:

- run the mail program
- send mail
- read incoming mail
- save your mail to a folder
- reply to mail
- forward mail
- delete mail
- save mail
- exit the mail program

You might want to set up your login procedure to start your preferred mail program whenever you log in.

Here are some slightly more advanced things that you'll also probably want to do:

- create aliases (shortcuts) for mail addresses
- make a signature file that will be attached to the end of your outgoing mail
- tag several of the messages in your inbox and then perform the same action on all of them at once.

Handling E-Mail with elm

elm is neither the most common mail program on UNIX systems nor the easiest one to use, but it is the most common easy mail program around. It's a full-screen program and it shows you a menu of the most useful commands at the bottom of the screen.

To read the manual pages for elm, type **man elm** and press Enter.

Sometimes you'll want to include the original message when you reply to mail. Other times, you'll want to reply to everyone who was sent a copy of the original message. I'll show you how to do both.

You might also want to transfer files or search databases using the e-mail equivalents of ftp and gopher (if you don't have ftp or gopher available on your system). Throughout this book I will explain the e-mail equivalents of more complicated procedures, when they exist.

There is a Usenet newsgroup on elm, called **comp.mail.elm**. (See Chapters 7 and 8 for more on Usenet.) There is also an elm FAQ posted to **comp.mail.elm**, **comp.answers**, and **news.answers** once a month. You can get the elm FAQ sent directly to you by sending e-mail to **mail-server@cs.ruu.nl** with no subject and the words **mail-server@cs.ruu.nl** and **end** each on their own lines.

Starting elm

You start elm, easily enough, by typing **elm** at the command prompt and pressing Enter. The program will clear the screen and list the ten most recent messages you've received, followed by a menu of suggested commands (see Figure 3.1).

FIGURE 3.1

The elm screen. Messages are listed in the order they were sent, from most recent to oldest.

This is the most recent mail message. This is the number of lines.
This is the date it was sent. This is the subject.
This is the sender.

```
                              Terminal - NETCOM.TRM
File  Edit  Settings  Phone  Transfers  Help

              Mailbox is '/usr/spool/mail/xian' with 11 messages [ELM 2.4 PL23]

     1   Jun 29  Jeffrey Matthew Eh (23)   Re: my picks
     2   Jun 28  John Fail           (24)   Re: typos
     3   Jun 28  GoMedia             (53)   Re: Brit Hume in WINDOWS magazine
     4   Jun 28  pjpg1258@uxa.cso.u  (25)   Trade?
     5   Jun 27  Glee Harrah Cady    (22)   Re: Wanted: NetCruiser Support Staff
     6   Jun 27  Gary Wickboldt     (21)   chicago
     7   Jun 16  pms@buphy2.bu.edu  (202)   SM on CRx2 (fwd)
     8   Jun 8   CASSELL            (311)   Greetings and salutations
     9   Jun 6   HT3832@ALBNYVMS.bi (46)    Re: Setlists verified
    10   Jun 3   HT3832@ALBNYVMS.bi (46)    Re: belated reply

         You can use any of the following commands by pressing the first character;
         d)elete or u)ndelete mail, m)ail a message, r)eply or f)orward mail, q)uit
            To read a message, press <return>.  j = move down, k = move up, ? = help

Command:
```

To have elm start automatically, put the word **elm** on a line by itself in your .login, .profile, or .cshrc file. (If your UNIX system uses a different startup file, you'll have to ask your system administrator what it is.)

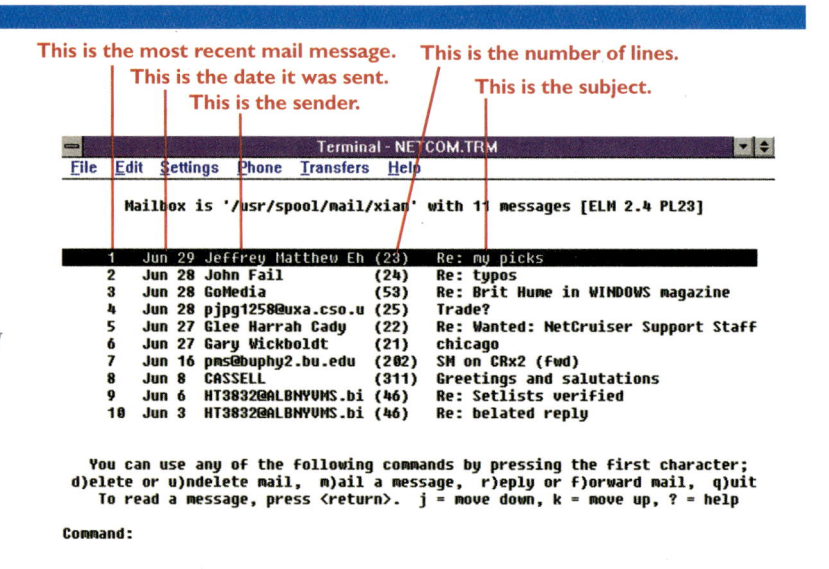

Sending Mail with elm

The easiest way to send mail to someone is to reply to mail that they've sent you. If you're not sure exactly how to form someone's e-mail address, ask them to send you some mail and then simply reply to it. That's what I always do.

To send mail, first press **m** (it has to be lowercase). The word **Mail** will appear next to the **Command:** prompt at the bottom of the elm screen, and another prompt will appear below it: Send the message to:. Type the address of the person to whom you wish to send the mail and press Enter. The person's address must be of the form *login@address.domain*, where *login* is the person's identifier, the name the log in with, *address* is the identifier of the person's network and or machine on the network (it might consist of several words—the *host* and

Handling E-Mail with elm

subdomain—separated by dots), and *domain* is the three-letter code indicating whether the address is a business (.com), a non-profit (.org), a university (.edu), a branch of the government (.gov), a part of the military (.mil), and so on.

My address is xian@netcom.com (you pronounce the @ sign as "at," and the . as "dot"). I log in as xian, my service provider is Netcom, and Netcom is a commercial business.

The name of your recipient will appear over to the right and another prompt will appear: **Subject of message:**. Type a subject (keep it short) and press Enter. This will be the first thing the recipient of your mail sees. (If you make a mistake while typing the subject, use Delete to erase the incorrect characters. Backspace will not work.)

Then the prompt **Copies to:** will appear. Type any additional addresses you want to send copies of your mail to (separated by commas), if any. Or just press Enter.

The words **Invoking editor...** will appear, and then the screen will go blank and you'll be plopped into some clumsy UNIX text editor to compose your message, most likely the editor called vi.

If you're used to decent word processors such as Microsoft Word or WordPerfect, you will find vi frustrating and limited. For one thing, you have to press Enter to end your lines. For another, you have to type special characters before you can even begin writing (because vi starts you off in command mode, not in text-editing mode).

To start typing your message, press *i*.

The insertion commands you need to know about are *i*, *a*, and *o*. Press *i* to insert text before the character the cursor is on. Press *a* to insert text after the character the cursor is on. Press *o* to start a new line below the line the cursor is on.

> Would you rather write up your message ahead of time and then just pull it in when it comes time to send it? See Chapter 5 for how to include a text file you've already prepared.

> If you've typed the wrong address or pressed **m** by mistake and don't actually want to send mail (I do this all the time), simply leave the Subject line blank and press Enter. elm will then give you the option of canceling the message.

> Having trouble with vi? I don't blame you. This is what passes for easy on UNIX systems! See Chapter 5 for complete instructions on editing with vi or pico.

E-MAIL—THE LIFEBLOOD OF THE INTERNET

Sending Mail to People on Other Networks

Many people have Internet addresses even though they are not, strictly speaking, on the Internet. Most other networks have "gateways" that send mail to and from the Internet. If you want to send mail to someone on another network, you'll need to know their identifier on that network and how their network address appears in Internet form. Here are examples of the most common:

Network	Username	Internet Address
America Online	Mang	mang@aol.com
AT&T Mail	Mang	mang@attmail.com
CompuServe	75555,5555	75555.5555@compuserve.com
Delphi	Mang	mang@delphi.com
Fidonet BBSs	1:2/3	f3.n2.z1@fidonet.org
GEnie	Mang	mang@genie.com
MCI Mail	555-7777	555-7777@mcimail.com
Prodigy	Mang	mang@prodigy.com

As you can see, the only real tricky ones are CompuServe, for which you have to change the comma in the CompuServe address to a dot in the Internet address; and Fidonet, for which you have to reverse the order of the three numbers and then put them after f, n, and z. (If you are only given two numbers, in the form a/b, then assume that they are the n and f numbers and that the z number is 1 [one].)

If you're not sure of an MCI Mail patron's number, you can send mail to **lastname@mcimail.com**, and you'll receive back a list of MCI Mail users with that last name and their correct e-mail addresses.

Handling E-Mail with elm **21**

When you get near the end of the line (or even earlier—it's better to have short lines than long lines because other people might read your mail in smaller windows), press Enter. Write whatever you want to write (see Figure 3.2).

FIGURE 3.2

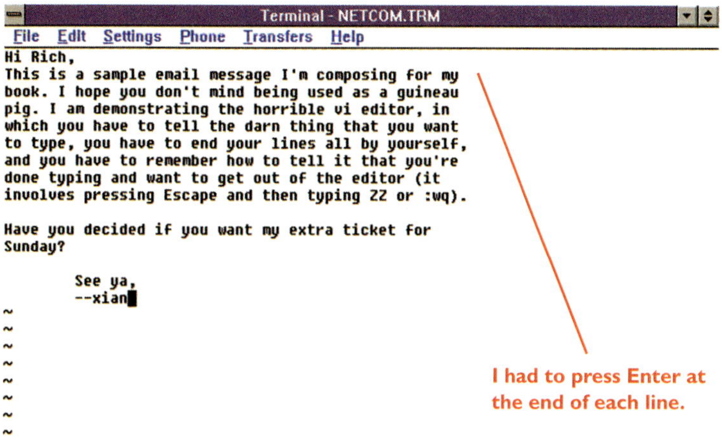

A short e-mail message to a friend.

I had to press Enter at the end of each line.

When you are done, press Escape (to go back to command mode) and then type ZZ or :wq to exit vi and return to elm.

You will then be given the choice of editing the mail, editing the headers (the addressee, the subject, the cc: line, etc.), sending it, or canceling it (see Figure 3.3).

FIGURE 3.3

elm always gives you these four options when you finish editing a message.

Press s or Enter to send the message

Press s or Enter to send the message. elm will tell you Sending mail... and then return you to the main menu and list of received mail. The words mail sent! will appear at the bottom of the screen until you take another action.

Reading Your Mail with elm

Whenever I log into my Internet account, the first thing I always do is check my e-mail. It's like checking your mailbox when you get home, except the contents are usually more interesting. To check your mail with elm, again start by typing elm and pressing Enter. Whatever mail has come in since the last time you checked will appear with the letter N (for *new*) in the left margin. If you've run your mail program without reading all your new mail, unread mail will have O (for *old*) next to it.

In addition, any mail that you've read but not moved to another folder will still appear in the first elm screen. Figure 3.4 shows my "inbox" with old and previously read mail.

I keep my read mail around until I've replied to it. I could save it to a folder (as I'll explain presently) but then I might forget about it. When my inbox gets too cluttered, I bite the bullet and reply to mail I've been putting off, and then delete most of it.

FIGURE 3.4

My inbox as seen in elm. I haven't read the first piece of mail. I've read all the other mail shown but I'm keeping it around until I reply.

This is an "old" message. I haven't read it yet, but it came in last time I ran elm.

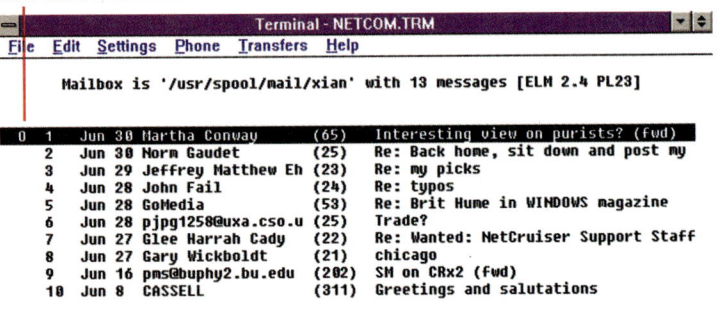

```
                    Terminal - NETCOM.TRM
 File  Edit  Settings  Phone  Transfers  Help

      Mailbox is '/usr/spool/mail/xian' with 13 messages [ELM 2.4 PL23]

 O   1   Jun 30  Martha Conway          (65)   Interesting view on purists? (fwd)
     2   Jun 30  Norm Gaudet             (25)   Re: Back home, sit down and post my
     3   Jun 29  Jeffrey Matthew Eh      (23)   Re: my picks
     4   Jun 28  John Fail               (24)   Re: typos
     5   Jun 28  GoMedia                 (53)   Re: Brit Hume in WINDOWS magazine
     6   Jun 28  pjpg1258@uxa.cso.u      (25)   Trade?
     7   Jun 27  Glee Harrah Cady        (22)   Re: Wanted: NetCruiser Support Staff
     8   Jun 27  Gary Wickboldt          (21)   chicago
     9   Jun 16  pms@buphy2.bu.edu      (202)   SM on CRx2 (fwd)
    10   Jun  8  CASSELL                (311)   Greetings and salutations

      You can use any of the following commands by pressing the first character;
       d)elete or u)ndelete mail,  m)ail a message,  r)eply or f)orward mail, q)uit
          To read a message, press <return>.  j = move down, k = move up, ? = help

 Command:
```

You may also be able to use ↑ and ↓ to scroll through the list of messages, depending on your terminal-emulation settings.

Handling E-Mail with elm   23

To view the contents of a mail message, highlight it in the menu and then press the spacebar or Enter. To move the highlight down, press **j**. To move the highlight up, press **k**. (These options are listed in the menu at the bottom of the elm screen.)

The screen will go blank and the message will appear on the screen. The top line on the screen will show basic information about the message, when it was sent, and its place in your inbox. Then there will be a blank line and then some header information with the sender's return address, the date the message was sent (again), the subject, and your address. After that will appear the body of the message (it might continue off the bottom of the screen), and then usually a signature at the end.

Figure 3.5 shows a message in elm.

If the message continues beyond the bottom of the screen, press the spacebar or Enter to see the next screenful (when you are ready).

FIGURE 3.5

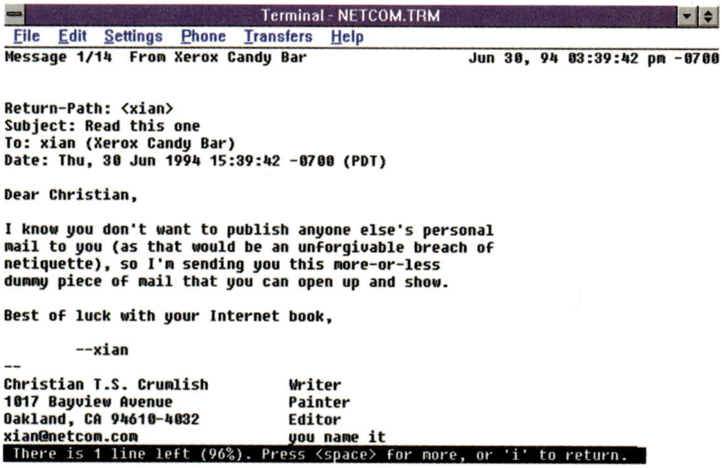

Here's an e-mail message I sent myself.

```
┌─────────────── Terminal - NETCOM.TRM ───────────────┐
 File  Edit  Settings  Phone  Transfers  Help
 Message 1/14  From Xerox Candy Bar         Jun 30, 94 03:39:42 pm -0700

 Return-Path: <xian>
 Subject: Read this one
 To: xian (Xerox Candy Bar)
 Date: Thu, 30 Jun 1994 15:39:42 -0700 (PDT)

 Dear Christian,

 I know you don't want to publish anyone else's personal
 mail to you (as that would be an unforgivable breach of
 netiquette), so I'm sending you this more-or-less
 dummy piece of mail that you can open up and show.

 Best of luck with your Internet book,

         --xian
 --
 Christian T.S. Crumlish          Writer
 1017 Bayview Avenue              Painter
 Oakland, CA 94610-4032           Editor
 xian@netcom.com                  you name it
 There is 1 line left (96%). Press <space> for more, or 'i' to return.
```

24 E-MAIL—THE LIFEBLOOD OF THE INTERNET

j and **k** move you up and down here too.

elm automatically prompts you to save all your read messages to your received mail folder when you quit elm. I almost never want to do this because I check my received mail folder so rarely that stuff gets moldy in there.

If you want to reply to everyone else who was also sent a copy of the message, press **g** (for group reply), instead of **r**.

If you pressed **r** by mistake (I do this a lot, too), press Ctrl-U to delete the Subject line and then press Enter. elm will ask you if you want to continue with no subject. Press **n**.

After reading the message, you can press **i** to return to the index (the list of messages), **r** to reply to the message, **f** to forward the message to another address, or **m** to mail an unrelated message.

Saving Your Mail with elm

If you want to save a piece of mail for future reference, press **s** either in the index or while reading the mail. elm will suggest the sender's login as a folder name, but you can replace it with anything you like, or type **>** to save the mail to your "received mail" folder.

To look at the contents of a folder from the index, press **c**, and then type the name of the folder.

Replying to Mail with elm

To reply to mail, either from the index or while reading it, simply press **r**.

elm will prompt you with Copy message? (y/n) n. If you want the text of the original message to be included in your reply, press **y**, otherwise press **n** or Enter.

elm will then prompt you for a subject. It will suggest "**Re:** " followed by the subject of the original message. Press Enter to accept this, or press Ctrl-U and type a new subject.

People often fail to change the subject line of messages, even when the conversation has evolved its way onto a new topic.

Again you are given the choice of sending copies to other people. After you press Enter again, you are unceremoniously dumped into your text editor. If you chose to include the text of the original message, it appears preceded by "**>** " on each line (see Figure 3.6).

Try to minimize the amount of quoted text that you keep in your return message. To move down a line, press **j**; to move up, press **k**.

Handling E-Mail with elm **25**

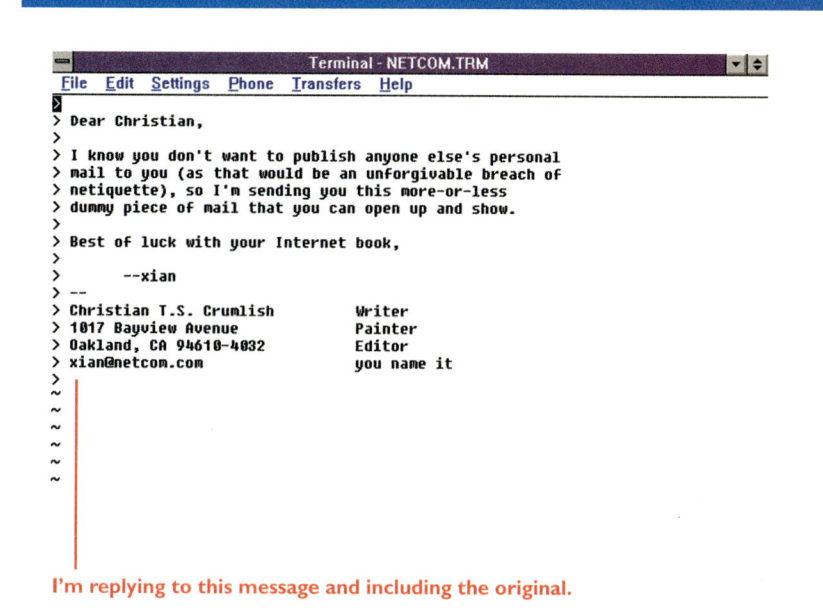

FIGURE 3.6

My reply to myself, with the original message included. (I haven't added anything yet.)

```
┌─────────────── Terminal - NETCOM.TRM ─────────────┐
 File  Edit  Settings  Phone  Transfers  Help
>
> Dear Christian,
>
> I know you don't want to publish anyone else's personal
> mail to you (as that would be an unforgivable breach of
> netiquette), so I'm sending you this more-or-less
> dummy piece of mail that you can open up and show.
>
> Best of luck with your Internet book,
>
>         --xian
> --
> Christian T.S. Crumlish        Writer
> 1017 Bayview Avenue            Painter
> Oakland, CA 94610-4032         Editor
> xian@netcom.com                you name it
>
~
~
~
~
~
~
```

I'm replying to this message and including the original.

To delete a line completely, press **dd**. To delete a single character, press **x**. To begin inserting text, press **i** to insert before the cursor, **a** to insert after the cursor, or **o** to insert on a new line below the line the cursor is on. To switch back to command mode (so you can move around some more, for example), press Esc.

When you are done editing the message, press Esc, and then type **ZZ** or **:wq**. Then press **s** to send the reply.

Forwarding Mail with elm

If someone sends you mail and you'd like to send a copy of it to someone else, you can forward it by pressing **f**. elm will respond with **Edit outgoing message? (y/n) y**.

Press **y** or Enter to edit the message or add an explanation of why you are forwarding it to the beginning. Press **n** to have the message forwarded without explanation. elm will ask who to send the message to. Type the person's address and press Enter. It will

If you want to add some explanatory text before the forwarded message, but you don't want the forwarded message to have the ">"'s before each line, then first press **n** to forward the message without editing it. Enter the address as normal, but then, instead of pressing **s** to send the message, press **e** to edit it. Add your explanation, exit the editor, and then send the message.

then suggest a subject—the previous subject with "**(Fwd)**" added at the end. You can press Enter to accept this subject or press Ctrl-U and type a new one (and then press Enter).

Press Enter again, or add other addresses to receive copies and then press Enter. Then edit the message (if you opted to), or press **s** or Enter to send it.

Deleting Mail with elm

If you have read a piece of mail and have no need to save it, you should delete it so it doesn't clutter up your inbox (and waste precious hard-disk storage space). To delete a message, place the highlight on it and press **d**. A **D** will appear in the left margin next to the message, indicating that it will be deleted when you quit elm.

If you change your mind, press **K** to go back up to the message (if you just press **k**, you will go to the line above it), and then press **u** to undelete the message.

To delete (or mark for deletion) all messages with a certain word, or any string of characters really, in the From or Subject lines, press Ctrl-D and then type the word you have in mind and press Enter. All messages with that word will be marked for deletion.

You will have a final chance to change your mind about deleting messages when you exit elm.

Exiting elm

When you are finished sending, reading, and replying to mail, you should quit elm. To do so, press **q**. if you've marked messaged for deletion, elm will ask you **Delete messages? (y/n) y**. Press **y** or Enter to delete the marked messages, or press **n** to change your mind. Then, elm will ask you **Move read messages to "received" folder? (y/n) n**

---

*Capital **J** and **K** will allow you to move to a message marked for deletion, although lowercase **j** and **k** will not.*

See Tagging Messages in elm, ahead, for how to tag any number of messages and then perform an action on all of them at once (such as deleting them, er, marking them for deletion).

*To skip the one or two questions elm asks you when you quit, you can exit by pressing **Q** instead of q. This automatically accepts the default answers, deleting marked messages and keeping read messages in your inbox. This is how I always quit elm.*

Press **y** if you want your read messages moved to the received folder, or press **n** or Enter if you want to keep them in the inbox for the time being.

Then elm will tell you how many messages were deleted (if any), how many are left, how many were moved to the "received" folder, or that the folder was unchanged. Then you'll be back at the UNIX prompt.

Usually when I'm done checking my mail, I next run my newsreader and try to get caught up on Usenet news (an impossible task, for sure). See Chapters 7 and 8 for more on Usenet.

*If you press **y** by mistake, to move the messages back into your inbox, run elm again, type **c**, Enter, **>**, Enter (then type **n** and press Enter if you're asked if you want to move any more messages). Highlight the first message to move back and type **t** repeatedly. Then type **>**, Enter, **!**, Enter. Then type **Q** to quit.*

Creating Aliases in elm

If there are people with whom you correspond regularly through e-mail, or people whose e-mail addresses are hard to remember or difficult to type correctly, you can create aliases for these people. Aliases are shorter words that you type instead of the actual address. elm then converts the alias that you type into the correct e-mail address.

To make an alias in elm, press **a** while at the main screen. This brings up the alias screen. Figure 3.7 shows my second screenful of aliases. If you have none, the screen will be blank in that area.

To make a new alias, press **n**.

Now type an abbreviation. Then press Enter. elm will prompt you for a last name and then a first name of the person for whom you are creating an alias. Then it allows you to add an optional comment. Whatever. Next you have to type the actual Internet address to which the alias will correspond. Finally, it will check all the information with you:

You can also use a single alias for a list of addresses, so you can send mail to a group of people all at once. I've got a group alias of people to whom I send stupid stuff I find on the Net. No one's complained yet.

```
You can use any of the following commands by pressing the first character;
     a)lias current message, n)ew alias, d)elete or u)ndelete an alias,
     m)ail to alias, or r)eturn to main menu.  To view an alias, press <return>.
                   j = move down, k = move up, ? = help
Alias: Add a new alias to database...         Accept new alias? (y/n)
New alias: andy is 'Andy Nisbet'.
Messages addressed as: natron@aol.com (Andy Nisbet)
```

*To make an alias for the sender of the current message (the one highlighted in the index, press **a**).*

FIGURE 3.7

*The elm alias screen.
(I hit j ten times.)*

This alias corresponds to a list of e-mail addresses.

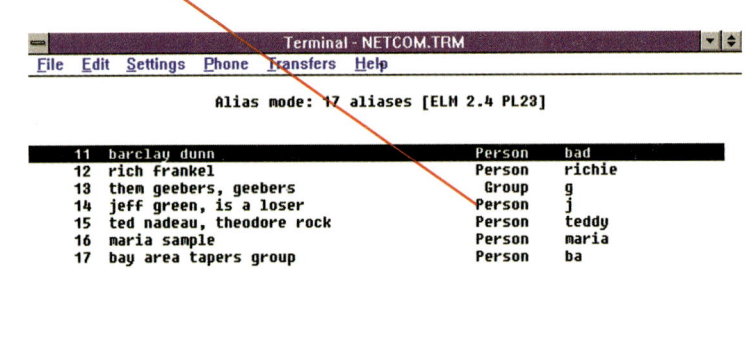

```
                        Terminal - NETCOM.TRM
 File   Edit   Settings   Phone   Transfers   Help

                  Alias mode: 17 aliases [ELM 2.4 PL23]

       11  barclay dunn                           Person    bad
       12  rich frankel                           Person    richie
       13  them geebers, geebers                  Group     g
       14  jeff green, is a loser                 Person    j
       15  ted nadeau, theodore rock              Person    teddy
       16  maria sample                           Person    maria
       17  bay area tapers group                  Person    ba


   You can use any of the following commands by pressing the first character;
        a)lias current message, n)ew alias, d)elete or u)ndelete an alias,
        m)ail to alias, or r)eturn to main menu. To view an alias, press <return>.
                        j = move down, k = move up, ? = help
Alias:
```

Keep it short—the whole point is to save you some typing—and try to make it memorable (although you can always look it up if you forget).

If it all looks okay, press **y** or Enter. Otherwise, press **n** and start over. Then press **i** to return to the index (the main screen).

Now, whenever you want to use the alias, just type it instead of the full Internet address. elm will do the rest. If you forget it, press **a**, highlight the one you want on the alias screen, and then press **m** to mail to that alias.

Using a Signature file with elm

The required location of your signature file might vary from one system to the next, so if your signature file does not appear at the end of your messages, ask your system administrator where it should be stored.

If there's a standard signature, tagline, or quotation that you would like to attach to the end of all your outgoing mail messages, you can create something called a signature file. The file should be put in your .elm directory and named **signature**.

With elm, you can create a different signature file for your posts to Usenet newsgroups. This can be useful if you want different information in your e-mail messages (which are relatively more private) and your Usenet posts (more public).

See Chapters 7 and 8 for more on Usenet and posting.

To create the file, first switch to the .elm directory. Type **cd** .elm at the UNIX prompt and press Enter. Then type **vi signature** and press Enter to create the file. Press **i** to insert text. Keep your sig under four lines, as traditional netiquette dictates. When you are done, press Esc, and then type **:wq** and press Enter.

Your signature will appear at the end of all your e-mail messages. When you reply to a message and include the original text, your signature will appear after the quoted message, and you might not notice it right away, because elm will start you off at the top, before the quoted message.

> Confused about UNIX files and directories? Been there, done that. See Chapter 5 for more on editing text files and Chapter 9 for more on directories and files in general.

Tagging Messages in elm

In elm, you can *tag* a number of messages and then perform an action on all of them at once (such as deleting them, saving them, or moving them to another folder). To take the current message, press **t**. To untag it, press **t** again. To tag a message and have the highlight move down to the next message, press **T** instead.

That's it for elm. If you're not interested in how to use other mail programs, skip ahead to *Recovering Lost Messages*, later in this chapter.

> To tag all messages with a certain word, or any string of characters really, in the From or Subject line, press Ctrl-T and then type the word and press Enter.

Handling E-Mail with pine

Probably the easiest UNIX mail program around is pine. If it's available on your system, then you should at least check it out, because it might be right for you.

Starting pine

You start pine by typing **pine** at the command prompt and pressing Enter. The screen will clear and the pine Main Menu will fill the screen (see Figure 3.8).

FIGURE 3.8

The pine main menu. Press i to view messages in your inbox.

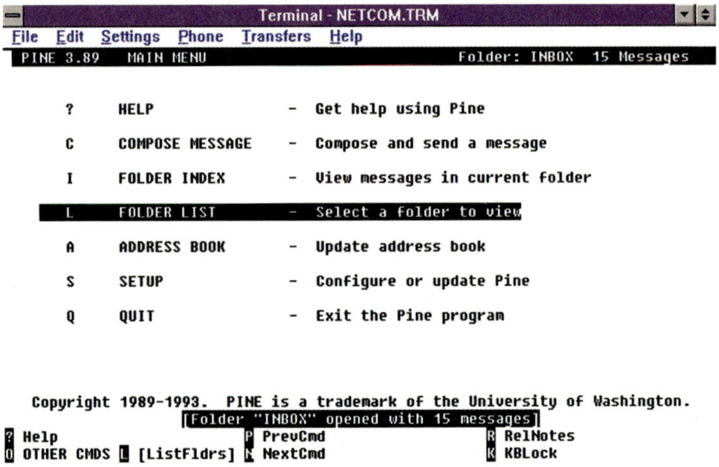

```
                Terminal - NETCOM.TRM
 File  Edit  Settings  Phone  Transfers  Help
 PINE 3.89      MAIN MENU              Folder: INBOX   15 Messages


          ?    HELP              -  Get help using Pine

          C    COMPOSE MESSAGE   -  Compose and send a message

          I    FOLDER INDEX      -  View messages in current folder

          L    FOLDER LIST       -  Select a folder to view

          A    ADDRESS BOOK      -  Update address book

          S    SETUP             -  Configure or update Pine

          Q    QUIT              -  Exit the Pine program


       Copyright 1989-1993.  PINE is a trademark of the University of Washington.
                         [Folder "INBOX" opened with 15 messages]
  ? Help                    P PrevCmd                       R RelNotes
  O OTHER CMDS L [ListFldrs] N NextCmd                      K KBLock
```

To have pine start automatically, put the word **pine** on a line by itself in your .login, .profile, or .cshrc file. See Chapter 5 for how to create and edit files.

Want to write your message ahead of time and then just pull it in when it comes time to send it? See Chapter 5 for how to include a text file you've already prepared.

"sent-mail" is a folder that contains copies of all the mail that you send.

Sending Mail with pine

To send mail, first press **c**. This will bring up the Compose Message screen (see Figure 3.9).

First type the address of the person to whom you are sending the mail.

Then press Tab. If you want to send copies to others, type their addresses on the Cc line. Otherwise, just press Tab again. Press Tab again to go down to the Subject line and then enter a subject. You can press Enter as well as Tab to jump from line to line.

Then press Tab again and begin writing your message.

The pine text editor knows how to word-wrap, so you can just type away and let it worry about the line breaks. Write whatever you want to write.

When you are done, press Ctrl-X to send the message. (If you change your mind and don't want to send it, press Ctrl-C—try Ctrl-Shift-C if Ctrl-C doesn't work—and then press **y**.)

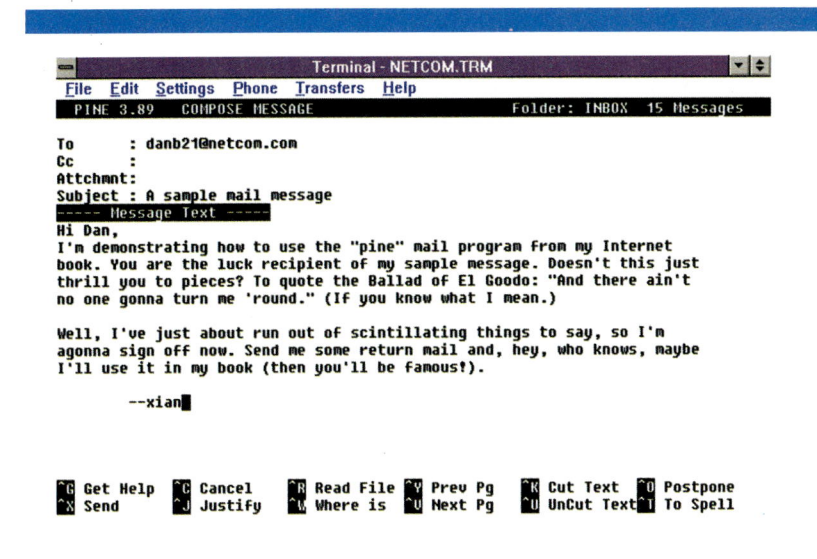

Handling E-Mail with pine

FIGURE 3.9

The pine Compose Message screen. Enter the address and subject and then type your message.

See the sidebar titled *Sending Mail to People on Other Networks* earlier in this chapter for help with addressing messages.

pine will respond with Send message? [y] :. Press y or Enter to send the message. pine will tell you [Sending mail...] and then return you to the Main Menu. The words [Message sent and copied to "sent-mail"] will appear near the bottom of the screen until you take another action.

Reading Your Mail with pine

From the pine Main Menu, press *i* to view messages in your inbox folder. The index screen for the inbox folder will appear (see Figure 3.10).

Whatever mail you haven't read will appear with the letter *N* (for *new*) in the left margin.

To view the contents of a mail message, highlight it in the menu and then press the spacebar or Enter. To move the highlight down, press *p*. To move the highlight up, press *n*. (These options are listed in the menu at the bottom of the pine screen.)

The screen will clear and the message will appear on the screen. The message begins with some header information

I keep my read mail around until I've replied to it. I could save it to a folder (as I'll explain presently) but then I might forget about it. When my inbox gets too cluttered, I bite the bullet and reply to mail I've been putting off, and then delete most of it.

Your arrow keys also might help you move up and down.

FIGURE 3.10

The pine folder index screen. Messages are listed in the order they were sent, from oldest to most recent.

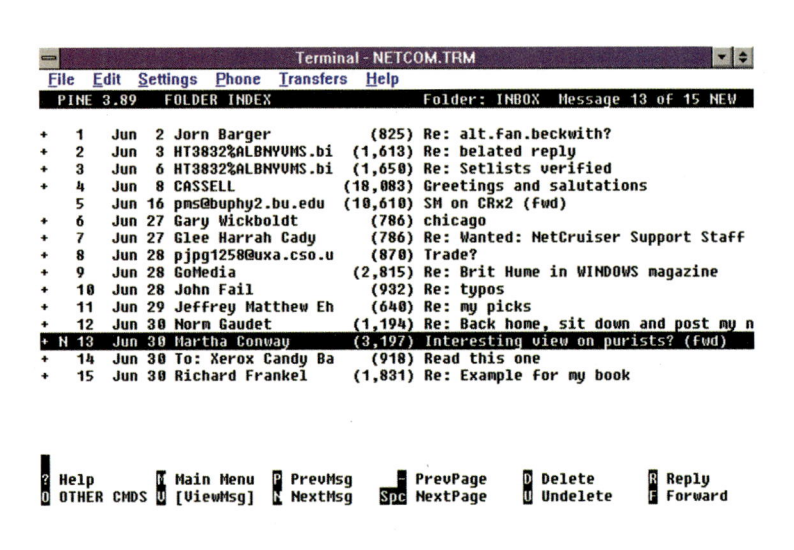

```
                       Terminal - NETCOM.TRM
 File  Edit  Settings  Phone  Transfers  Help
 PINE 3.89      FOLDER INDEX              Folder: INBOX  Message 13 of 15 NEW

 +   1   Jun  2  Jorn Barger          (825)   Re: alt.fan.beckwith?
 +   2   Jun  3  HT3832%ALBNYVMS.bi   (1,613) Re: belated reply
 +   3   Jun  6  HT3832%ALBNYVMS.bi   (1,650) Re: Setlists verified
 +   4   Jun  8  CASSELL              (18,083) Greetings and salutations
     5   Jun 16  pms@buphy2.bu.edu    (10,610) SM on CRx2 (fwd)
 +   6   Jun 27  Gary Wickboldt       (786)   chicago
 +   7   Jun 27  Glee Harrah Cady     (786)   Re: Wanted: NetCruiser Support Staff
 +   8   Jun 28  pjpg1258@uxa.cso.u   (870)   Trade?
 +   9   Jun 28  GoMedia              (2,815) Re: Brit Hume in WINDOWS magazine
 +  10   Jun 28  John Fail            (932)   Re: typos
 +  11   Jun 29  Jeffrey Matthew Eh   (640)   Re: my picks
 +  12   Jun 30  Norm Gaudet          (1,194) Re: Back home, sit down and post my n
 + N 13  Jun 30  Martha Conway        (3,197) Interesting view on purists? (fwd)
 +  14   Jun 30  To: Xerox Candy Ba   (918)   Read this one
 +  15   Jun 30  Richard Frankel      (1,831) Re: Example for my book


 ? Help       M Main Menu   P PrevMsg        - PrevPage    D Delete     R Reply
 O OTHER CMDS V [ViewMsg]   N NextMsg      Spc NextPage    U Undelete   F Forward
```

We'll get to replying and forwarding in a minute.

with the date the message was sent, the sender's return address, your address, and the subject. After that will appear the body of the message (it might continue off the bottom of the screen), and then usually a signature at the end.

If the message continues beyond the bottom of the screen, press the spacebar to see the next screenful (when you are ready). To go back to the previous page, press -.

After reading the message, you can press **m** to return to the Main menu, **r** to reply to the message, or **f** to forward the message to another address.

Saving Your Mail with pine

If you want to save a piece of mail for future reference, press **s** either in the index or while reading the mail. pine will suggest [saved-messages] as a folder name, but you can replace it with anything you like.

Handling E-Mail with pine

To look at the contents of a folder, press l to see a folder list, press Tab to get to the folder list you want to see, and then press Enter. When you are done, press l to get back to the folder list and choose the INBOX folder.

Replying to Mail with pine

To reply to mail, either from the index or while reading it, simply press r. pine will prompt you with Include original message in Reply? (y/n/^C) [n]:. If you want the text of the original message to be included in your reply, press y, otherwise press n or Enter.

pine will then plop you into the compose screen. If you chose to include the text of the original message, it appears preceded by ">" on each line.

pine supplies a subject ("Re: " followed by the subject of the original message). To change the suggested subject, press Ctrl-P until you are up to the subject line, then Ctrl-K to erase the contents of the subject line. Then type whatever you like and press Tab (or Enter) until you are back in the Message Text area of the screen.

When you are done editing the message, press Ctrl-X to send it.

Forwarding Mail with pine

If someone sends you mail and you'd like to send a copy of it to someone else, you can forward it by pressing f. pine will clear the screen and put you in the Forward Message screen, which is exactly the same as the Compose Message screen. The only difference is that there will be a line that reads ----------Forwarded Message---------- in the Message Text area before the original message. Proceed as you would with a normal message.

> You can always go back to your inbox folder by pressing g (for Go to) and then Enter to accept the default.

> Try to minimize the amount of quoted text that you keep in your return message. This saves your recipient the work of rereading material unrelated to your response. To move down a line, press Ctrl-N, to move up, press Ctrl-P. To delete a line completely, press Ctrl-K.

Deleting Mail with pine

If you have read a piece of mail and have no need to save it. You should delete it so it doesn't clutter up your inbox (and waste precious hard-disk storage space). To delete a message, go to the index (press i), place the highlight on it, and press d. A D will appear in the left margin next to the message, indicating that it will be deleted when you quit pine.

If you change your mind, press u to undelete the message.

> You will have a final chance to change your mind about deleting messages when you exit pine.

Exiting pine

When you are finished sending, reading, and replying to mail, you should quit pine. To do so, press q. if you've marked messages for deletion, pine will ask you Expunge the 1 deleted message from "INBOX"? (y/n) [y]: (or 2 or more as the case may be). Press y or Enter to delete the marked messages, or press n to change your mind.

Then pine will tell you how many messages were kept and how many were deleted (if any). Then you'll be back at the UNIX prompt. Usually when I'm done checking my mail, I next run my newsreader and try to get caught up on Usenet news (an impossible task, for sure).

> See Chapters 7 and 8 for more on Usenet.

Creating a pine Address Book

To create an address book—a list of e-mail addresses you regularly send mail to—press a. This brings up the Address Book screen.

To add a new address to the address book, press a. pine will prompt you with New full name (last, first) :. Type the last name, a comma, and then the first name of the person whose Internet address you want to add to your address book. (Then press Enter.) Then pine will prompt you with Enter new nickname (one word and easy to remember): .

> To automatically add the sender of the current message to your address book from the Folder Index screen, press t and then type a nickname for the sender and press Enter. Then press Enter twice to accept the full name and address of the sender.

Handling E-Mail with mail

Type a short nickname and press Enter. Then pine will ask you Enter new e-mail address :. Type the address and press Enter. The new address will be added to the address book. Press i to return to the inbox folder index or press m to return to the Main Menu.

Now, whenever you want to use the nickname in the address book, just type it instead of the full Internet address. pine will do the rest.

Using a Signature File with pine

If there's a standard signature, or tagline, or quotation that you would like to attach to the end of all your outgoing mail messages, you can create something called a signature file. The file should be named ".signature". (pine will use the same signature file that you use for posting news to Usenet.)

To create the file, type pico .signature and press Enter. Type whatever you want for your signature (but keep it under four lines as traditional netiquette dictates). When you are done, press Ctrl-X.

Your signature will appear at the end of your mail messages. When you reply to a message and quote the text in your reply, pine will put your signature at the beginning of your new message, before the quoted text. The idea is for you to write your message before the signature and then delete as much of the quoted text as possible.

That's it for pine. If your not interested in how to use other mail programs, skip ahead to *Recovering Lost Messages*, later in this chapter.

The required location of the .signature file might vary from one system to the next, so if your signature file does not appear at the end of your messages, ask your system administrator where it should be stored.

UNIX files and directories getting you down? See Chapter 5 for more on editing text files and Chapter 9 for more on directories and files in general.

Handling E-Mail with mail

If you have neither of the excellent mail programs elm and pine, you might have to do with the most basic mail program of all, the one called mail. This comes with every UNIX system, so you're sure to have it (but ask your system administrator if there's anything better around). It's really bare bones compared to the other programs, and it has no menus and offers you no hints about what to do.

Press Enter after each of these commands.

To Do This	Type This
Send mail	m *username@address*
Type a message	*just type it*
End a message	*. (period)*
Read a message	*message-number (or just press Enter for the current message)*
Save a message	s *filename*
Reply to a message	r
Delete a message	d
Undelete a message	u
Exit mail	q

Windowed Mail Programs

As I outlined earlier in this chapter, you might be lucky enough to have available to you a windowed mail program that runs on your normal operating system. With full Internet access, you can swing this with an offline mail reader (see *Offline Mail Readers*), a SLIP or PPP account, or a network connection to the Internet from your desktop PC or Macintosh. With commercial services such as America Online and CompuServe, the windowed mail programs are built in.

Offline Mail Readers

If you are charged by the minute for your connect time, you might want to look into using an offline mail reader. Offline mail readers connect to your Internet account, download your mail to your home computer, and then allow you to read and respond to your mail in your own good time. When you have composed your responses, the offline mail reader will then connect again to your Internet account and send the mail you've written.

The most common offline mail reader for the Macintosh is called Eudora, and is available as freeware or shareware (for more advanced versions) all over the Net. There is no one single standard offline mail reader for IBM PCs and compatibles, but there are standard formats, such as QWK, HDPF, and ZipNews.

Handling E-Mail with Eudora

Eudora, the Macintosh mail program, can function as either an offline mail reader or as an online reader for SLIP, PPP, and network accounts. It works about the same either way. To run Eudora, click the Eudora icon.

This will bring up windows representing your inbox (In), your sent mail (Out), and your saved mail (Saved Mail).

When you double-click on a message in any of those windows, it will open up in a window of its own (see Figure 3.11).

Most of the useful Eudora commands are available on the Message menu (shown here).

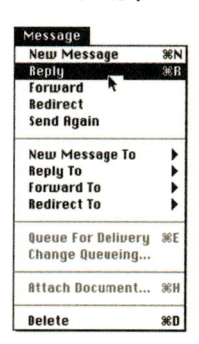

The only difference you'll notice if you run Eudora as an off-line reader is that it will use your modem to connect to your shell account when you first run it (to download your new mail) and when you exit it (to send any messages you've written).

FIGURE 3.11

In Eudora, messages appear in their own windows.

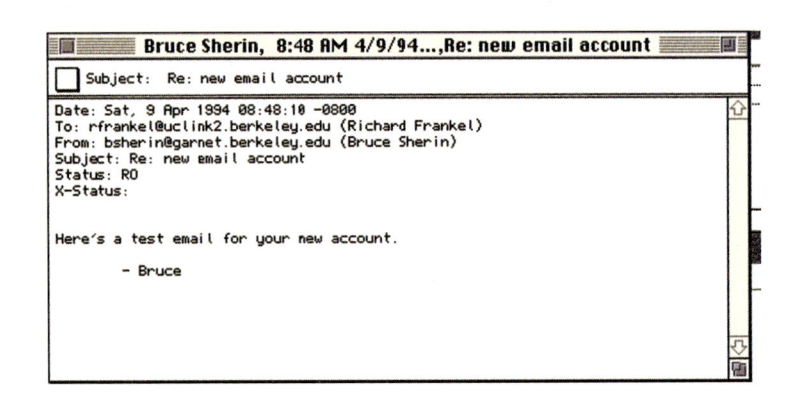

```
Bruce Sherin, 8:48 AM 4/9/94...,Re: new email account
Subject: Re: new email account
Date: Sat, 9 Apr 1994 08:48:10 -0800
To: rfrankel@uclink2.berkeley.edu (Richard Frankel)
From: bsherin@garnet.berkeley.edu (Bruce Sherin)
Subject: Re: new email account
Status: RO
X-Status:

Here's a test email for your new account.

        - Bruce
```

CompuServe lets you compose any number of messages offline and put them in your outbasket. You can then use the Mail ➤ Send/Receive All Mail command to send and receive all your mail as quickly as possible and get back offline. You can also arrange file transfers this way.

E-Mail with an Online Service

America Online and CompuServe are the two most popular online services today. Both of them have easy-to-use mail interfaces both for sending mail to other members of the service as well as for sending Internet mail. Figure 3.12 shows what the America Online mail program for Windows looks like.

With America Online, choose Mail ➤ Compose Mail to send mail. To read mail, click the You've Got Mail icon, then double-click the title of the message in the New Mail dialog box.

With CompuServe, choose Mail ➤ Create Mail to send mail. In the Recipient dialog box, choose your recipients and then click the OK button. Write your message in the Create Mail dialog box (see Figure 3.13). Then click the Send Now button or the Out-Basket button.

To retrieve mail on CompuServe, choose Mail ➤ Get New Mail. Double-click on a message to read it.

Windowed Mail Programs 39

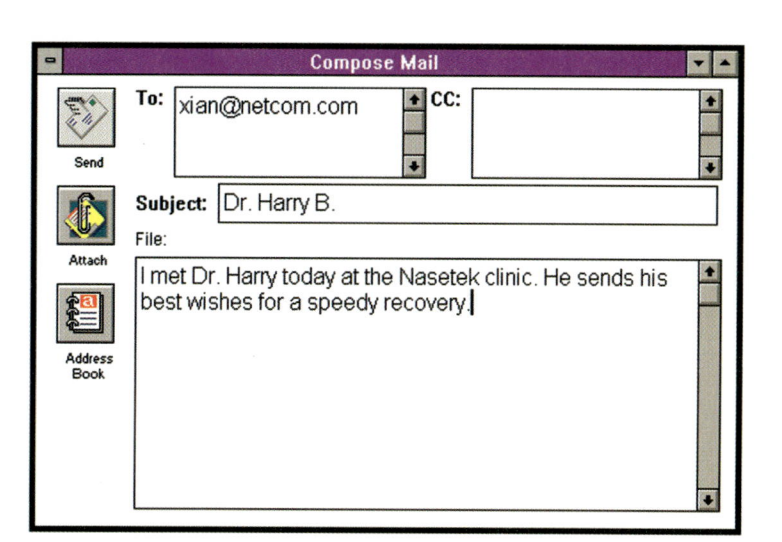

FIGURE 3.12

America Online's Windows e-mail program is very easy to get the hang of.

America Online lets you compose messages off-line, then log in and send them, so you're not paying for connect charges while racking your brains over what to write.

FIGURE 3.13

With CompuServe, click the Send Now button to send immediately or the Out-Basket button to store the message until you next connect.

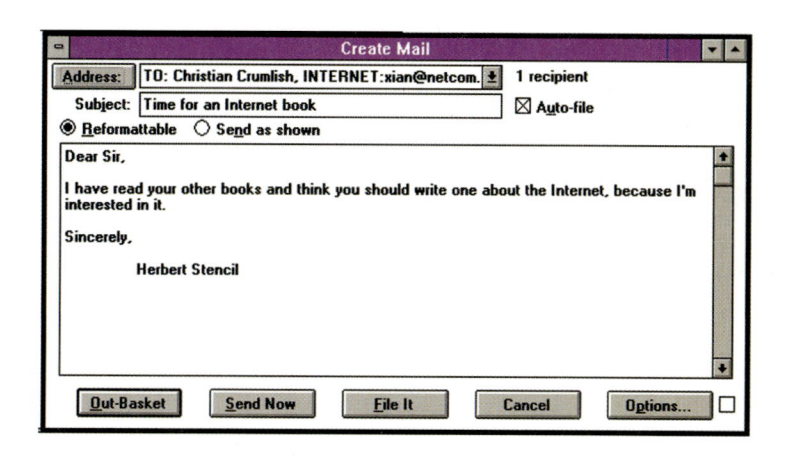

E-MAIL—THE LIFEBLOOD OF THE INTERNET

See Chapter 5 for more on composing mail and including files in your mail messages.

This section discusses how to manipulate your mail with a UNIX-based account. If you have another kind of account, look at the options in your mail program or ask your system administrator for the equivalent commands, if they exist. If your e-mail access comes through an online service, ask the authorities if you have these capabilities.

E-mail mailing lists are explained in Chapter 6.

Recovering Lost Messages

Sometimes your UNIX system will crash while you're in the midst of composing mail. Usually your message, or most of it, will be saved and then loaded again the next time you run your mail program. You might also get an automatic message sent to you telling you where to find the preserved version of the mail.

Just to be safe, though, if your connection stops responding while you are in the middle of composing a mail message, you should go ahead and copy the text you've written (using your PC's normal selection and copying function), and save it to a text file. Then, when you reconnect, you can paste it into the terminal window after running the mail program again.

Going on Vacation

If you go on vacation for more than a couple of days, you'll want to temporarily unsubscribe to any mailing lists you belong to. You'll also want people who send you e-mail to know that you're not around to answer it, so they don't think you're ignoring them. You can do this by creating a vacation message.

Unsubscribing to Mailing Lists

For person-administered mailing lists, send mail to the -request - address asking to be unsubscribed, and then send mail when you return to the same address asking to be subscribed again. For robot-administered lists, send mail to the listserv@ (or major domo@) address, with: **set** *list* nomail in it(substituting the name of the mailing list for *list*, of course).

When you return, send the message **set** *list* mail to start up your subscription again.

Setting Up a Vacation Message

To have an automatic reply sent to anyone who sends you e-mail while you're on vacation, run the vacation program. To do so, type *vacation* at the UNIX prompt and press Enter.

If you've never run it before, the vacation program will put you into your text editor so you can edit your vacation message. It starts you off with some generic information, as shown in Figure 3.14.

You can add more information to the outgoing message—say the dates of your vacation. When you're done, exit your text editor.

vacation then tells you *You have a message file in home-directory/.vacation.msg. Would you like to see it?* This seems weird, since you just edited the message file, but vacation is a simple program and doesn't know any better. It looks for a file called .vacation.msg, and if it finds one, offers to show it to you, whether or not it just helped you create it. Type *n* and press Enter. vacation will then prompt you *Would you like to edit it?*

Run the vacation program the day you're leaving, or as close to it as possible, because it takes effect right away.

See Chapter 5 for details on editing text files.

FIGURE 3.14

The vacation program helps you set up an outgoing message and a .forward file.

42 E-MAIL—THE LIFEBLOOD OF THE INTERNET

*If you already have a .forward file, vacation will mention it to you and show you its contents. Press **n** and Enter repeatedly to get out of the vacation program and then rename your .forward file to something like .forward.old. Then run vacation again.*

Type **n** and press Enter again. Then vacation tells you To enable the vacation feature a ".forward" file is created. Would you like to enable the vacation feature? Type **y** and press Enter. vacation signs off with Vacation feature ENABLED. Please remember to turn it off when you get back from vacation. Bon voyage. Now anyone who sends you mail will get the message you created.

When You're Back from Vacation

When you get back, run vacation again. It will tell you that you have a file called .vacation.msg and ask if you want to see it or edit it. Type **n** and press Enter after each question. Then it will tell you You have a .forward file in your home directory containing: \your-login, "l/usr/ucb/vacation your-login" Would you like to remove it and disable the vacation feature? Type **y** and press Enter. vacation will tell you Back to normal reception of mail.

Forwarding Your E-mail

If you have more than one e-mail account, you might not always get around to checking each one, so you might want to forward all your mail to one account. As discussed in the previous section, the vacation program uses a .forward file to send the return messages, but .forward files have many uses. The simplest is to send mail to another address. If you have more than one e-mail address but you only want to check one regularly, you can have all your mail forwarded to that one address. It's simple.

Be very careful not to create infinite loops by forwarding mail back and forth between two accounts or among a larger number of accounts.

For any account whose mail you want forwarded, create a file called .forward (to do it in vi, type **vi .forward** and press Enter).

In the file, just list the e-mail address you want the mail to go to. Then exit the file. Now, all mail sent to that address will be forwarded to the address in the .forward file.

To keep a copy of the mail in the mailbox it was sent to, while forwarding another copy to your central mail account, put a line of the following form in your .forward file:

>   \this-account, central-account

This will forward the mail to two places—this same account (the one the .forward file is in) and the central account that you check regularly. The backslash before the first address prevents .forward from re-forwarding the mail when it comes around again. It is therefore very important. If you leave the backslash out, you can get an infinite number of mail messages flooding into your mailbox, until it's full.

Don't Fly Off the Handle

In this book I'm trying not to give you too much advice about how to behave on the Net, for several reasons. First, I assume you are an adult and can decide for yourself how to behave. Secondly, the Net has a strongly interactive culture and you will receive plenty of advice and cues from others if you overstep the bounds of good behavior.

Nevertheless, I will point out that e-mail is a notoriously volatile medium. Because it is so easy to write out a reply and send it in the heat of the moment, and because text lacks many of the nuances of face-to-face communication, the expression- and body-cues that add emphasis, the tones of voice that indicate joking instead of insult, and so on, it has become a matter of course for many people to dash off ill-considered replies to perceived insults and therefore fan the flames of invective.

Issues of *netiquette* (as it's called) arise even more frequently when you are communicating with millions over Usenet. See Chapter 7 for more details.

This Internet habit, called "flaming," is widespread and you will no doubt encounter it from one end or the other. All I can suggest is that you try to restrain yourself when you feel the urge to fly off the handle. (And I have discovered that apologies work wonders when people have misunderstood a friendly gibe or have mistaken sarcasm for idiocy.)

CHAPTER 4

Reach Out and Touch Someone

Featuring

- Collecting people's e-mail addresses
- Looking for people on the Net
- How to use finger
- How to make a .plan file
  Finding people with Whois, Netfind, and the Knowbot
- "Chatting" with people in realtime on the irc

E-mail communication is as useful as phone communication (and better in some ways) but it's not yet as common, not yet universal, not yet standardized. As I mentioned in Chapter 3, there are many different ways to have an Internet e-mail address. Unfortunately, because of this, there are no comprehensive listings of e-mail address, nothing equivalent to white pages, yellow pages, or directory assistance. There are some ways to look for people or verify e-mail addresses, but they are all unreliable in one way or another.

Once you do find people or build an address book of e-mail addresses, you might also want to check and see when people have last logged on, if they've read their mail recently, and so on. If someone is logged onto a computer on the Net at the same time that you are, you may also attempt to communicate with them in "realtime." I'll also explain *talk* and *chat* in this chapter.

Say "Send Me E-Mail"

If you're not sure how to send mail to someone but you know they're on the Net, ask them to send you some mail (tell them your e-mail address). Once their mail comes through okay, you should have a working return address. Either copy it and save it somewhere, or just keep their mail around and reply to it when you want to send them mail (try to remember to change the subject line if appropriate, not that I ever do).

> Really, the best way to collect e-mail addresses is from people directly. Many people now have their e-mail addresses on their business cards, so you can capture people's addresses this way.

Finding People on the Net

If you know someone's out there but you don't know their address, or if you know an address but you're not sure it's the right person, there are a few things you can try to find or verify e-mail addresses. (I explained how to convert e-mail addresses from other online services into Internet format in Chapter 3.)

> The Internet is a sprawled out anarchy consisting of many smaller networks. There is no sure way to find a given address, especially if it has not been registered with InterNIC.

Mailing Postmaster@

If you know someone's domain (such as the company where they work) but not their login, you can try sending mail to **postmaster@***address* (this will be a real person) and asking politely for the e-mail address.

Finding People with finger

The *finger* command is a standard UNIX command for checking the status of a machine (or network) or of an individual. Designed to tell you who's logged onto a single machine or network, finger works across the Internet. However, it is unreliable, as not all networks keep the information up to date or accurate.

> For more information on finger, type **man finger** at the UNIX prompt and press Enter.

finger a Whole Domain

If you just type finger at the UNIX prompt and press Enter, you are fingering your own network, and you'll get a list of who is currently logged in. Type finger *host.subdomain.domain* and press Enter to finger another domain.

> There are limitations to fingering. The information you get back is only as accurate and up to date as the particular network makes it. I've fingered my address and gotten back an indication that I was not logged in at the time!

finger a Single User

Type finger *username@address.domain* and press Enter to finger a specific e-mail address. Figure 4.1 shows the result when I finger xian@netcom.com.

Among other things, the finger command returns the "real name" of the person to whom the Internet address belongs. The real name is a variable that can be changed on most systems, so what comes up as the real name may actually be a pseudonym, a joke, or anything really.

> If you are interested in changing your own real name, type **chfn** at the UNIX prompt and press Enter. You will be asked to type a new real name, and then you'll have to enter your password.

Making .plans for Nigel

Try fingering yourself and see what happens. In the area headed "Plan:," you'll see the words "No plan" or something similar. What does this mean? It means you have no .plan file. And what's a .plan file? It's just a text file named ".plan" whose contents are printed under "Plan:" when someone fingers you. The idea is that you'll write what you're up to there. Many people use them like a signature file, to tell jokes, spread pet information, or whatever.

FIGURE 4.1

Fingering xian@netcom.com, I get my real name and the name of the machine I'm currently logged on to (under Host). Then there's my "Plan."

```
                    Terminal - NETCOM.TRM
 File  Edit  Settings  Phone  Transfers  Help
cougar      Phillip Lee            t4    3 Fri 12:53  hpccoa.corp.hp.c
mld         Matthew Deter          t5      Fri 11:38  NETCOM-sac2.netc
pwd         Philip W. Dalrymple    t7      Fri 12:53  NETCOM-at12.netc
jshunter    James                  ta   13 Fri 12:55  www.net.effects.
{netcom12:35} finger xian@netcom.com
[netcom]

Christian T.S. Crumlish (xian)
Home: /u39/xian
Shell: /bin/csh
New mail since Fri Jul  1 12:57:55 1994
Has not read mail for  0:13:20.
     User       Real Name                    Idle  TTY  Host         Console Location
     xian       Christian T.S. Crumlish                 p9 netcom12  (NETCOM-al3.netco)

Plan:
Right now I'm working on
_A_Guided_Tour_of_the_Internet_
for SYBEX, beta testing Netcom's
upcoming NetCruiser for Windows[TM]
software, and experimenting a lot
with the WorldWide Web.

{netcom12:36}
```

My real name

My plan

Some versions of finger also look for a .project file. This is also a text file. It's there for describing your current project.

See Chapter 5 for more on creating text files, especially if you don't have access to vi.

To make a plan file in vi, just type **vi .plan** (yes, including the period) and press Enter. Press **i** to start inserting text, and then type your plan. When you are done, press Esc, then type **:wq** and press Enter.

Once you've created a .plan file, finger your address again to see if it shows up. If not, you have to make it readable to others. At the UNIX prompt, type **chmod a+x $HOME** and press Enter, then **chmod a+r $HOME/.plan%** and press Enter again.

The first command lets people look at files in your home directory when they specify them by name. The second command specifically makes your .plan file readable to others.

Finding People with Whois

Another (equally unreliable) way to look for people is to consult a Whois database. You do this by typing **whois *name*** at

Finding People with Netfind   **49**

> ### finger the Pop Machine
>
> There's a story going around Internet and Usenet circles about a Computer Science department at a university, at which some clever person set up a fingerable address that could give current information on the status of the soda pop machine down the hall. It would tell how cold the sodas were in each slot (or how long it had been since they were refilled) and how many sodas were left.
>
> It turns out this story is true, and soda machines are on the Net at more than one university. To finger the soda machine at RIT, for example, type **finger drink@drink.csh.rit.edu** at the UNIX prompt and press Enter.

the UNIX prompt and pressing Enter. (Use the person's real last name.) To search for a first and last name, type it like so: **whois ' lastname, firstname ' .**

If you have to specify the Whois database you want to consult, you put **–h** and then the address of the host database. For example, **whois -h rs.internic.net crumlish**.

Finding People with Netfind

Yet another unreliable service for seeking people out on the net is Netfind. Netfind is a program that looks in databases of users for matches to your search criteria. You run Netfind by logging on to one of the sites that hosts the program.

There are different versions of the program, but for each of them, you're usually just making choices off menus, so they're fairly easy to use.

> For more information on whois, type **man whois** and press Enter at the UNIX prompt.

To run Netfind, telnet to one of the following addresses (type **telnet *address*** and press Enter) and log in as **netfind** (no password required).

> I'll explain telnet in Chapter 13. For now you'll just have to trust me and do *exactly* what I tell you.

archie.au	Melbourne, Australia
bruno.cs.colorado.edu	Boulder, CO
dino.conicit.ve	Venezuela
ds.internic.net	S. Plainfield, NJ
eis.calstate.edu	Fullerton, CA
hto-e.usc.edu	Los Angeles, CA
krnic.net	Taejon, Korea
lincoln.technet.sg	Singapore
malloco.ing.puc.cl	Santiago, Chile
monolith.cc.ic.ac.uk	London, U.K.
mudhoney.micro.umn.edu	Minneapolis, MN
netfind.anu.edu.au	Canberra, Australia
netfind.ee.mcgill.ca	Montreal, Canada
netfind.icm.edu.pl	Warsaw, Poland
netfind.if.usp.br	Sao Paulo, Brazil
netfind.oc.com	Dallas, TX
netfind.sjsu.edu	San Jose, CA
netfind.vslib.cz	Czech Republic
nic.nm.kr	Taejon, Korea
nic.uakom.sk	Banska Bystrica, Slovakia
redmont.cis.uab.edu	Birmingham, AL

Figure 4.2 shows me telnetting to netfind.sjsu.edu.

Finding People with Netfind

FIGURE 4.2

```
{netcom12:48} telnet netfind.sjsu.edu
Trying...
Connected to pascal.SJSU.EDU.
Escape character is '^]'.

SunOS UNIX (pascal)

login: netfind
```

I telnet to netfind.sjsu.edu and log in as netfind.

Netfind spews out a partial list of other Netfind telnet sites and then gives me five choices.

In this version of Netfind, choose 1 for help, 2 to start your search, or 5 to quit (and press Enter). I press 2 and enter what Netfind calls "search keys." You can string together any number of words for Netfind to search for, all separated by spaces. To have Netfind search for two or more words together, you have to put them in double quotation marks. The only way to specify a host address, such as netcom.com, is to put it in quotes without the period, as in Figure 4.3. Don't forget to press Enter.

FIGURE 4.3

```
                    Terminal - NETCOM.TRM
File  Edit  Settings  Phone  Transfers  Help
         monolith.cc.ic.ac.uk (Imperial College, London, England)
         mudhoney.micro.umn.edu (University of Minnesota, Minneapolis)
         netfind.anu.edu.au (Australian National University, Canberra)
         netfind.ee.mcgill.ca (McGill University, Montreal, Quebec, Canada)
         netfind.if.usp.br (University of Sao Paulo, Sao Paulo, Brazil)
         netfind.oc.com (OpenConnect Systems, Dallas, Texas)
         netfind.vslib.cz (Liberec University of Technology, Czech Republic)
         nic.nm.kr (Korea Network Information Center, Taejon, Korea)
         nic.uakom.sk (Academy of Sciences, Banska Bystrica, Slovakia)
         redmont.cis.uab.edu (University of Alabama at Birmingham)

I think that your terminal can display 24 lines.  If this is wrong,
please enter the "Options" menu and set the correct number of lines.

Top level choices:
         1. Help
         2. Search
         3. Seed database lookup
         4. Options
         5. Quit (exit server)
--> 2
Enter person and keys (blank to exit) --> crumlish "netcom com"
                                          Search Keys
```

I type 2 to start a search and then enter my last name and the host address of my service provider, Netcom.

To return to the first menu after a search, just press Enter. To quit from the main menu, press 5 or q and press Enter.

Asking the Knowbot

*To get a Knowbot manual e-mailed to you, put the word **man** on a line by itself in your message.*

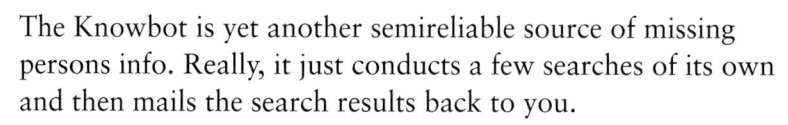

The Knowbot is yet another semireliable source of missing persons info. Really, it just conducts a few searches of its own and then mails the search results back to you.

You contact the Knowbot by e-mail, by sending a message to kis@nri.reston.va.us —it doesn't matter what you put in the subject line of the message. In the body of the message, type query *username@host.subdomain.domain*. You can include as many query lines as you like.

Figure 4.4 shows my message to the Knowbot. I'm querying after my username and my "real name," and I'm asking for a Knowbot manual.

FIGURE 4.4

A message for the Knowbot. Two queries and a request for a manual.

```
                    Terminal - NETCOM.TRM
File  Edit  Settings  Phone  Transfers  Help
query xian
query christian crumlish
man
--
Christian T.S. Crumlish         Writer
1017 Bayview Avenue             Painter
Oakland, CA 94610-4032          Editor
xian@netcom.com                 you name it
~
~
```

Chatting in Realtime

This is also where the mass media goes hunting for stories of "computer sex." Watch out if you have a female sounding login or "real name."

If you're in the mood for immediate communication, rather than tag games in e-mail or mass-market publication on Usenet, then you can look for people with similar interests and "chat" with them in realtime.

"Talking" from Screen to Screen

There is an even more intrusive form of communication possible across a lot of the Net, called talk. With the talk command (**talk username@address**), you send words directly to someone's screen. Actually, first they'll get a "talk request" from a server (called a "daemon"). They'll have to type **talk your-address** to get the line of communication open. I recommend that you use this only for emergencies and announcements.

Chatting is a form of immediate communication. With a chat program, you join conversations, and then whatever you type appears on the screen of everyone else in the conversation (you can also direct messages to specific people). It's not unlike talking over the telephone with teletype machines. With too many people, conversations degenerate into what net.folk call "noise." With the right amount of people, a sort of conversation or debate can take place.

The geeky terms for the difference between chat and e-mail is that chat is *synchronous* (happening for all participants at the same time) and e-mail is *asynchronous* (taking place variously at different times). Telephones are synchronous, answering machines are asynchronous, beepers are synchronous, and voice mail is asynchronous. U.S. Mail is totally asynchronous.

I prefer e-mail to chat, because I like considering my replies in writing and responding when the time is best for me.

Bull Sessions on the irc

To check out chat, type **irc** at the UNIX prompt and press Enter. (irc stands for "internet relay chat.") If this command is not recognized, try typing **chat** at the prompt and pressing Enter. The program called chat is older than irc and has been replaced on most systems, but if it's all you've got, give it a try.

If your provider does not offer irc or any chat program, you can telnet to a host that does. Chapter 13 explains telnet.

People will also be able to see your "real name" (or whatever you've set it to with chfn), with the /who command. To change that, you have to type **setenv ircname "the real name you want between quotation marks"** at the UNIX prompt and press Enter. (You can also put this command in any of your startup files, such as .login, .profile, or .cshrc.)

Some conversations are kept open by what are called "bots" or "'bots." These are robotic (participants in the conversation). Some of them are not bad conversationalists compared with a lot of real people.

Some conversations are "invitation only." This means someone in the conversation has to give you a password or invite you to join.

The program will start. It will tell you if your login conflicts with any other one currently on the system. If so, you'll have to change your irc nick (name). You may want to change it anyway. To do so type **/nick** *newnickname* at the irc prompt. All irc commands start with /.

See What's Going On

Use the /list command to see what conversations are out there going on. Conversation names all start with #. You can specify a minimum and maximum number of participants for the groups the /list command should list. For example, try **/list –min 3 –max 4** and press Enter.

Join a Conversation

To join a conversation, type **/join #***conversation*.

Type **/who #***conversation* to get a list of who else is "on."

Your End of the Conversation

To talk to the whole group, just type and press Enter. To send a message to one person, type **/***their-nick your message*.

To leave the conversation, type **/join 0**. To quit irc, type **/quit**.

For more information on irc, see the irc FAQ that is posted regularly to the comp.answers Usenet newsgroup. There is another irc FAQ put together by Undernet that is also posted regularly to comp.answers. See Chapters 7 and 8 for more about Usenet newsgroups.

At any point, you can get help by typing **/help** and pressing Enter. People will help you out usually if you just ask questions.

CHAPTER 5

Composing Mail and Creating Files with Text Editors

Featuring

- Different ways to compose mail messages
- Changing your text editor
- Writing messages in vi
- Writing messages in pine or pico

When it comes to writing, UNIX provides text editors, not word-processing programs. If you ever complain to a UNIX geek about the quality of vi, for example, you'll be told that it's not supposed to be a word processor—just a text editor. You know, for writing code. The fact is that you have to use these programs as word processors, and they're basically throwbacks to the stone age of text editing, when just being full-screen was state of the art.

Composing Mail

When it comes to composing mail (or Usenet posts), there are really three different ways to write the text. There's the easy way, the familiar way, and the advanced way:

- **The easy way:** Run the mail program, get dumped into a text editor, write the mail, exit the editor, and send the mail. This approach is explained in Chapter 3.

- **The familiar way:** Compose your mail on your own computer in your favorite word processor, save the message as a text file, run the mail program, get dumped into a text editor, and then "send" the text file to it with your terminal program. (You can also try cutting and pasting directly through Windows or uploading a big file ahead of time.)

- **The advanced way:** Compose mail first in a UNIX editor, run your e-mail program, get dumped into a text editor, read in the completed file, exit the editor, and send the mail.

> With what I explain in this chapter, you'll also be able to run a text editor and create a text file, even when it has nothing to do with mail.

Using a Word Processor

You can write your message in your favorite word processor and then cut it and paste it into the terminal window (once you have your e-mail and text-editor programs running). However, cut and paste does not always work. You can exceed the buffer of your modem by trying to squeeze too much text through it too fast, and your selection might also have some special hidden characters in it that will screw up your connection.

Another problem with putting word-processed text into e-mail messages is that some word processors substitute special characters for apostrophes and quotation marks. These special characters come out as garbage characters that make your mail harder to read. Also, there are sometimes problems with

> If you're writing your message in a word processor, planning to eventually insert it into a message from elm, use a large font size in your word processor. This will ensure that your lines aren't too long.

Using a Word Processor

line breaks, either with lines being too long, or with extraneous ^M characters appearing at the end of each line.

So cut and paste is a little crude for our needs here. Fortunately, communications programs have a built-in way to send text files, usually on a menu called Transfer. There are four kinds of transfers: sending a binary file, receiving a binary file, sending a text file, and receiving a text file. Binary files may consist of anything. Text files must be text only.

In Chapter 10 I explain more about sending and receiving files.

First save your message as a text file. Figure 5.1 shows a text file I created in Word for Windows 6.0.

Then close the file, so it is available to other programs. Then switch back to your terminal window and run your mail program. Get a message started, make sure you're in insert mode, and then choose to send a text file. Specify the text file you just created.

FIGURE 5.1

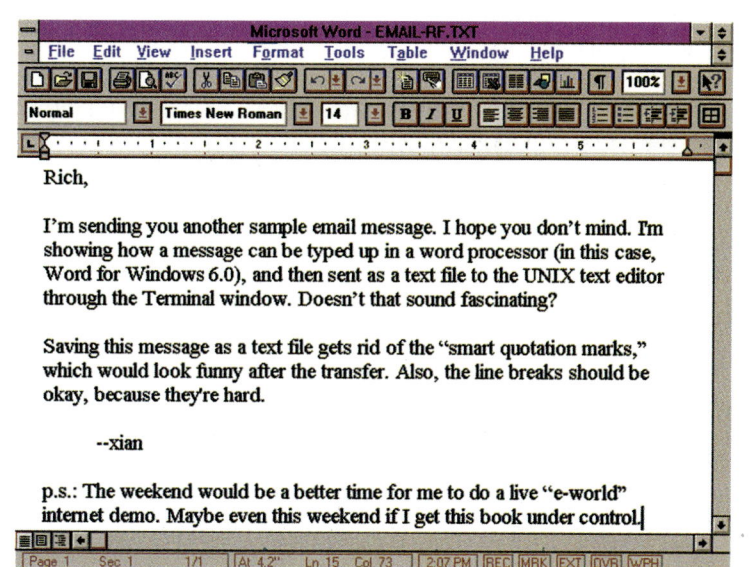

I created this file in Word for Windows 6.0. Now I'm going to save it as a text file.

For elm, put hard line breaks at the end of each line (press Enter). That way the lines won't run together when you transfer the file to your text editor in UNIX.

COMPOSING MAIL WITH TEXT EDITORS

Uploading is explained in Chapter 10. Reading files into text editors is explained in this chapter.

The text will appear in the text editor as if you typed it there.

Another way to handle a text file edited on your home computer, especially a long one, is to upload it (send it as a binary file), and then read it into your text editor. One way to upload a file is to type **kermit –r** at the UNIX prompt and press Enter. Then, from within your communications program, choose to send a binary file and select the text file to upload.

Changing Your Editor

As you saw in Chapter 3, as soon as you start creating a mail message, your mailer program dumps you into a text editor, without asking you which one you prefer. For elm and for every other mail program, you can specify a different editor if you wish.

You can also change your newsreader's default editor. See Chapter 8 for details.

To set a different text editor as your default, first figure out where exactly the text editor is located. You'll need its full path—the directories and subdirectories that lead to it.

To change the default editor for all mail programs besides elm, put the line **setenv EDITOR /full-path/filename** in your .login file (or .profile or .cshrc).

If you use elm, run it. Then press **o** (for options). This brings up the Options Editor. Press **e** to go to the Editor (primary) line. Type the path and filename of the editor you want as the default. Then press Enter. Then type **>** to save the change.

See Chapter 9 for an explanation of paths, files, directories, and so on.

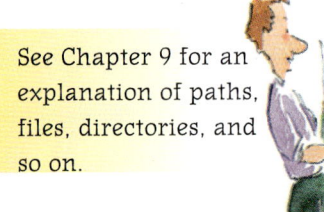

General Text-Editor Stuff

There's a fairly short list of things you need to know, no matter what text editor you use. You have to know how to

- start the program
- type

- save your work
- exit the program
- get help
- continue with a preexisting file
- start a new file
- move around
- do cut-and-paste editing

You also might want to know how to

- make simple corrections *and*
- check your spelling

I'll explain how to do all of these things in the two most popular and common UNIX editors, vi and pico. There are many other text editors floating around the Internet world, such as ed, a line-at-a-time editor; joe, which uses WordStar-style commands; ee, another visual editor; and emacs, which is more of a full UNIX environment than a text editor. They all have their staunch defenders and they're all good for something (except maybe ed, which is good for nothing). If you prefer another editor, search the **man pages** *or help information for how to do all of the above.*

vi Basics

The next few sections cover the basics of vi, one of the most common UNIX text-editing programs.

Starting vi

To start vi, type **vi** at the UNIX prompt and press Enter. To start vi and open up a file at the same time, type **vi *filename*** and press Enter. It doesn't matter if *filename* exists yet: vi will create it if necessary.

Typing in vi

To start typing in vi, press **i**, **a**, or **o**. Type **i** to *i*nsert text before the character the cursor is on. Type **a** to insert text *a*fter the character the cursor is on. Type **o** to insert text *o*n a new line.

You don't need to start vi if your e-mail program starts it for you.

You have to press Enter when you get near the end of a line.

To stop typing and start editing, press Esc.

Saving Your Work in vi

To save the file you're working on, press Esc, and then type **:w** and press Enter. To give the file a new name, press Esc, and then type **:w** *newfilename* and press Enter.

The w stands for write. Programmers call saving "writing to a file" and retrieving "reading from a file."

Exiting vi

To exit vi, press Esc and then do one of the following: To quit without saving, type **:q** and press Enter (if you've made changes, and you still want to quit without saving them, type **:q!** and press Enter).

To quit and save, type **:wq** or **ZZ** and press Enter.

Getting Help in vi

There is no built-in help for vi, so you're stuck struggling with man pages and asking people if you get stuck. There are some good quick-references floating around the Net, and there are even real books you can buy in stores. This section of this chapter should cover most of your questions, though.

*Some systems have a built-in tutorial that runs vi and gives you examples to try. To see if you have that tutorial available, type **teachvi** at the UNIX prompt and then press Enter.*

Opening Files in vi

To continue working on a preexisting file with vi, just press Esc, and then type **:r** *filename* and press Enter. To start working on a new file, quit and run the program again.

Moving Around in vi

Here is a chart of cursor-movement commands for vi.

To move	Press
To the beginning of a line	^
To the beginning of the document	1G
To the end of the document	G
Up 11 lines	Ctrl-U
Down 11 lines	Ctrl-D
Up one screenful	Ctrl-B
Down one screenful	Ctrl-F
One character to the left	h *or* Backspace *or* ←
One character to the right	l *or* the spacebar *or* →
One line down	j *or* Enter *or* ↓
One line up	k *or* – *or* ↑
Back one word	b
Forward one word	w

For all of these commands, you must press Esc first. For most of them, you can type a number first and have the movement or action take place that number of times.

Simple Editing with vi

To go from typing to editing in vi, you have to first press Esc. To delete a single character, place the cursor on it and type **x**. To delete more than one character, place the cursor on the first one you want to delete and type *nx*, with *n* being the number of characters you want to delete. For example, **7x** would delete seven characters, starting with the one the cursor's on.

To delete a single word, put the cursor on it and type **dw**. (You can precede dw with a number to delete that number of

If you are in the middle of a line when you press Esc, the cursor will move one character to the left. Remember to press the spacebar to move back one to the right, if you intend to delete or insert characters where the cursor was.

words: **9dw** would delete nine words, starting with the one the cursor's in, for example.)

To delete a single line, put the cursor on it and type **dd**. (You can precede dd with a number to delete that number of lines from the current line downward.)

Cut-and-Paste Editing with vi

You can only cut and paste an entire line at a time with vi. To cut a line, put the cursor on it and type **Y**. To paste the cut line, move the cursor. Then, to put the line after the current line, type **p**. To put the line before the current line, type **P**.

Checking Your Spelling with vi

vi has no built in spellchecker, but elm does. When you have completed editing your message and have quit vi, you will be returned to elm. Then, before sending the message, type **i**. This will start a spellchecking routine.

It can get real confusing switching from one kind of word processor to another. Usually after I've been working with vi a lot, I make all kinds of strange errors in Word for Windows, such as typing jjjjjjjj when I want to go up a few lines.

Don't Look Like a Newbie

Looking like a newbie is forgivable, as we've all been there at one time or another. Nevertheless, no one wants to be caught with their digital pants down, so here's a couple of things to look out for:

Typing vi commands into your file: If you forget to press Esc first, your message might end up with the word ":wq" on the bottom line. If so, delete it.

The first few characters are missing: If you forget to press **i**, **a**, or **o** to start typing, the first few characters you type will not appear—not until you hit **i**, **a**, or **o** by mistake. Reread the beginning of your mail to see if you're missing anything (and again any time you switch back from editing).

pico Basics

The e-mail program pine has a built-in text editor. People liked it so much that it was spun off into a text editor called pico. The next few sections cover the basics of pico.

Starting pico

To start pico, type *pico* at the UNIX prompt and press Enter (unless your e-mail program has already started it for you). To start pico and open up a file at the same time, type *pico filename* and press Enter. If *filename* doesn't yet exist, pico will create it.

Typing in pico

Typing is easy in pico. Just type. Press Enter only to start new paragraphs. pico will handle the normal word-wrapping.

Saving Your Work in pico

To save the file you're working on, press Ctrl-O. This, along with most other useful commands, is listed at the bottom of the screen.

If Ctrl-V doesn't work, try Ctrl-Shift-V. (If you're in Windows, your comm program might interpret Ctrl-V as Paste.)

Exiting pico

To exit pico, press Ctrl-X. You will be asked if you want to save the file you're working on. Type *Y* or *N*.

Getting Help in pico

To get help in pico, type Ctrl-G. Then press Ctrl-V to see each following page of the help text.

Opening Files in pico

To continue working on a preexisting file with pico, press Ctrl-R and then name the file you want "read" in.

To work with a new file, exit pico and then start over.

Moving Around in pico

Here is a chart of cursor-movement commands for pico:

To Move	Press
To the beginning of the line	Ctrl-A
To the end of the line	Ctrl-E
Up one screenful	Ctrl-Y
Down one screenful	Ctrl-V
One character to the left	Ctrl-B or ←
One character to the right	Ctrl-F or →
One line down	Ctrl-N or ↓
One line up	Ctrl-P or ↑

Depending on your terminal-preference settings, you might be able to move around in pico with your arrow keys.

Simple Editing with pico

To delete a single character, place the cursor on it and press Ctrl-D.

To delete a selection, first mark it. Mark the beginning of the selection with Ctrl-^. Then move the cursor past the end of the selection. (The end of the selection is the character to the left of the cursor.) Then press Ctrl-D to delete the selection.

Cut-and-Paste Editing with pico

To cut text, first select it. Put the cursor on the first character of the selection and press Ctrl-^. Then move the cursor past the end of the selection. (The end of the selection is the character to the left of the cursor.)

Then press Ctrl-K to cut the selected text. If nothing is selected, Ctrl-K cuts the line the cursor is on.

Move the cursor to the character you want to insert before, and then press Ctrl-U.

You can press Ctrl-^ again to deselect a selection.

Checking Your Spelling with pico

To check your spelling with pico, press Ctrl-T.

Attaching Files to E-mail

Internet mail generally consists only of straight text files, although there are some "protocols" for sending other forms of information. For example, some mail programs use MIME (Multipurpose Internet Mail Extensions) to send other kinds of data. If you are sent e-mail with a MIME attachment, you may not be able to see the pictures, hear the music, or view the movies, but the text in the attachment should come through just fine. You'll be asked if you want to view it or save it.

Nevertheless, you *can* still send other types of files as attachments to e-mail. The trick is that you have to *uuencode* (pronounced "you-you-encode") them. Converting files with uuencode turns them into a string of regular characters. Once you've done that, the characters can be included in regular mail. Then the recipient simply needs to uudecode the file you've sent and the transfer is complete.

Unencoding makes files about one-third longer, so they take longer to transfer and can cost you more in phone bills and connect time.

See Chapter 10 for a thorough explanation of uploading and downloading files.

Sending Uuencoded Files

To send a file through e-mail, first compress it as much as possible with an archiving program, such as PKZIP, LHARC, or BinHex. Make sure that you use a program that your recipient also has, so they can expand the archive file at their end. Next, upload the file to your Internet account through your terminal program.

One way to do this is to set your binary transfer protocol to Kermit in your terminal program. Then, at the UNIX prompt, type **kermit –r –i** (the –r means receive, the –i means a binary file) and press Enter. Then, in the communications program, choose to send a binary file. (In Terminal, that's Transfers ➤ Send Binary File.) Then wait.

Once the file is uploaded, you can uuencode it. The basic form of the uuencode command is as follows:

uuencode old-filename new-filename > text-filename

where *old-filename* is the name of the file you've just uploaded, *new-filename* is the name the file will get after the recipient uudecodes it (usually the same as *old-filename*), and *text-filename* is the name of the temporary text file that contains the uuencoded file.

Then you simply "read" the uuencoded file into a mail message and send it. The recipient will either be prompted to uudecode the file or be given the file automatically uudecoded.

Receiving Uuencoded Files

If you receive a mail message with a uuencoded inclusion, save the message to a file. (In elm, you type **s** and then specify a file name.) Then leave the mail program and type **uudecode** *file-name* at the UNIX prompt (using the file name you just assigned) and press Enter. You don't have to specify the name the uudecoded file will have—that's specified on the begin line of the uuencoded file.

Then, if necessary, send the file back to your home computer and decompress it.

Receiving Other Kinds of Files

For most other forms of attached files (such as BinHex, which comes from Macintoshes), your mail program will prompt you to decide whether you want the file to be displayed on the screen or saved to a file.

See Chapter 9 for more on managing your files.

Privacy and Security

Internet e-mail is *not* secure. When you send mail to someone else on the Net, it passes through many other networks and computers along the way. There's nothing to stop administrators on any of those intervening machines from reading the contents of your mail message. In a sense, e-mail messages are a lot more like postcards than like letters. To start with, then, don't write anything in an e-mail message that you couldn't afford to have strangers read.

Encrypt Your E-mail

If you do want to send secure e-mail, you'll need to *encrypt* your messages. To encrypt them means to convert them with a cipher into an unreadable form. In one type of encryption popular on the net, you have two keys, a *public* key and a *private* key. You give the public key to anyone who asks. Anyone with your public key can send you a message only you can decrypt. Also, you can "sign" your mail with your private key, and then anyone with your public key can verify that it came from you.

One of the best-known encryption packages is PGP (it stands for Pretty Good Privacy), a shareware program that is available for UNIX, the Macintosh, and DOS, and will eventually be available for Windows also. If you dial-up to a UNIX

Read the Usenet newsgroups alt.security, alt.privacy, comp.eff.talk, comp.security.announce, and comp.security.misc to find out more about specific encryption software and other issues of privacy in the world of electronic communications. I should warn you that some pretty kooky people post to some of these groups. Chapters 7 and 8 discuss Usenet.

PGP is somewhat controversial. The U.S. Government has asserted that its easy availability on the Internet violated federal laws against the export of encryption software. There are different versions of PGP around and not all of them raise the same hackles. The trick is to get your copy from a site on the same side of the U.S. border that you're on. For up-to-date information on this subject, read the alt.security.pgp Usenet newsgroup.

Some people are opposed to anonymous remailers because they might allow people to hide behind anonymity while harassing or attacking others on the Net. On Usenet, some people will criticize anonymous posters for not signing their names to their posts. But people have their own reasons for wanting their privacy, and anonymity is essential to newsgroups such as alt.sexual.abuse.recovery.

account through a Windows communications program, you'll have to compose your mail offline, switch to a DOS prompt to encrypt your mail with PGP for DOS, and then upload your mail messages to send them.

To find ftp sites with the latest version of PGP for your desktop computer, point your Web browser at http://www.mantis.co.uk/pgp/pgp.html or run an archie search for the word *pgp*. An article called *Where to get the latest PGP (Pretty Good Privacy) FAQ* is posted monthly to alt.security.pgp, news.answers, and alt.answers.

E-Mail and Post Anonymously

Another form of privacy available on the Net is anonymity. There are a number of servers on the Net that function as anonymous remailers. This means you send mail to them, indicating the ultimate destination, and they remail your message with all identifying headers and signatures stripped off. If someone replies to your mail (or Usenet post), the reply likewise goes through the remailer and is "anonymized."

The most well known anonymous remailing service is anon.penet.fi. For information on how to use it, send mail with any subject, any contents to help@anon.penet.fi. If you're serious about anonymity, don't rely on just one remailer. To get information about another remailer, send mail to remailer@soda.csua.berkeley.edu with remailer-info as your subject.

CHAPTER 6

Getting on Mailing Lists

Featuring

- Finding interesting lists
- Subscribing to lists
- Unsubscribing to lists
- Putting in your two cents

Another benefit of e-mail is that it gives you the ability to participate in mailing lists. The computer makes it easy to send the same piece of e-mail to any number of addresses. The simplest kind of a mailing list is an alias (or address book entry) that corresponds to a list of e-mail addresses, but the more interesting kind of mailing list (or just "list") allows anyone to send mail to a single address and have it forwarded to everyone on the list. These lists function as discussion groups for any subject you can imagine, with subscribers all over the globe.

Anyone with an Internet mailing address can participate in lists of this sort. And every subscriber can be a contributor as well. Sending a message to a mailing list is called *posting*.

Not sure what I mean by aliases and address books? They're explained in Chapter 3.

Mailing Lists versus Usenet Newsgroups

Another way for people to share common interests by exchanging messages over the Internet is by participating in Usenet newsgroups.

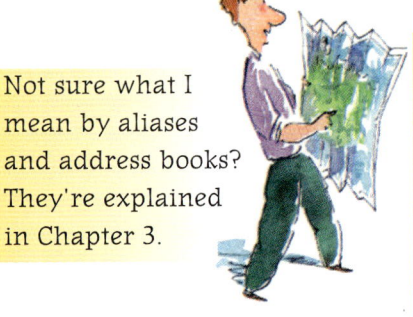

Mailing lists have been around longer than Usenet and are more universal, as anyone with Internet access, even without Usenet, can participate in mailing lists. Lists generally have less traffic (fewer "posts") than newsgroups, but there are some very large, very busy lists and some pretty dead newsgroups. Busy lists fill up your mailbox, whereas newsgroup posts are not sent to you directly. Chapter 7 explains Usenet and Chapter 8 tells you how to "read" it.

Sometimes mailing lists "become" newsgroups. Usually this means that there is a "gate" between a list and a corresponding newsgroup, and all posts are shared between them. Most of these decisions are made by plebiscite, by polling the readership. Some people feel that lists are more private, even when they are open to anyone, because they are harder to find—if you don't know where to look.

Some lists are available as digests. This means that posts are grouped together and sent out less often. You might receive, say, ten posts in a single mailing. If you subscribe to a list and then find that the traffic is too much for you to handle—look into whether it is also available in a "digestified" form.

There are moderated lists, for which a volunteer reviews each submitted post and decides first whether it is relevant or "on-charter" for the list. Most lists are unmoderated and rely on peer pressure to keep posts in line.

If you subscribe to a busy list or several lists and then don't read and clear out your mail box for a while, it can fill up and even exceed your system's limitations. This could result in your losing mail. So if you *do* subscribe to some lists, be sure to check your mail regularly.

Finding Mailing Lists

So how do you find the lists you'd be interested in? There's no single way. To some extent, all information on the Net flows by word of mouth (or e-mail, more likely). People will tell you about mailing lists. I've heard about some of the lists I subscribe to in Usenet newsgroups. There are also some large "lists of lists" out there that you can consult and peruse.

General Lists of Lists

I know of two e-mail addresses you can send to so as to have lists of lists mailed back to you. The first one is so large that it is broken into eight parts. Send mail to **mail-server@rtfm.mit.edu**. The Subject: line can be anything—blank is fine. The message should contain just this line:

> send usenet/news.answers/mail/mailing-lists/part1

You will receive part1 as e-mail. Save the message to a file and then browse it in a text editor, or by typing **more part1** and pressing Enter, and then pressing the spacebar to see each next screenful.

Send the same message, but substitute **part2**, **part3**, and so on, all the way up to **part8**, to obtain the entire list.

For another good list of lists, send e-mail to

> bbslist@aug3.augsburg.edu

The Subject: line and contents of the message can be anything. It doesn't matter. In addition to the lists of lists, you'll get a lot of other useful Internet information sent to you. Save the e-mail you receive in return and skim it as I just explained.

> These lists are long and will take up a lot of disk space. If you find what you're looking for, delete them. You can always get the updated versions in the future with the same method.

> Look for a fairly thorough list of lists posted regularly to the news.announce.new users newsgroup, with the subject "Publicly Accessible Mailing Lists." See Chapters 7 and 8 for more on Usenet newsgroups.

Specific Lists of Lists

You can seek out lists that relate to a specific topic by sending mail to listserv@bitnic.educom.edu. Leave the subject blank. Include the line list global / topic in your message and use whatever word you want for *topic*. (Also, delete your signature if you've got one. The listserv will try to interpret it as commands.)

Figure 6.1 shows the mail I got in response when I sent the message list global / bicycle to the bitnic listserv.

If you are interested in music, you might want to see the musical list of lists, which is updated regularly. Send mail to mlol-request@wariat.org and the current list will be sent to you.

> You *can* send mail to this address and just include the line list global without specifying a topic, but then the message sent back to you will be incredibly long. You're much better off limiting the responses in some way.

FIGURE 6.1

Well, there's at least one cycling list out there.

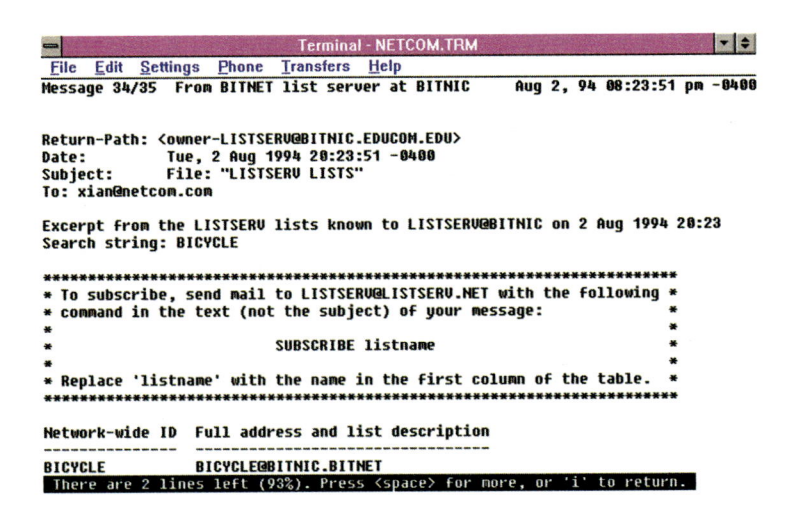

```
                    Terminal - NETCOM.TRM
File  Edit  Settings  Phone  Transfers  Help
Message 34/35  From BITNET list server at BITNIC    Aug 2, 94 08:23:51 pm -0400

Return-Path: <owner-LISTSERV@BITNIC.EDUCOM.EDU>
Date:          Tue, 2 Aug 1994 20:23:51 -0400
Subject:       File: "LISTSERV LISTS"
To: xian@netcom.com

Excerpt from the LISTSERV lists known to LISTSERV@BITNIC on 2 Aug 1994 20:23
Search string: BICYCLE

************************************************************************
* To subscribe, send mail to LISTSERV@LISTSERV.NET with the following   *
* command in the text (not the subject) of your message:                *
*                                                                       *
*                      SUBSCRIBE listname                                *
*                                                                       *
* Replace 'listname' with the name in the first column of the table.    *
************************************************************************

Network-wide ID   Full address and list description
---------------   ---------------------------------
BICYCLE           BICYCLE@BITNIC.BITNET
There are 2 lines left (93%). Press <space> for more, or 'i' to return.
```

Subscribing to Lists

The first and most important thing I can tell you is that to subscribe to a mailing list, you send a message to an address *different from the mailing list address.* People constantly make the mistake of sending their subscription requests directly to the lists in question. This results in everyone on the list having to read your mistaken post.

The next thing you need to know is that there are two different kinds of lists. Once you're on the list, it won't make any difference to you. There are lists administered by real live people and there are automated lists—lists that are run by programs called "listservs."

You'll need to know what sort of list you're subscribing to ahead of time. If the address you've found for subscribing to a list is of the form *list*-request@*address* (with *list* being the name of the mailing list), then the list is handled by a person. If the address starts with listserv@ or majordomo@, then the list is handled by a program (or robot or 'bot).

It's embarrassing to you and annoying to everyone else on a mailing list when you send your requests to the list itself instead of to the administrative address. Be careful.

People-Administered Lists

To subscribe to a person-administered list, send e-mail to the "request" address for the list. This address should be of the form **list-request@address**.

Since this message will be read by a human being, write a normal sentence to the effect that you'd like to subscribe to the list. Include your e-mail address, just to be sure it comes through okay.

The administrator will acknowledge your mail and send you the actual address (for posting) of the list. She might also send you some additional information.

So, for example, to join the campervan-etc list, to discuss the now-defunct rock band Camper van Beethoven and related groups, I sent to the address **campervan-etc-request@list. Stanford.EDU** a message that said something like "Hi, I'd like to subscribe to the campervan-etc list. My e-mail address is xian@netcom.com. Thanks!"

There's another popular list-server program out there called majordomo. The instructions for subscribing to a majordomo-administered list are the same, but the e-mail address you send to starts with the word **majordomo**, naturally enough, instead of **listserv**.

GETTING ON MAILING LISTS

No human will read your message. Only a computer program. So don't gussy up the language to make it sound natural. Include only the key words listed here. To get help, send a message to the same address with just the word *help* in it.

For a constant update of the newest listserv lists, send e-mail to **listserv@ndsuvm1.bitnet**. Include only the line **subscribe NEW-LIST Your Name**. You can also read the Usenet newsgroup bit.listserv.new-list for the same information. Usenet newsgroups are explained in Chapters 7 and 8.

Robot-Administered Lists

The listserv program runs on IBM computers and mailing lists handled by listserv originate from Bitnet—a different network from the Internet. Because Bitnet sends mail to and from Internet without problems, you can subscribe to these lists from your Internet account.

To subscribe to a listserv list, send mail to the contact address of the list, which should be of the form **listserv@*host.bitnet*** (or **majordomo@*address***). Leave the subject line blank. Include in your message only the line **subscribe** *list Your Name*. Use the name of the list for *list*. Put your real first and last name on that line, not your e-mail address. You will receive a confirmation and a welcome message in response.

So, for example, to join the Top-Ten list, whose moderator sends out the David Letterman Top Ten list each night, I sent to the address **listserv@tamvm1.tamu.edu** a one-line message, reading **subscribe TOP-TEN Christian Crumlish**.

Unsubscribing to Lists

If you tire of a list, you can simply unsubscribe to it. Again, it's different for people and robots.

People-Administered Lists

Send e-mail to the original *list*-request address, asking "Please unsubscribe me," or words to that effect.

Robot-Administered Lists

Send e-mail to the original listserv@ address, with no subject and only the line **signoff** *list*, substituting the name of the list for *list*, of course.

Temporarily Unsubscribing

If you're going on vacation, you can temporarily cancel your subscription by sending to the listserv@ address the message **set** *list* **nomail**. When you return, send the message **set** *list* **mail** to start up your subscription again.

Posting to Lists

There are two ways to post to mailing lists. The first is to send mail to the list address. The other way is to reply to a message from the list, when the return address is set to the list itself. This varies from list to list, so watch out you don't do this by mistake when you mean to reply to someone directly.

Remember that you always have the option of sending mail just to the person whose post you're replying to, though you may have to copy that person's address and then mail to it directly.

Participation

Everybody was a newbie once, and there's no such thing as a dumb question, but there are such things as frequently asked questions. Most lists eventually get around to compiling a FAQ, a document of answers to *f*requently *a*sked *q*uestions. Look for or ask for the relevant FAQ and read it before posting the first questions that come to mind. FAQs are usually fun and interesting to read—they are one of the best resources of the Net.

I highly recommend "lurking," reading the list without posting to it for a while, to get caught up on the various threads of conversations that are going on. Once you've made these reasonable efforts to get up to speed, plunge right in and start gabbing. Many people lurk most or all of the time. It's easy to

In Chapter 3, I explain what to do when you go on vacation—how to send replies telling people when you'll be back.

In general, remember that many people will read your post. If you post, it is like speaking in public. You never know who is listening, or saving what you've written. Try to ensure that your posts are "on-topic."

Always look at the header of a message before replying to it. Normally, your reply will go to the return address, but sometimes there's a "Reply-To" line, and then your reply will go to the address there.

Some people just like to make trouble and post messages designed to arouse indignation, resentment, or anger. After a while, it's easy to tell when someone has posted "flame bait," and you learn to just ignore it until it goes away. Unfortunately, there are always too many people too ready to jump in and "debate" even the most obviously insulting posts. Oh well. Fortunately, this seems to happen on mailing lists less often than it does on Usenet.

forget how many people are out there when only a small number of them post regularly.

Lists are like communities and often have their pet peeves, their unassailable truths, their opposing parties, and so on. You might experience some campaigning if someone is taking a poll or a vote. Rules of e-mail etiquette become especially important in a one-to-many forum such as a mailing list. Bear in mind that sarcasm and other subtleties that are so easy to communicate when face-to-face do not translate well in cold, hard, ASCII text. Try to say exactly what you mean and read things over before posting them. Ask yourself if what you've written might be misinterpreted.

CHAPTER 7

Usenet News

Featuring

- Usenet explained
- Newsgroups and their hierarchies
- Posts, trolls, and flames
- Usenet culture

For many people, Usenet *is* the Net. Usenet is a network of other networks, BBSs, and computers, all of which have made bilateral agreements with other members of Usenet to share and exchange "news." So what's *news*? Usenet is divided up into *newsgroups* topic areas. Newsgroups consist of *articles,* posted by their readers/contributors. The word *news* is confusing in this context, because Usenet news articles are posted by whoever wants to write them, not by a staff of reporters. The term *news* suggests that it might replace your habit of reading or skimming a daily newspaper every morning or evening.

If you have Internet access, you probably have access to Usenet. This chapter discusses what Usenet is. Chapter 8 explains how you can read news yourself.

Where Everybody Knows Your .signature

As soon as I log in to my Internet account, I immediately check my mail. After that, I compulsively run my newsreader and skim the newsgroups that I'm currently hooked on. In a sense, Usenet is where I "hang out" on the Net. I'm on some mailing lists as well, but Usenet is the mother lode of discussion groups.

Sometimes, fast-breaking real-world events appear on Usenet before they appear on TV or in the newspaper, but generally, Usenet is not the information source "of record," the way some newspapers are. Look for tabloid-style gossip in talk.rumors or among the alt.fan groups (such as the recently created alt.fan.ojsimpson.drive-faster).

People post about what they find interesting. If you post to a newsgroup looking for some information, you might be told to "go to a library" to look it up for yourself. Every newsgroup sees its share of posts that begin something like "I'm

It's been said that the fastest way to get information on Usenet is to post incorrect information, because people will immediately post to correct you or flood your e-mail inbox with the correct information. I don't recommend this, because people out there skimming the newsgroups might only see your erroneous post and none of the corrections, but it gives you an idea of the culture of Usenet.

Some Newsgroups Are Mailing Lists Too

Some Usenet newsgroups, particularly those which evolved from mailing lists, maintain something called a "gateway" with a list, so that all posts to the newsgroup or the list are shared between both. Even if you don't have Usenet access, you should still be able to join lists that correspond to Usenet newsgroups. See Chapter 6 for more on lists and Chapter 8 for how to post to Usenet through e-mail.

writing a high-school paper on..." and end with "... please reply to me by private e-mail, since I don't read this group."

On the other hand, there are plenty of "wizards" out there who believe there's no such thing as a dumb question and who are willing to share their knowledge with anyone who asks.

What Is Usenet?

Usenet has been called the biggest bulletin board in the world. It can be more entertaining than television (hard to imagine?). I think of it as an enormous magazine rack, filled with magazines, each of which have infinitely long letters-to-the-editor pages and no articles.

It's been called a huge writing project, and enthusiasts claim that we are right now involved in a renaissance of the written word, as a direct result of e-mail and Usenet communication.

Fundamentally, Usenet is a way of sharing information. Many newsgroups that are technically not part of the Usenet hierarchy flow through the same *servers* (computers that store and share news) and are passed along as part of the *newsfeed* (electronic mailpouch) from computer to computer (not unlike other long-distance carriers traveling on AT&T wires).

Your provider is not obliged to supply you with a full newsfeed. Many networks carry an incomplete feed, usually more for reasons of disk-storage limitations than corporate censorship, though some of the more controversial or shocking-sounding alt groups certainly experience a limited distribution because of their topics. Many system administrators refuse to carry "binaries" newsgroups, which generally contain huge posts each comprising part of a large binary file, as much because of the enormous storage requirements as because of the pornographic nature of some of those binary files.

Usenet is also an anarchy—with rules. Nobody reigns from above, but the entire community is knit together through customs, traditions, and "netiquette." More and more, this culture is coming under attack, most recently by greedy advertisers, deliberately misinterpreting the acceptable use of the medium. If you are interested in Usenet, familiarize yourself with the existing culture and become a net.citizen (or netizen), not one of the net.barbarians beating down the gates.

Most providers do carry all of the newsgroups in the Usenet hierarchy proper, as there are complicated plebiscite mechanisms in place to limit the proliferation of new newgroups. In the alt hierarchy, pranksters create joke newsgroups every week, some of which are probably only carried by those providers that carry everything.

What Is a Newsgroup?

So what exactly is a newsgroup? A newsgroup is an "area" for posting articles on a given topic. The topic names are arranged hierarchically, in order that people might be able to look for and find newsgroups of interest in a systematic way. This means, for example, that there's no newsgroup called nintendo, nor is there one called rec.nintendo, but there is one called rec.games.nintendo.

There are seven official Usenet hierarchies: comp, misc, news, rec, sci, soc, and talk:

> Ideally, your *newsreader* would help you work your way through a hierarchy tree to find the newsgroups you are interested in. Unfortunately, most of them just list them all flat out or allow you to search the list for key words. I'll explain all about newsreaders in Chapter 8.

Newsgroup Hierarchy	Meaning
comp	Computers—from the extremely technical to help for beginners to geek wars between Mac enthusiasts and Amiga diehards.
misc	Miscellaneous—anything that doesn't fit into the other hierarchies.
news	News—information about Usenet itself, discussion of new newsgroups, advice for Usenet newbies.
rec	Recreation—games, sports, music, entertainment, etc.
sci	Science—discussions of research, developments, techniques, policy.
soc	Social—both in the sense of socializing and in the sense of talking about society.
talk	Talk—some think this hierarchy should be called "argue"; these newsgroups house some of the eternal polarized debates, such as those about gun control and abortion.

One Way Not to Look Like a Newbie

Not that there's anything wrong with looking like a newbie, but here's one way not to give yourself away (besides confusing Usenet and the Internet): Call a newsgroup a newsgroup. Don't call it a forum, a board, a bboard, a SIG, an echo, a file, a conference, a list (well, except for the ones that also are lists), an America Online folder, or a Prodigy folder.

On the other hand, who cares if you do, besides Usenet snobs?

In addition, there's alt, the alternative hierarchy; biz, the business hierarchy, in which advertising is explicitly acceptable; gnu, for discussion of the Free Software Project; bitnet, for newsgroups "gated" to bitnet listservs, bionet, for biologists; local hierarchies for geographical regions (such as ca, uk, de—California, United Kingdom, Germany [Deutschland]); k12 for grade-school students, teachers, parents, and so on; and others.

why.group.names.look.weird

So newsgroup names are in the form of two or more words or abbreviations, separated by periods.

The words between the dots correspond to UNIX directories on the machines that store the Usenet postings. If more than one word is needed to describe something, the two words are joined by hyphens, not periods. There can be at most fifteen characters between two periods.

So how do you pronounce these names? The proper geeky way to do it is to pronounce a period "dot," so that comp.sys.mac.games is pronounced comp-dot-sys-dot-mac-dot-games. While that's the traditional pronunciation, many people drop the "dots" and would pronounce that newsgroup name comp-sys-mac-games. Regulars in a newsgroup often refer to the group's name by its initials—c.s.m.g or csmg or CSMG, for example. It's up to you whether to pronounce soc "soak," or "soash."

Newsgroup Names Are Not Always Obvious

Unfortunately, the hierarchical system does not always help you find the newsgroup you're looking for. For instance, the jazz newsgroup is called rec.music.bluenote—look for the perennial "rap is not music" *flamewar* there. Likewise, you'd never know that the newsgroup alt.fan.warlord is devoted to reposting and spoofing monstrous signatures from other Usenet newsgroups. Sometimes you have to ask around a bit.

Especially in the alt hierarchy, there are also sometimes two or more newsgroups that cover the same topics but have slightly different names. There's alt.coffee, alt.food.coffee, and alt.drugs.caffeine. A similar debate surrounded the formation of newsgroups named alt.philosophy.zen, alt.religion.zen, and alt.zen.

> Purists hate to see a specific word like coffee as a first-level hierarchical distinction, but coffee lovers know that coffee is a basic element of life—comparable to music and sex.

What Is an Article?

An article, also called a *post*, is a message "sent" to a newsgroup. Posts are very similar to e-mail messages, although the header information at the top is different. An article can be posted apropos of nothing or as a reply, in regard to a previous post. A series of articles and replies is called a *thread*.

Eventually articles expire, meaning they are deleted from the directory in which they are stored. How long after they were posted varies from site to site. On my system, articles expire after two weeks. When you start reading a newsgroup for the first time, your newsreader program will probably tell you that it's "skipping unavailable articles" or something like that. This means that it is discovering that some of the articles posted from the beginning of time have expired.

> You can also cancel your own articles after you post them (though you can't cancel anyone else's). This won't prevent some people from seeing the canceled article in the meantime because some machines will already have propagated it beyond your network's server. Eventually, it will disappear from everywhere, but the cancel message has to chase the heels of the original post.

Replying to Posts

There are two ways to reply to someone's post. One way is to post a follow-up article, including some or none of the previous post, and append your comments. The other way is to send e-mail to the poster directly to discuss the post further. You have to decide when your follow-up is appropriate for the entire newsgroup (the thousands of invisible readers) or for the one person whose ideas caught your fancy.

Ignoring Flamers

Arguments that rage on for a while or become more and more incoherent or ad hominem are called *flamewars*. After you've been on the Net for a while you'll recognize flamewars in the making and learn how to avoid them. They might be entertaining at first but they follow such regular patterns that they inevitably become boring.

Some people enjoy flaming and causing flamewars. Some of these people post deliberately inflammatory articles designed to incite flamewars. Such posts are called *flamebait*. Often the instigator will eventually drop out of the conversation and watch how long the fire rages on its own. You'll also learn to

If somebody's post angers you, think twice before dashing off a reply, especially if you intend to post the reply to the entire group. It is easy to take people's writings in a spirit different from the intent of the writer. Most disagreements can be worked out in private e-mail a lot more easily than as gladiatorial contests in front of the rest of the group. Angry, insulting posts are called *flames*.

Usenet Puts the R in James R. Kirk

A more subtle net.pastime than flamebaiting is called trolling. To troll is to deliberately post information so egregiously incorrect that anyone with half a brain will see that it's a joke. Then everyone with less than half a brain, and a strong desire to correct people and go on record with the right information, will post follow-ups insisting that Bing Crosby and David Crosby are not actually father and son. (Everyone knows that David Crosby's father is Bill Cosby.)

Anxious to get going with Usenet? See Chapter 8 for specific instructions on how to run the most common newsreaders.

Remember when you're reading Usenet that not everyone else is seeing the exact same things that you are seeing. Other readers may be getting their feed more slowly or their articles in a different order. They may be reading a newsreader with a different number of characters per line or different keyboard shortcuts from yours.

This "semi-anonymity" I speak of should not be confused with true anonymity, which can be used to disguise the origins of a post or e-mail message. For more on anonymous remailers, see Chapter 5.

recognize *flamebait* after a while. By then there will be other newbies taking up the gauntlet every time it's thrown down.

What Is a Newsreader?

A newsreader is a program you run to read Usenet news. With any newsreader you can:

- See which newsgroups are available
- Subscribe to newsgroups
- Read articles in a newsgroup
- Post articles to a newsgroup

There are many popular newsreader programs. There are at least four in common use on UNIX systems, and then many more written for Macintosh and other computers connected to SLIP accounts or networks attached to the Internet. There are also offline newsreaders, much like offline mail programs, which allow you to download the news you want to read and then browse it at your leisure without incurring connect-time charges.

Semi-Anonymity

Because you'll never see the vast majority of people whose posts you read on the net, this creates a veil of semi-anonymity. As I've already mentioned, people fly off the handle more easily, misunderstandings proliferate, and people simply behave in ways that would be much more difficult, if not impossible, in a face-to-face encounter. Bear that in mind and try to ignore the occasional vicious geek who attacks you in print for no reason.

Unfortunately, this same semi-anonymity makes it possible for losers to harass females (or anyone with a female-sounding name) on the net. For this reason, some women may prefer to use a genderless login or real name when posting.

Usenet as a Public Forum

While not completely public, Usenet is essentially a public forum, and you should consider anything you post to have been published. Your words may be noted or ignored by thousands or hundreds of thousands of readers. Anything you write will be available to strangers anywhere in the world. Some people say you should never post anything to the Net that you wouldn't want to see on the front page of a newspaper.

For the same reason, you should probably not put your telephone number in your .signature file or in your posts in general. Strangers still might be able to figure out your phone number if you give your name and address or by fingering your account or looking you up in the membership directory of your online service, but at least you will not seem to be inviting people to call.

Being a Good Netizen

Try to get yourself up to speed before you start contributing to Usenet. Read the newsgroups you're interested in for a while to get caught up and avoid posting something that's been repeated so often it's become nearly a mantra in that group.

Also, read the newsgroup's FAQ before jumping in. One of the purposes of a frequently-asked-questions list is to save people the trouble of answering the same few questions over and over to the end of time. A newsgroup's FAQ will be posted to the newsgroup on a regular basis, anywhere from every two weeks to every two months. FAQs are built and maintained by volunteers, just like every other institutional aspect of Usenet.

There are also a set of answers newsgroups—misc.answers, comp.answers, rec.answers, etc.—which consist only of posted and reposted FAQs (and similar informational postings). Look there if you can't find the one you need.

If you are concerned about issues of privacy and security on the Net, see Chapter 5.

Reading a group without posting is called lurking, *and there's no shame in it. It's easy to forget that many people are lurking out there and think in terms of the few hundred or more people who post regularly, but most newsgroups have more lurkers than contributors.*

You can also ftp to rtfm.mit.edu *and look in the* /pub/usenet *directory for FAQs. Chapter 11 explains ftp.*

Shooting Stars and net.spewers

Once you've been reading a newsgroup long enough, you will recognize a certain phenomenon of the eager new contributor. This should not be confused with the September flood of new .edu postings from university students with their first Internet accounts. When a new contributor starts posting to a group, often they will spew hundreds of posts, following up every thread that's around and attempting to start new ones. (I'm not really criticizing, I did this myself.) Eventually, though, they will run out of bottled-up ideas that have been waiting years for an audience and settle down to become regular or occasional contributors.

A newsgroup is a sort of community. The people in the group interact with each other in a recognizable way. Once you are familiar with the dynamics of a newsgroup, you will find it easier to contribute. Remember that, just as with mailing lists, sarcasm and other subtleties of spoken communication do not translate well into black-and-white text. Try to say exactly what you mean and read things over before posting them. Ask yourself if what you've written might be misinterpreted.

IMHO Hep

Inevitably, as you start reading Usenet newsgroups, you'll notice certain abbreviations showing up in people's posts. Most of these have come about as shorthand—to save typing. Although others were invented as jokes or to sow confusion. Some are used as disclaimers. You'll often see IMHO (in my humble opinion) attached to comments that are anything but. I'm waiting

Being a Good Netizen

for IMOO (in my obsequious opinion) and IMUO (in my unctuous opinion) and a host of others, but I haven't seen them yet. Here's a brief and arbitrary listing of some common acronyms:

Acronym	What It Stands For
BTW	by the way
FAQ	frequently asked questions
FOAF	friend of a friend
FQA	frequently questioned acronyms
FUQ	frequently unanswered questions
FWIW	for what it's worth
IMO	in my opinion
IMHO	in my humble opinion
IMNSHO	in my not-so-humble opinion
LOL	laughing out loud
MOTAS	member of the appropriate sex
MOTOS	member of the opposite sex
MOTSS	member of the same sex
ROTFL	rolling on the floor laughing
SO	significant other
UL	urban legend
WRT	with respect to
YMMV	your mileage may vary

What Kinds of Groups Are Out There?

Since most of the original Usenet readers were scientists, researchers, or computer programmers, the range of topics available on Usenet is still skewed toward techie interests, even among recreational topics. There are at least seven newsgroups devoted to some aspect of Star Trek, including one called alt.sex.fetish.startrek. The misc.writing newsgroup leans heavily towards science fiction and fantasy writing. And, of course, there are entire hierarchies devoted to computers and science.

This is just a brief sampling of the sorts of topics that are discussed on Usenet. There are over four thousand newsgroups, and more are created all the time.

There are newsgroups on art, entertainment, writing, just about every hobby you can imagine, games, sports, sex, politics, pets, science, school, computers, television shows, music, theater, cooking, want ads, religion, net.personalities, and so on.

If you can't find a newsgroup on the specific topic you're interested in, look for a more general newsgroup whose topic would include yours. Then post to that group about the subject you're interested in. Someone may point you toward a mailing list. Or you'll start a series of threads about your subject. If the interest is high enough, you can look into creating a splinter newsgroup for your particular interest. There is a long-standing procedure for broaching this topic on the Net, starting with something called a "request for discussion"—of course, there's an acronym for that too, RFD—and working up to a "call for votes" (CFV).

The Quality of Usenet

When newsgroups get very popular or are filled with single-thread posts asking general or repetitive questions, they are said to have a low "signal-to-noise ratio." To deal with this, some newsgroups are moderated. Usually, they will have the word *moderated* at the end of the newsgroup name (as in soc.history.moderated), but not always (as in alt.folklore.suburban, the moderated version of alt.folklore.urban—it's a play on words). This means that all posts first go to a volunteer moderator, who decides if they are on-topic and then posts the articles that are to the newsgroup. Some people prefer the messiness of open debate to the clarity of moderated discussion.

Imminent Death of the Net Predicted —Film at 11

With participation in the Internet, and Usenet, growing at an exponential rate, there is never a shortage of Chicken Littles out there decrying the state of the Net now that the philistines have arrived, and predicting the imminent demise of the medium. Such dire warnings have become so common, and reports of the Net's death have been so often exaggerated, that the expression "Imminent Death of the Net Predicted—Film at 11" has arisen to parody the jeremiads. The "—Film at 11" tag is also sometimes appended to old news that's been breathlessly posted to the Net as if it's timely.

You will also notice that the quality of writing varies greatly from post to post. Some people are just better writers (or better fast writers) and some people are in too much of a hurry to worry about style or typos. As you already know by now, editing your messages in UNIX can be frustrating and there is a certain amount of tolerance for typos and common errors such as confusing they're and their, or spelling separate *seperate*.

The type of writing done on Usenet is different from other kinds of writing. In some ways it is closer to spoken language—especially in its immediacy and informality. It is also constrained by typical line lengths and screen heights. An idea that can be expressed in one screenful is more likely to convince people than one that drags on for ten. If you spend time reading Usenet, though, you'll see that there are some experts out there who are quite adept at this new medium of communication.

It's considered very bad form to correct someone's spelling or usage—it implies that you are unequipped to counter the substance of their post.

Getting Help

If there's something going on with Usenet, or your feed, or your newsreader, just ask people flat out. Sure, some people will tell you to RTFM ("read the fucking manual") or call you a clueless newbie, but we were all clueless newbies once and most manuals are tortuous to read. Just go ahead and ask. Some people are very kind.

So enough on the "what" of Usenet. On to the "how." You'll learn much more about the Net through the medium of Usenet itself than I could ever tell you.

CHAPTER 8

Newsreaders

Featuring

- Prepping your newsreader
- Reading and replying to articles
- Posting your own articles
- Crossposting
- Filtering out bozos
- Reading news with trn, tin, nn, rn, and windowed newsreaders

Before I get into the details of newsreading, let me mention that your newsreader program will probably seem very complicated to you at first—the screen display won't make total sense, you'll be trying to memorize a new set of commands, and so on. Try not to let this discourage you. You'll be over the threshold in no time, and once you've set things up, you'll do most of your newsreading by just pressing a few keys over and over.

NEWSREADERS

Eventually, you'll discover more complicated things you'll want to do to fine-tune your newsreading, such as filtering out unwanted articles, but that's nothing to worry about for now.

Newsreaders have some things in common with e-mail programs. The UNIX types all "shop out" the text editing to programs such as vi and pico (you can change this), they allow you to append a signature to your messages, they allow you to reply automatically. Any good newsreader will have the capacity to send mail as well as post articles for you. See Chapter 3 for more about e-mail.

As with almost everything else on the net, there are many different newsreaders available. Even on UNIX machines, the only common denominator of the net, there are at least four popular programs. People with SLIP or PPP accounts and those who get their access through networks at universities or at work have another whole raft of newsreaders available to them, many with windowed, point-and-click interfaces.

Nevertheless, newsreading is more or less the same no matter what program you use to do it. As with e-mail, I'll first sketch out the "generic" newsreading process—the things you'll do

Net News by Mail—
If You Don't Have Usenet Access

If your system does not provide you with Usenet access, you can still read newsgroups and even post articles via e-mail. (In general, not all newsgroups are supported by any of these methods, though many are.) This is easiest for newsgroups that are gated to mailing lists. For them, you just subscribe to the list or digest and read and post as you would with any mailing list (Chapter 6 explains mailing lists).

To receive a list of mailing lists that are gated to newsgroups, ftp to rtfm.mit.edu, go to the /pub/usenet-by-group/news.announce.newgroups directory and get the files Mailing_Lists_Available_in_Usenet and Changes_to_Mailing_Lists_Available_in_Usenet.

To read newsgroups via e-mail, send mail to listserv@blekul11.bitnet with /nnhelp in the body (delete your signature too). You'll receive an informational file telling you how the listserv/usenet gateway works. Read this carefully before starting, save it, and keep it around for future reference. Start off by replying to the listserv mail with just /newsgroups in the body of your

Net News by Mail

mail. You'll be sent a list of groups. To subscribe to one, reply to the mail, deleting all extraneous text and keeping only the /group lines for newsgroups you want to read. Next you'll be sent mail including list of available articles. Again reply, delete as much as you can, and keep the /article lines for articles you want to read.

Another way to read Net news by e-mail is to subscribe to a filtering service. To do so, first send mail to netnews@db.stanford.edu with any subject or none, and help in body of the message. You'll be sent an introductory file. Essentially, you send mail to the same address with any subject (blank OK), and include the lines

> subscribe *keyword1 keyword2 etc.*
> period *n*
> end

Choose your keywords carefully to limit the mail you get. The number n is the number of days between mailings to you. You'll receive just the first 20 lines of any Usenet articles that match enough of your keywords to exceed some statistical threshold. If you want an entire article, you can send another message with the line **get news.group.name.article-number**. All that information is in the Subject: line of the article abstract.

If you have a Web browser (see Chapter 15), you can point it at http://sift.stanford.edu and subscribe to the news filtering service by filling out a form.

Finally, if you want to post to a Usenet newsgroup via e-mail, send your article to one of the following addresses:

> *newsgroup-name*@cs.utexas.edu
> *newsgroup-name*@news.demon.co.uk
> *newsgroup.name*.usenet@decwrl.dec.com
> *newsgroup.name*@undergrad.math.uwaterloo.ca
> *newsgroup.name*@nic.funet.fi

Use dots or hyphens as indicated above.

no matter what newsreader you use. Then I'll explain the specifics of the most popular UNIX programs and a typical Mac newsreader.

Newsreading Basics

Here are the basic things you'll do with any newsreader:

- **0** (That's right, step zero.) Prep the newsreader, set up your reading list.
- **1** Start the newsreader.
- **2** Select a newsgroup to read (you can do this in step 1).
- **3** Select articles to read.
- **4** Browse the articles:
  - Read articles.
  - Save articles.
  - Reply to articles by e-mail.
- **5** Post responses.
- **6** Start a new thread.
- **7** Quit the newsreader.
- **n** (Any time.) Get help.

Prep the Newsreader

This is the boring complicated thing you shouldn't get too worried about. There are over 6000 newsgroups out there, depending on which ones you count. The first time you run your newsreader, it doesn't know what you want to read about: fly fishing or macrobiotic cooking? Urban legends or international conspiracies? So you're stuck with a massive "all or nothing" problem. Most newsreaders start you off *subscribed*

Newsreading Basics

to every single newsgroup. It's up to you then to unsubscribe to the ones you don't want to read. This will mean repeating some keystroke or mouse-click thousands of times. The upside of this is that you'll see all the newsgroups (if you don't fall asleep).

Some newsreaders start you off without subscribing you to any newsgroups. You then browse through a list and add the newsgroups you're interested in. I think this is the better approach, so in newsgroups that start you off subscribed to everything, I recommend first prepping the .newsrc file.

What's the .newsrc file? It's a text file on UNIX systems that keeps track of what newsgroups you are subscribed to and which articles you've read. (Mac or PC newsreaders will have a file like this but with another name.) If you run a newsreader and it doesn't find a file like this, it will immediately create one—and that's when most newsreaders subscribe you to every newsgroup. Here's how to create a starter .newsrc:

1 Type **vi .newsrc** and press Enter.

2 Type **i** to start inserting text.

3 Type **news.announce.newusers:** (including the colon) and press Enter.

4 Press Esc. Type **:wq** and press Enter.

> The process of subscribing or unsubscribing to newsgroups is instantaneous and completely reversible. Your list of newsgroups will most likely shrink and grow in some organic fashion. You'll realize that you never read certain groups and possibly unsubscribe to them. You'll hear about new ones and add them.

The Other Way to Prep Your Newsreader

You could also just run the newsreader and quit immediately (type **q**, repeatedly if necessary). Then edit the .newsrc file that was created. To edit it, type **vi .newsrc** and press Enter. Then type **:%s/:/!/** and press Enter to change all ":" (subscribed) to "!" (unsubscribed). Then manually change back the ones you actually do want to subscribe to.

Start the Newsreader

Starting the newsreader is just a matter of typing a short UNIX command and pressing Enter, or clicking an icon on a Mac or Windows based newsreader. When you start the program, it will first let you know if any new newsgroups have been created since you last ran it. You can subscribe to any of the new groups at this point.

Select a Newsgroup

The newsreader will show you a list of the newsgroups you subscribe to and allow you to choose one to start reading. If you want to add a newsgroup to your available list, you can search for it, or just add it if you know its exact name.

Select Articles

Once you've chosen a newsgroup to read, you'll be shown a list of the unread articles in the newsgroup, listed by Subject line and usually author as well. (Some newsreaders may just show you the first unread article.)

Many newsreaders provide filtering capabilities, so you can screen out topics and authors or autoselect some you're especially interested in.

You can choose, ignore, or delete articles.

Browse the Articles

Once you've selected the articles (or the first article), you can start reading them. The first article you selected will appear on the screen (or in a window). It will start with a bunch of header lines, similar to those in an e-mail message. The article itself starts after a blank line. Figure 8.1 shows the first screenful on an article I selected in the rec.humor.oracle newsgroup.

Newsreading Basics

FIGURE 8.1

Reading an article with trn

I pressed the spacebar (or Enter) to start reading the articles I'd selected in trn. This one is longer than one screenful. I'll have to press the spacebar to read the next "page."

If you get way behind in a newsgroup and don't want to wade through all the intervening posts, you can usually "catch up" the newsgroup, marking all current articles as read.

Read Articles

If an article is longer than one screenful, you press the spacebar to see each successive page, for UNIX programs. For windowed programs, you can usually scroll by clicking the vertical scroll bar to see more of the post.

Save Articles

If an article looks interesting, you can mark it as "unread" (most newsgroups delete articles after you read them—otherwise, simply don't delete any article you want to read later). If you actually want to save it to a file to read later or store, you can use the save command.

When I say that you're deleting articles, I mean that you are only deleting them from your list of unread articles. You are not actually deleting them from their source or even from the newsfeed that supplies your newsreader.

Not everyone's postings point back to their e-mail addresses properly. Sometimes, when you try to reply to a post by e-mail, the message "bounces." If so, it's probably not your fault.

Keep your lines down to 75 characters each (or 80 at the most). Many people, probably including you, can only get 80 characters on the screen at once, and any more will wrap to the next line and look bizarre. I recommend 75 instead of 80 so people can quote you without starting the bad-wrap problem.

What Does "Ob" Mean?

You may notice at the end of some posts, a cryptic line starting with Ob, such as ObDylan:. The Ob stands for obligatory. The idea is that if you post something to a newsgroup, there must always be some content relevant to the topic of the group. When a post seems to lack that sort of content, the author will add an obligatory comment or quotation to satisfy the requirement. This is usually done tongue partly in cheek.

Reply to an Article

When you reply to the author of an article by e-mail, you have the choice, in most newsreaders, of quoting the text of the post you're responding to or not.

Your newsreader will then allow you to write and edit an e-mail message, probably by dropping you into a text editor.

When you are done, exit the text editor if necessary and then send the mail.

Post a Response

When you post a response to an article, your post becomes part of the thread the original article was in. Usually, you keep the same Subject line, although you can edit it if you like. As with replying by e-mail, you also have the choice of including the text of the preceding article, or not.

Most newsreaders will give you a last chance to change your mind and not post. Some will try to convince you not to, to save the resources of the net.

Newsreading Basics **99**

Your Identity on Usenet

There are three ways people will identify you on Usenet. The first is by your e-mail address, or at least the login part of it before the @ sign. The second is by your "real name." This will appear in the author column of the article listing in a newsreader. (Although some put the e-mail address there.) Third, people will see your .signature file, if you have one, attached to the end of your posts.

The .signature file is a bit like a bumpersticker on a car. People use them to make jokes, to quote other people, to strike political poses, and so on.

The alt.fan.warlord newsgroup exists only to mock ridiculous or overlong .sigs, especially those with ASCII art such as enormous swords, crude Bart Simpsons, and maps of Australia with Perth pointed out on them. Read that newsgroup to find out what "tab damage" is.

If you include text from the article you're responding to, trim it down to the minimum text necessary for the context of your reply. It's just as bad to quote an entire message, just to add your short reply, as it is to post a reply without any context, so the meaning is lost.

Start a New Thread

In any newsreader, there will be a separate command for posting a new article without any reference to previous posts. This is starting a new thread, although it may grow no longer than your one post. (Even interesting posts do not always evoke follow-ups or even e-mail replies.)

Before letting you post, trn asks: Are you absolutely sure that you want to do this? [ny] n. Most newsreaders give you a last chance to change your mind.

When you post, your newsreader will prompt you for the "Distribution." The default is **world**. Your choices range from **local** (just your domain) to geographical abbreviations such as usa, na (North America), ny, ca, uk, and so on.

Quit the Newsreader

When you are finished reading news (for now), it's time to quit the newsreader. With some newsreaders, you have to quit the current article, then quit reading articles, then quit selecting newsgroups. Some just let you quit immediately from any part of the program. If you've mucked things up and deleted articles you still want to read, you can usually quit without keeping any changes from the current session.

Get Help and Avoid Problems

Most newsreaders have some kind of help, even if it's only a list of available commands. If you're stuck, try pressing **h** or **?**, or looking for a Help menu.

> In the worst-case scenarios, you can open up your .newsrc file in a text editor and edit it.

If you've deleted articles by mistake or done anything else to change the newsgroups you subscribe to or the articles you've read, and you want to scrap all your changes and go back to things the way they were before you ran the newsreader, you can usually quit without saving your changes.

Some Advanced Stuff

Here are some things you might not want to do right away but with which you should at least be familiar.

Crossposting

You can post articles to more than one newsgroup, if they are relevant to all of them. This is better than posting the same article more than once because it will only really be stored in one place even though it will be available to all the newsgroups it's posted to.

If you follow-up someone else's article, be sure to check which newsgroups your reply is going to, and edit the line (or the Follow-Up line) if necessary. Look out for pranksters who've directed follow-ups to *.test newsgroups. Newsgroups such as misc.test, alt.test, and so on, exist so that you can test the propagation of articles that you post through your newsreader. If you post to them (on purpose or accidentally), automated UNIX programs called daemons will send you e-mail verifying that your posts are getting through. This can easily overflow your mailbox as daemons from around the world send you electronic postcards.

Articles can also have a Follow-Up line that may specify different newsgroups from the ones it was originally posted to.

Killing and Autoselecting

Not all newsreaders allow you to kill or autoselect posts automatically, but the best ones all do. The file of automatic commands that gets created when you do this is called a killfile, because most people use them to filter out unwanted posts, not to automatically select their favorite topics and authors. Killfiles are also sometimes called "bozo filters" because they allow you to filter out some of the bozos who fill newsgroups with their bleatings.

Types of Newsreaders

The main distinction worth noting between newsreaders is whether they are *threaded* or *unthreaded*. Threaded newsreaders are better. They allow you to follow conversations from post to reply to follow-up. Unthreaded newsreaders don't keep track of which posts are related to which. You have to figure this out from context or from the quoted text at the beginnings of some posts.

As I've already mentioned, UNIX character-based newsreaders are a lot different from the kinds of windowed newsreaders you can use if you can get your access through a Mac or Windows-based account.

The last distinction is between online newsreaders and offline newsreaders. Offline newsreaders download all the current

102 NEWSREADERS

> ### The WorldWide Web Might Be the Best Newsreader Someday
>
> It is possible to read Usenet on the WorldWide Web. (The Web is explained in Chapter 15.) Currently, you can't post or reply to posts with Web browsers, but eventually this feature will also be added. Some people are already prepared for Web Usenet readers, and include hypertext codes in their signatures of messages. If you are not using the Web to read Usenet, these codes will appear as characters inside angle brackets (<>), such as <a href="gibberish">. Ignore them.

articles in all the newsgroups you subscribe to and then log off. Then you can browse through the downloaded posts at your leisure without running up your phone bill or connect-time charges; compose posts and replies; and then log in again to send your replies. Still, offline newsreaders function more or less the same way online readers do, from your perspective.

We'll start with some of the threaded newsreaders for UNIX—trn and tin. First, trn.

> If you want to read just one specific newsgroup, you can type **trn newsgroup.name** and press Enter.

Reading News with trn

trn is the threaded version of a popular old UNIX newsreader called rn. trn is available on most UNIX systems.

Start trn

To start trn, you type **trn** and press Enter. Figure 8.2 shows what you should see.

If any new newsgroups have been created since the last time you ran trn, you'll see a message like this before the listing of

Reading News with trn

FIGURE 8.2

```
~
~
~
~
~
~
".newsrc" 1 line, 25 characters
{netcom3:8} trn
Unread news in news.announce.newusers          325 articles

====== 325 unread articles in news.announce.newusers -- read now? [+ynq]
```

I've created a .newsrc file and am now running trn. It shows me that there are such-and-such unread news articles in news.announce.newusers and then asks me if I want to read that newsgroup now.

subscribed newsgroups Newsgroup alt.silly-group.beable not in .newsrc -- subscribe? [ynYN]. Type **y** to subscribe to this new group, type **n** not to subscribe, type **Y** to subscribe to this group and any other new ones, or type **N** not to subscribe to any of the new ones (and to keep them from even being listed in your .newsrc).

To go to a specific newsgroup (and subscribe to it if you don't already), type **g newsgroup .name** and press Enter. Try this by typing **g news. newuser.questions** and pressing Enter.

Select a Newsgroup

If you don't want to read the first newsgroup on the list, press **n**. If you do want to read the current newsgroup, press the spacebar. To go back to the previous newsgroup, press **p**.

To search for any newsgroups containing a word, type **a** *word* and press Enter. Try this now.

1. Type **a answers** and press Enter. trn will prompt you with the name of the first newsgroup with the word "answers" in its name, such as: Newsgroup news.answers not in .newsrc -- subscribe? [ynYN]. (Newsgroups with "answers" in the name are places where FAQs are posted.)

2. Type **y** (lowercase). trn will ask you where to put it: Put newsgroup where? [$^.Lq]

3. Press Enter (to put it at the end of the list).

Don't worry if what you type goes off the right edge of the screen.

NEWSREADERS

As you find that you read some groups more often than others, you can move them to the top, so you see them first. To move a group, type **m**. Then to put the group at the top of the list, type **1** and press Enter. To see your other options, press **h**.

4 Go through the rest of the list, pressing **y** or **n** depending on your preferences. I recommend saying yes to rec.answers and alt.answers, at least.

5 Type **a** and press Enter, to remove the restrictions.

At any point, you can see all the newsgroups you subscribe to by pressing **L**. To see all the newsgroups you don't subscribe to, press **l**. If you get tired of pressing the spacebar to get through this list, press **q**.

Select Articles

Once you've pressed the spacebar to start reading a newsgroup, you'll be shown a list of the unread articles and you can choose articles to read, delete, or save for later.

1 Press **n** until you are back at the news.announce.newusers line.

2 Press the spacebar. Figure 8.3 shows the available articles in this newsgroup.

FIGURE 8.3

Turns out there are only 14 articles available right now in this newsgroup. All of the topics look worth reading, especially if you are a beginner.

If the number of articles listed is fewer than the number mentioned when you first ran trn, some articles have expired since you last checked this group.

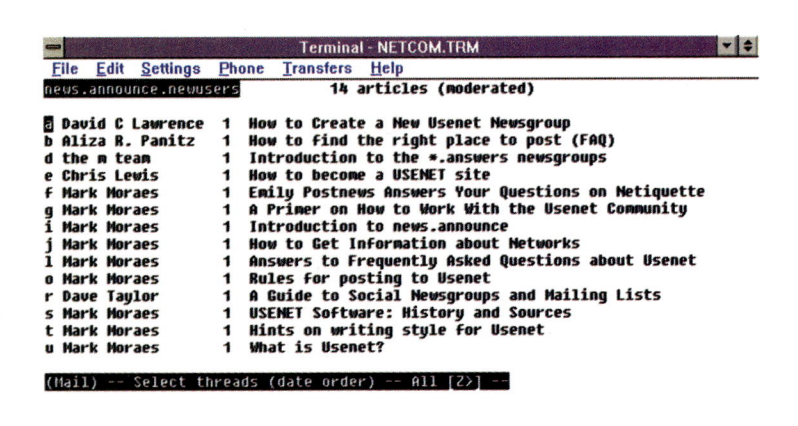

To choose an article you want to read, either type its letter, or move the cursor to it (n for next, p for previous, or ↑ and ↓ if they are working) and then press +. To skip over an article for now, just ignore it. To delete an article, move the cursor to it and press – or k.

3. I'm selecting "Answers to Frequently Asked Questions about Usenet" by pressing l.

If there are more articles than one screenful, you can press the spacebar or > to go to the next screen, and < to go back to the previous screen.

If you start reading a newsgroup and there are far too many articles, Press c to "catch up" (mark as read) all the current articles. trn will ask you to press y if you're sure. Then the newsgroup will appear empty until someone posts something new.

> If you'd rather see the most recent articles first in this newsgroup, press R. This will switch the order. Press R again to switch back. The order you choose in one newsgroup will carry over to others.

Browse the Articles

To start reading a newsgroup after selecting articles, press the spacebar (repeatedly if necessary) or Enter. If the article is longer than one screenful, press the spacebar to see the next page. The bottom of the screen will tell you how much of the article you've seen so far, expressed as a percentage.

> To go to a specific newsgroup (and subscribe to it if you don't already), type g newsgroup.name and press Enter. Try this by typing gnews.newusers.questions and pressing Enter.

Read Articles

When you get to the end of an article, press n or the spacebar to go to the next selected article. Press p to go to the previous selected article. Press [to go to the parent article of the current one in this thread. Press] to go to the first child article of the current article in this thread.

The upper-right corner of the screen shows a somewhat graphical display of the thread the current article belongs to. Watch that display as you move up and down the thread with [and], and side to side with (and).

You may notice that when people post controversial articles, they sometimes warn others ahead of time, which is fine. What's annoying is when they add something like: "If you don't want to read this post, just press n." What's annoying about this is that the author has assumed that all readers are using trn, rn, or a similar UNIX-based newsreader. Remember that most people are not doing things the same way you're doing them.

Save Articles

To mark an article as unread, so you can read it later, press **m**. trn will respond with something like Article 287 marked as still unread. To save an article as a file, type **s** *filename* and press Enter. trn will ask whether to save it in mailbox format. Type **n** and press Enter. The file will be saved to your News directory. See Chapter 9 for more on files and directories.

Reply to an Article

To send an e-mail reply to someone whose post you're reading, press **r** (to send a message without including the original post) or **R** (to send a message including the original post—this is a better idea because it will help the person remember what they were writing about).

trn will drop you into a text editor. Write your message and exit the editor. Then press **s** to send the mail or **a** to cancel it.

Post a Response

To post a follow-up, press **F** or **f**. If you press F, your article will have the same subject, will appear in the same thread, and will include the text of the original message, under a line identifying the author. Always make sure the attribution is correct and not misleading. People hate to be misquoted. Then reduce (or paraphrase) the original text as much as you can without losing the gist of what you're replying to.

If you press f, no text will be included and you'll be asked if your reply will be unrelated to the previous post. Press **n** to keep the reply in the same thread. The subject line will still be the same. (You can always edit any of the header lines—they're just regular text. But if you botch them up, you will confuse the newsreader when it tries to send the post.)

Press **y** when trn asks if you're really, really sure you want to do this. Then edit your message in the text editor it sends you to, exit the editor, and press **s** to send the message or **a** to cancel it.

If you plan to post a reply to a message, mark it as unread first and read the rest of the thread. You never know when someone else has already made the point you were planning to make. You'll get your chance. Then, if you do actually reply, check the Newsgroups: and Follow-up to: lines in the post to which you're replying to make sure you know where your post is going. Edit them in your reply if necessary.

Start a New Thread

To start a new thread, press f while reading any post. trn will ask you Are you starting an unrelated topic? [ynq] y. Type y or press Enter. trn will then prompt you for a subject line. Type one and press Enter. Remember, this is the first thing people will see and some people will decide whether or not to read your post based on it. When trn asks you about distribution, press Enter. Then type y when trn asks you Are you absolutely sure that you want to do this? [ny] n unless you've changed your mind. Then edit your message in the text editor it sends you to, exit the editor, and press s to send the message or a to cancel it.

Quitting trn

To quit trn, press q. If you are reading an article, the first q will just take you to the end of the article, so you'll have to press q again to go back to newsgroup selection, and then press q a third time to actually quit trn.

If you've deleted articles you didn't mean to, you can quit by pressing x. This will make no changes to your .newsrc, and next time you run trn, everything will be like it was at the beginning of the previous session.

Get Help and Avoid Problems

To get help, or at least a list of commands, press h. You will see different options depending on whether you are choosing newsgroups, choosing articles, reading an article, or at the end of an article.

Crossposting

To post to more than one newsgroup, simply edit the Newsgroups line among the headers of your post. Put a comma between each pair of newsgroup names. Don't overdo crossposting—people get annoyed if you post messages to inappropriate groups.

NEWSREADERS

Killing and Autoselecting

If there's a subject you don't want to read about or a person out there who annoys you, you can create and edit a killfile that will screen out the topic or author you don't like before you ever see the posts. You can make a global killfile that performs the same commands in every newsgroup, or a local killfile that pertains to only one newsgroup.

To create a global killfile, press Ctrl-K while selecting newsgroups. trn will put you into an editor. The killfile commands all take the following form: /pattern/modifier:command.

The *pattern* is the word or string of words you don't want to see. The *modifier* tells the newsreader whether to search all or part of the articles (searches of entire articles take much longer). The *command* tells the newsreader what to do with the articles that meet the criteria.

You'll probably use one of these two modifiers:

- h   to scan the headers
- a   to scan the entire article

While in article selection, you can add the subject of current thread to your killfile automatically by typing **K**.

And you'll probably use **j** as the command. j is for junk. Junking an article is the same as deleting it. If you want to autoselect articles, use the + command instead.

To create a local killfile, press Ctrl-K while in the article selection or reading part of trn. The rest of the instructions are the same.

If you want to read just one specific newsgroup, you can type **tin newsgroup.name** and press Enter.

Reading News with tin

Another popular threaded UNIX newsreader is called tin. tin is also available on most UNIX systems.

Start tin

To start tin, you type **tin** and press Enter. tin will first respond with

> tin 1.2 PL1 [UNIX] (c) Copyright 1991-93 Iain Lea.
> Reading news active file...

Then the Group Selection screen will appear, showing all the groups you're subscribed to and how many new articles each group has. Figure 8.4 shows what you should see.

FIGURE 8.4

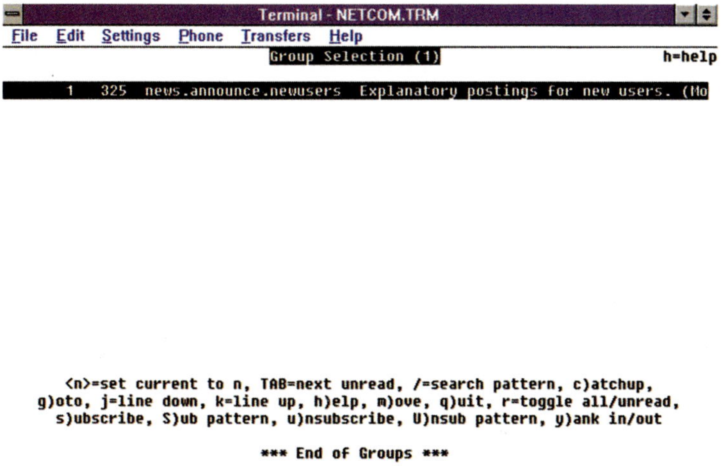

I've created a .newsrc file and am now running tin. It shows me that there are such-and-such unread news articles in news.announce.newusers.

Select a Newsgroup

If you don't want to read the first newsgroup on the list, press **j** to go down to the next line. If you do want to read the current newsgroup, press Enter. Press **k** to go up to the previous line. (Or try using ↑ and ↓.)

To go to a specific newsgroup (and subscribe to it if you don't already), type **g**. tin will respond with Goto newsgroup []>.

As you find that you read some newsgroups more often than others, you can move them to the top of your list, so you see them first. To move a newsgroup, type **m**. Then to put the newsgroup at the top of the list, type **1** and press Enter. To put it at the end, type **$**. In between, type the appropriate number.

NEWSREADERS

Don't worry if the number of articles listed is sometimes fewer than the number mentioned when you first ran tin—it just means that some articles have expired since you last checked this newsgroup.

Threads with a plus next to them have unread articles in them. Threads with numbers next to them have that many replies to the original article.

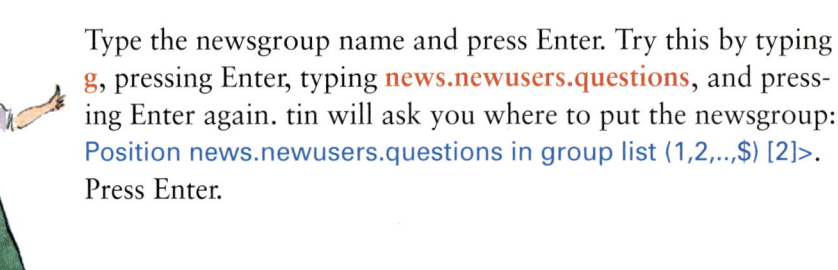

Type the newsgroup name and press Enter. Try this by typing **g**, pressing Enter, typing **news.newusers.questions**, and pressing Enter again. tin will ask you where to put the newsgroup: **Position news.newusers.questions in group list (1,2,..,$) [2]>**. Press Enter.

Select Articles

Once you've pressed Enter to start reading a newsgroup, you'll be shown a list of the unread articles and you can choose which articles to read, which to delete, and which to save for later.

1 Highlight the news.newusers.questions line (press **j** or **k** if you're not there already).

2 Press Enter. Figure 8.5 shows the available articles in this newsgroup.

To choose an article you want to read, either type its number and press Enter or move the cursor to it (**j** for down, **k** for up).

FIGURE 8.5

Here's the first screenful of unread articles (actually threads) in news.newusers.questions.

You're choosing whole threads here. Press **l** to list the articles in the current thread so that you can read the ones you're interested in. Press **q** to go back to thread selection when you've finished reading.

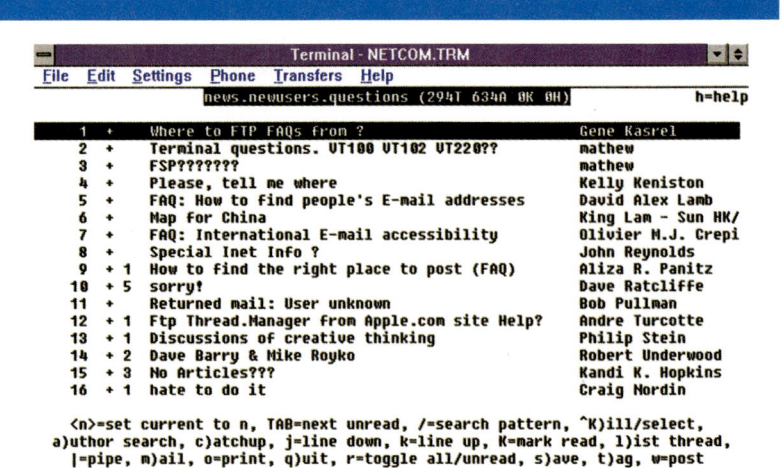

Then press *. To skip over an article for now, just ignore it. To delete an article, move the cursor to it and press **K**. At any point, you can read a thread by pressing Enter while it is highlighted.

To skip to the next screenful of articles, press the spacebar. To go back a screenful, press **b**.

3 I'm selecting "FAQ: How to find people's E-mail addresses" by pressing **5** and then Enter.

If you start reading a newsgroup and there are far too many articles, press **c** to "catch up" (mark as read) all the current articles. tin will ask you to press **y** if you're sure. Then the newsgroup will appear empty until someone posts something new.

Browse the Articles

To start reading a thread, press Enter. If the article is longer than one screenful, press the spacebar to see the next page. The bottom of the screen will tell you how much of the article you've seen so far, expressed as a percentage.

Read Articles

When you get to the end of an article, press the spacebar to go to the next unread article or press q to go back to thread selection.

> If you want more room on the screen for the articles you're reading, press **H**. This removes the menu of options at the bottom of the screen. Press H again at any time to bring it back.

Save Articles

To mark an articles as unread, so you can read it later, press **z**. tin will respond with something like Article marked as unread. To save an article as a file, type **s**, then type **a**, then type a file name and press Enter, and then press Enter again. See Chapter 9 for more on files and directories.

To mail an article to someone, press **m**, then press **a**, then type an e-mail address and press Enter, and then type **s** (or type **e** to edit the message first).

Before replying to a message, mark it as unread first and read through the thread. You never know when someone else has already posted what you were planning to post. Then, if you do actually reply, check the Newsgroups: and Follow-up to: lines in the original post so you know where your post is going. Edit these lines in your reply if necessary.

Reply to an Article

To send an e-mail reply to someone whose post you're reading, press **r**. tin will drop you into a text editor. Write your message and exit the editor. Then press **s** to send the mail or **q** to cancel it.

Post a Response

To post a follow-up, press **f**. tin will put you in a text editor and include the text of the original article with an attribution. Trim down the quoted text as much as you can without losing the context.

Write and edit your article. Then exit the editor. To post the article, press **p**. To cancel the article, press **q**. To go back and edit it again, press **e**. To check the spelling, press **i**.

Start a New Thread

To start a new thread, press **w** while reading any post (or while selecting threads). tin will ask you for a subject. Type one and press Enter. Remember this is the first thing people will see and some people will decide whether or not to read your post based on it. Then edit your message in the text editor tin sends you to, exit the editor, and press **p** to post the article. To cancel the article, press **q**. To go back and edit it again, press **e**. To check the spelling, press **i**.

Quit the Newsreader

To quit tin, press **q**. If you are reading an article, the first q will just take you back to thread selection, so you'll have to press q again to go back to newsgroup selection, and then press q a third time to actually quit tin.

Get Help and Avoid Problems

To get help, or at least a list of commands, press **h.** You will see a list of options appropriate to the part of tin you're in just now—choosing newsgroups, choosing articles, reading an article, or having reached the end of an article.

Crossposting

To post to more than one newsgroup, either edit the Newsgroups line among the headers of your post (put a comma between each pair of newsgroup names), or post by pressing **x** instead of **w** or **f.** If you press x, tin will prompt you for the newsgroups you want to post to and then let you edit the post you're crossposting if you want. (But don't go crazy with crossposting—people get annoyed when they find irrelevant messages in their newsgroup.)

Killing and Autoselecting

If there's a subject you don't want to read about or a person out there who annoys you, you can selectively kill topics or authors to screen them out before you ever see the posts.

To kill a subject, or author, press Ctrl-K with such an article selected. This will bring up the Kill / Auto-select Article Menu (see Figure 8.6).

On this screen, the spacebar switches between options and Enter selects the current option.

If you want to kill the subject or author, press Enter. To have this author or subject selected automatically in the future, press the spacebar and then Enter. Then press Enter again to get down to the Kill Subject line. If it's the subject you want to kill, press Enter; if not, press the spacebar and then Enter. If you want to kill articles by this author, press the spacebar and then Enter; if not, press Enter. Finally, if you want to kill articles

> Press **e** to edit the kill file directly. See the killfile entry under *Reading Usenet News with trn* above for more on killfile commands.

114   NEWSREADERS

> **FIGURE 8.6**
>
> *The Kill / Auto-select Article Menu. tin makes it very easy to kill or auto-select subjects and authors.*

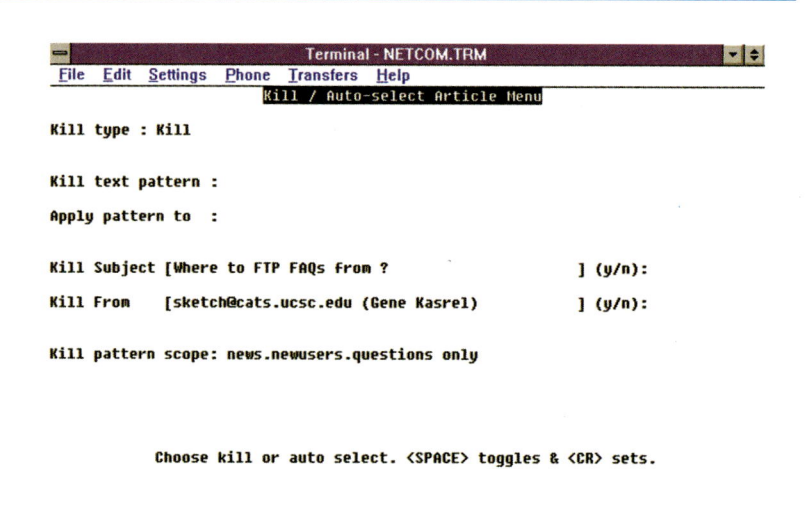

```
                    Terminal - NETCOM.TRM
 File  Edit  Settings  Phone  Transfers  Help
                    Kill / Auto-select Article Menu

 Kill type : Kill

 Kill text pattern :

 Apply pattern to  :

 Kill Subject [Where to FTP FAQs from ?                 ] (y/n):

 Kill From    [sketch@cats.ucsc.edu (Gene Kasrel)       ] (y/n):

 Kill pattern scope: news.newusers.questions only


              Choose kill or auto select. <SPACE> toggles & <CR> sets.
```

in the current newsgroup only, press Enter. If you want to kill such articles in all newsgroups, press the spacebar and then Enter.

Then press **s** to save the killfile entry (or **q** to cancel).

Reading News with nn

> If you want to read just one specific newsgroup, you can type **nn newsgroup.name** and press Enter.

Another popular UNIX newsreader is called nn. It's "sort of" threaded, because it arranges articles in order by thread and uses the > symbol to show related articles. Also, it does allow you to select articles before reading them. Like trn and tin, nn is available on most UNIX systems.

Start nn

To start nn, you type **nn** and press Enter.

Select a Newsgroup

nn will ask you if you want to "enter" the first newsgroup in your .newsrc: Enter news.announce.newusers (50 unread)? Press Enter. You'll be taken to an article-selection screen. If you want to skip to the next newsgroup, type N.

Select Articles

Once you've pressed Enter to start reading a newsgroup, you'll be shown a list of the unread articles and you can choose which articles to read, which to delete, and which to save for later.

To choose an article you want to read, either type its letter or move the cursor to it and press . (period). Selecting an article moves you down to the next line. Typing . will also unselect a selected article.

To skip to the next screenful of articles, press the spacebar or >. To go back a screenful, press <.

Browse the Articles

To start reading an article, press the spacebar to scroll until you get to the last screenful of articles and then press the spacebar again to start reading the articles you've selected.

If the article is longer than one screenful, press the spacebar to display the next page.

To read **selected** articles **and** then return **to** article selection **when you** are done, press **Z**.

Read Articles

When you get to the end of an article, press the spacebar to go to the next unread article or press = to go back to article selection. When you get to the end of the last article in a newsgroup, the spacebar will take you to article selection for the next newsgroup.

Save Articles

To save an article as a file, type **w**, and press Enter to accept the suggested file name (or delete the suggested file name, type the name you want, and then press Enter). Then press **y**.

Reply to an Article

To send an e-mail reply to someone whose post you're reading, press **r**. In response to the prompt, type **y** if you want to include the original article in your reply or **n** if you don't. nn will drop you into a text editor. Write your message and exit the editor. Then press **s** and then Enter (and then Enter to add your .signature, or **n** and Enter not to) to send the mail. To cancel the mail, press **a** and then Enter (and then **y**).

Post a Response

To post a follow-up to an article, press **f**. Type **y** if you want to include the original article in your follow-up or **n** if you don't. nn will put you in a text editor. Trim down the quoted text (if any) as much as you can without losing the context.

Write and edit your article. Then exit the editor. To post the article, press **s**. To cancel the article, press **a** (and then **y**). To go back and edit it again, press **r**. To cc someone, press **c**.

Start a New Thread

To start a new thread, type **:post** while reading any post (or while selecting articles). nn will ask you for the newsgroup to post to. Type one and press Enter. Then nn will ask you for a subject.

nn will also prompt you for Keywords:, Summary:, and Distribution:. You can press Enter for all of these. Then edit your message in the text editor it sends you to, exit the editor, and press **s** to post the message. To cancel the article, press **a** (and then **y**). To go back and edit it again, press **r**. To cc someone, press **c**.

Quit the Newsreader

To quit nn, press **Q**.

Get Help and Avoid Problems

To get help in nn, you have three choices. Press **?** at any point for a quick reference for whatever mode you're in (selection or reading). Type **:help** for more detailed help on specific subjects. Or type **:man** for an online manual of nn.

Crossposting

To post to more than one newsgroup, simply edit the Newsgroups line among the headers of your post. Put a comma between each pair of newsgroup names. Don't overdo crossposting—people get annoyed at such blanket-bombing of innocent newsgroups.

Killing and Autoselecting

Here's how to selectively screen out topics that bore you or authors that vex you before you ever see the posts.

To kill a subject in one newsgroup for 30 days, press **K** in a newsgroup with such an article selected. nn will prompt you with **AUTO (k)ill or (s)elect (CR=> Kill subject 30 days)**. Press Enter. nn will ask you which subject to kill. Choose the one you want.

If you want to kill a name, or a subject or name, for a different amount of time from 30 days, or if you want to kill a subject or name in all newsgroups, then press **K**. nn will prompt you: **AUTO KILL on (s)ubject or (n)ame (s)**. Press Enter for subject, or **n** and Enter for name. Then type a subject or name and press Enter. nn will prompt you now with **KILL in (g)roup 'current.newsgroup' or in (a)ll groups (g)**.

> Just choose **s** instead of **k** to select articles automatically instead of killing them automatically.

Press Enter to kill in just the current group, or **a** and Enter to kill in all newsgroups. Finally, nn will prompt you **Lifetime of entry in days (p)ermanent (30)**. Type a number of days and press Enter, or just press Enter to accept the 30-days default, or type **p** and press Enter to kill the subject forever.

Reading News with rn

rn is an old UNIX newsreader that's unthreaded. trn is the threaded version of rn. If you've got trn available, I'd recommend using that instead of rn, but if not, rn is perfectly usable.

For instructions on how to use rn, refer to the trn section of this chapter. The only difference is that there is no article-selection mode in rn. After you decide to start reading a newsgroup, you are presented with the articles one by one, subject first. Otherwise, the commands are all the same.

Table 8.1 gives a run down of the essential commands in rn.

TABLE 8.1

How to Read News with rn

In Order To…	Press…
Start the newsreader	Type **rn** and press Enter *or* type **rn** *newsgroup.name* and press Enter.
Select a newsgroup to read	Type **n** to go to the next newsgroup, **p** to go to the previous one. Type **g** *newsgroup.name* and press Enter to add a new newsgroup to your list.
Select articles to read	Press the spacebar to read an article, press **n** to skip to the next article, press **m** to mark an article as unread, or press **p** to skip to the previous article.
Read articles	Press spacebar to get to the next screenful.
Save articles	Type **s** *filename* and press Enter. Then type **n** and press Enter.

TABLE 8.2

How to Read News with rn

In Order To...	Press...
Reply to articles	Press **R** to reply by email, including the text of the original post. Press **r** to reply by email without that text.
Post reponses	Press **F** to post a responding article, including the text of the original post. Press **f** (and then press **n** and then Enter) to post a responding article without the text.
Start a new thread.	Press **f** and the press **y** and then Enter to post an article to a news thread.
Quit rn	Press **q** one, two, or three times to quit rn.
Get help	Press **h**.

A Windowed Newsreader

I can't cover every type of newsreader out there, but I want to cover windowed newsreaders in general. If your Internet account is a UNIX shell account, then the only kind of windowed newsreader you could run would be an offline reader that logged into your account, downloaded all the unread articles in all the newsgroups you subscribe to, and then logged off again.

If you have a SLIP or PPP connection, or if your connection is based on a network at your work or university, *and* you work on a Mac or PC (or an Xwindows terminal), then you should be able to run a windowed newsreader in real time. Either way the programs all function more or less the same way.

NewsWatcher

One such newsreader is Newswatcher for the Macintosh. You run the program by clicking on it. It first brings up a window showing the newsgroups you subscribe to. If there are any new newsgroups, it brings up a window listing them. You can click on any of the new newsgroups to add them to your subscription list.

Usenet Interfaces for Online Services

More and more of the mainstream online services are offering Usenet newsgroups—some only allow you to read, but most allow you to post as well. Delphi has been offering Usenet for around two years now, and America Online and CompuServe have recently followed suit. If you read Usenet through such an online service, then the commands necessary to do so will be particular to your service. America Online offers a nice Windows interface for its whole environment, including Usenet.

Time for a couple of mild warnings: First, the ease with which an integrated "look and feel" allows you to jump into Usenet can be misleading. Old-timers are irritated when someone from an online service implies that Usenet is "part of AOL" or "just another folder on Prodigy, the world's largest online service™" or shows a blatant ignorance of Usenet or a seeming unwillingness to learn.

At this writing, the America Online interface for Usenet contains an annoying bug. When someone follows up a post without including any of the original text, the AOL program still begins the article with an attribution line, crediting the previous writer. This makes it seem as if the AOL poster is putting words in someone else's mouth (pen? keyboard?). The solution is to delete the attribution line.

In general, tread lightly and read your own posts to make sure they're coming out the way you intended.

To look for other available newsgroups, simply click Windows ➤ Show Full Group List. You can click on any of the listed newsgroups to add them to the subscription list.

To start reading news, simply double-click on a newsgroup name in the window showing your subscribed newsgroups. Newswatcher will open a window for that newsgroup. Figure 8.7 shows a window containing unread articles in a newsgroup.

FIGURE 8.7

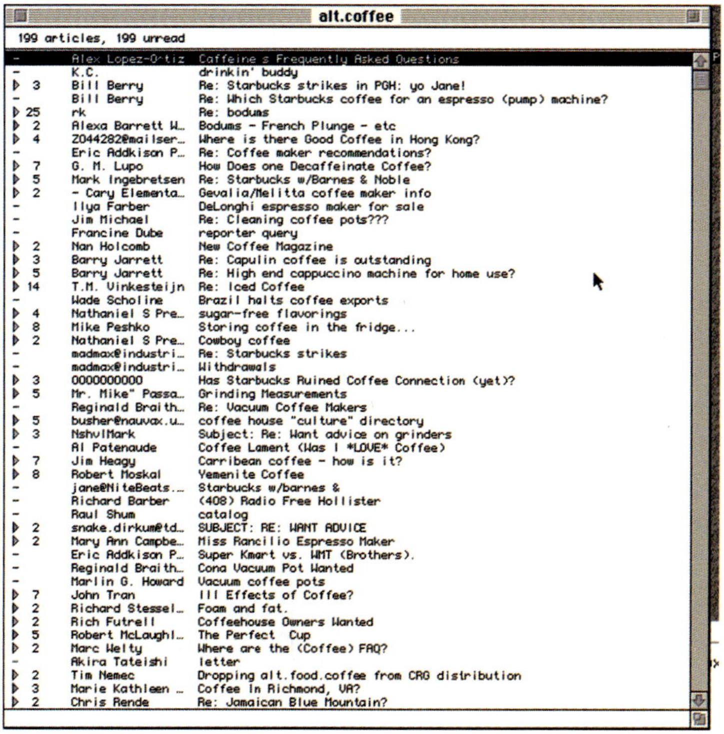

Unread articles in the alt.coffee newsgroup. The right triangles and numbers indicate threads and the number of responses. Click the triangle to see the whole thread.

To read an article, simply double-click the subject line. Newswatcher will open a new window with the contents of the post in front of the newsgroup window. To post an article, select the post option from a menu. Newswatcher will prompt you for a Subject and then open a new window in which you can write your post. (There is a separate menu option for following up the current article in a thread.)

To quit Newswatcher, select Quit on the File menu.

CHAPTER 9

Managing Your Files and Directories

Featuring

- Your home directory
- Moving around in directories
- Making and removing directories
- Listing, making, viewing, and removing files

If you get your access by dialing up a connection to a UNIX shell account, then you'll need to know a little bit about UNIX files and directories. You've encountered files already. E-mail messages are stored in files (they're called "folders" but they're just a special kind of file). When you save an e-mail message it is saved to a file. Usenet articles are files and if you save them you save them as files as well.

MANAGING YOUR FILES AND DIRECTORIES

But what are directories? Directories are just a way of organizing files. They are (imaginary) subdivisions of disks, and they're arranged into hierarchies. At the first level is the root directory, symbolized by a forward slash (/). All other directories branch off from the root or from other directories. If you trace a subdirectory's "path" back all the way, you always end up at the root. Let's deal with directories first. Figure 9.1 shows what a typical UNIX directory looks like (in fact, it's part of the directory tree of my own system).

FIGURE 9.1

This illustration shows part of a UNIX directory tree. In my system (from which it's drawn), there are many more directories that are children to the root directory (including usr and u1 through u38, all of which contain users' home directories).

If your computer is on a network connected to the Internet or you dial up with a SLIP or PPP account, then you store your Internet files on your regular computer and manage your directories (or folders) the normal way.

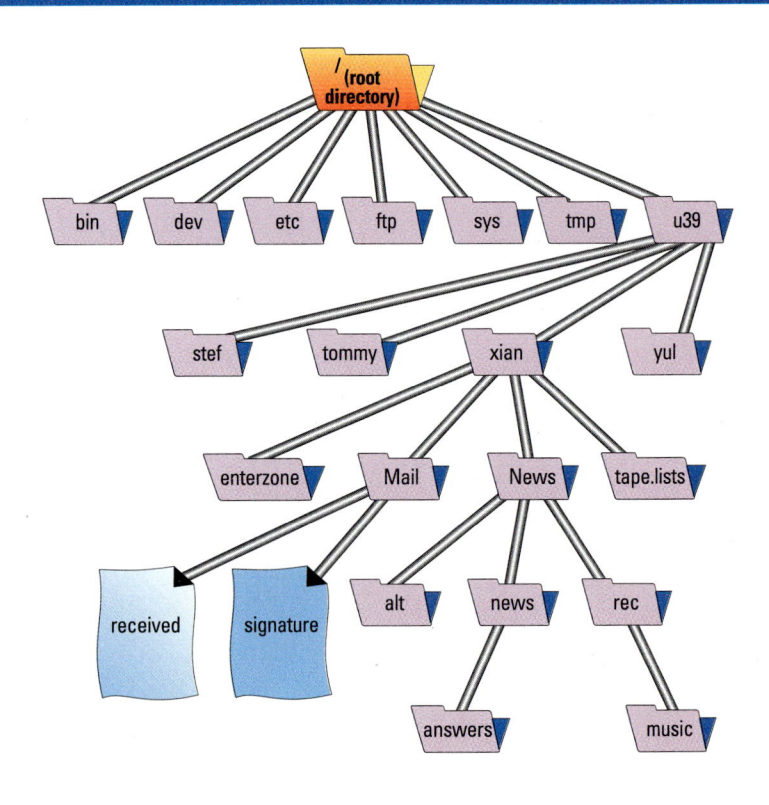

UNIX Directories

First, a little more terminology. There is no real difference between a subdirectory and a directory. Directories are just called subdirectories when they are discussed in terms of their *parent* directory. A parent directory is the directory one level above—closer to the root than—the current directory. A *child* directory is a subdirectory, a directory one level below—further from the root than—the current directory. The whole list of directories leading from the root to the current directory is called the *path*.

Home—Where You Hang Your Hat

UNIX keeps track of your working directory, the directory you're currently in. When you log in, your working directory should be one named for your login. This is your home directory. On some systems, this will be /usr/*your-login* or /home/*your-login*. Your home directory probably already has some subdirectories in it, such as Mail and perhaps News.

Comparing UNIX and DOS Directories

As I mentioned, UNIX directories are analogous to DOS directories (and to Mac folders, and to a lesser extent to Windows groups). The main difference is that the root directory is signified by a forward slash in UNIX, but a backslash in DOS. This same symbol is used to divide directories and subdirectories. Thus, in UNIX: /directory/subdirectory. In DOS: \directory\subdirectory. But if you're familiar with DOS, most of what you know about directories and how you expect them to behave will apply to UNIX directories as well.

Finding Out Where You Are

If at any point you're not sure what your working directory is, you can type **pwd** at the UNIX prompt and press Enter (pwd stands for "print working directory"). Figure 9.2 shows the result when I type pwd after logging on.

FIGURE 9.2

pwd shows that my home directory is /u39/xian

```
You have new mail.

This disk usage summary is for the last 22 days.
Your average usage to date is:     4.96 meg
At this rate your disk charge will be: $   0.00
Your account balance is:           0.00


Terminal type is vt100
{netcom:1} pwd
/u39/xian
{netcom:2}
```

Changing to Another Directory

You always start out with your home directory as your working directory, but you can change that easily. To change to another directory, type **cd *directory-name*** and press Enter. To change to a child directory of your working directory, you don't need to specify the entire path, just the part that comes after your working directory.

Remember, UNIX is case-sensitive. If your Mail directory is called Mail, then you can't refer to it as **mail** or **MAIL**. Likewise, the change directory command must be **cd**, not **CD**.

So if you're in your home directory, and you want to change to your Mail directory, type **cd Mail** and press Enter. You can always specify the entire path of a directory if you want. So I could change to my Mail directory just as easily by typing **cd /u39/xian/Mail** and pressing Enter.

You can always get back to your home directory by just typing **cd** and pressing Enter.

You can always go to the parent directory of your working directory by typing **cd ..** and pressing Enter. In fact, .. is an abbreviation for your parent directory and you can use it as part of a path. So if you change to your Mail directory and then want to change to your News directory, you could enter **cd** and then **cd News**, or type the entire path to the News directory after the cd, or, you could just type **cd ../News**, press Enter, and be done with it.

> You must include the space before the two periods. Otherwise, UNIX won't understand what you mean.

Making a New Directory

The command to make a new directory is mkdir. To make a new directory as a child of the current directory, just type **mkdir** *new-directory-name* and then press Enter. Try this now. Type **mkdir test** and press Enter. Then change to the new directory. Type **cd test** and press Enter. You're now in your new directory. To go back to your home directory, type **cd** and press Enter.

Removing a Directory

You can remove an empty directory by typing **rmdir** *directory-name* and pressing Enter. If you attempt to remove a nonempty directory, UNIX will respond with **rmdir:** *directory-name:* Directory not empty.

> I'll explain how to delete files later in this chapter.

What's in the Directory?

To see what files (and other directories) are in your working directory, type **ls** and press Enter. You can list the contents of a specific directory (other than the working directory) by typing **ls** *directory-path* and pressing Enter. The path can be relative to the working directory or absolute, starting with the root.

If you have so many files in a directory that the list scrolls off the screen, you can "pipe" the ls output through the more program to see one screen at a time. Type **ls | more** and press Enter. (The | symbol is called a pipe.) Press the spacebar to see the next screenful of files.

> You won't see files that start with a . (a period) when you list files with ls. To see them, type **ls -a** and press Enter.

MANAGING YOUR FILES AND DIRECTORIES

If you're interested in complete information (size, date, and other gibberish you won't understand) about each file, and you find plain ls doesn't give it to you, type ls –l and press Enter.

If you want to distinguish directories from files, type ls –F and press Enter. Directory names will appear followed by a slash.

UNIX Files

There are two kinds of files—text files and binary files. Text files, as you might imagine, are files containing text. You've already worked with text files if you've sent e-mail, posted to Usenet, or created a file with vi or pico. If you look at the contents of a text file, you'll see stuff you can recognize. Words. If you look at a binary file, you'll see gobbledygook. Stuff only a computer could understand. Binary files might contain data, art, compiled computer code, and so on. A word-processed letter consisting of only words and formatting would be a binary file (not a text file) because of the formatting information.

This is oversimplifying things a bit, but that's what I'm here for, right?

Including Wild Cards in File Names

For any UNIX command you can include wildcard characters when specifying file names, as a way of covering many possibilities at once (although for some commands it wouldn't make any sense to do this). The two wildcard characters are * (the asterisk, Shift-8) and ? (the question mark). Use * to represent any number of characters, ? to represent any single character. So r*t matches *report* and *rob.wasserman.duet*, b* matches *book-report* and *beatles.lyrics*, report? matches *report1*, *report2*, and *report3*, and so on. Just plain * all by itself matches everything. Be careful when deleting files!

Making Files

You already know how to make a text file. You can do it in any UNIX text editor. You won't need to make your own binary files, although you may end up schlepping them around from the Net to your UNIX account and from your UNIX account to your desktop computer. (See Chapters 10, 11, and 12 for more on moving files around.)

You can also send the output of a UNIX command to a text file by putting a > and a filename after the command. For example, to make a file with a list of the contents of your directory, type **ls >** *filename* and press Enter.

Unlike in DOS, files in UNIX can have nice long descriptive names. You can't put spaces in them, but most people use hyphens or underline characters or dots to break up words (such as january-widget-report, or january_widget_report or january.widget.report). Other than those, use just letters and numbers. Most other punctuation characters relate to UNIX commands and are either Not Allowed or will muck things up when you try typing them out. Remember, once again, that UNIX is case sensitive, so crucial.report and CRUCIAL.Report are different files.

> To append the results of a UNIX command to the end of a preexisting file, use ›› instead of ›.

Viewing the Contents of a File

To view the contents of a file (without editing it), type **cat** *filename* and press Enter. If the file is longer than one screenful, type **more** *filename* and press Enter.

Figure 9.3 shows the first screenful of a file in my home directory called net.legends.FAQ.

Printing a File

You can't print directly from your UNIX account to the printer attached to your desktop computer. If you try the

MANAGING YOUR FILES AND DIRECTORIES

FIGURE 9.3

more shows the first screenful of net.legends.FAQ. I have to press the spacebar to see more.

```
{netcom:39} more net.legends.FAQ
This... is the Net.Legends FAQ. Due to minutes^H^H^H^H^Hweeks of
unrelenting plagier^H^H^H^H^Hresearch, we have gathered together here
some descriptions of those net.phenomena that one hears about in passing,
and (due to the collective memory of the Net being about one week, maximum)
wishes one had more information about (such as "Who *was* McElwaine,
anyway, and *why* is he still being talked about?). What follows is a list
of some of the Legends of the Net, along with descriptions,
semi-explanations, and (in some cases) a parenthesized catchphrase for
easy identification... not all of the following are completely factual
entries: in some cases the true facts are known only to one person, or lost
in the mists of time, while in others the facts pale in relation to the
mythology. In any case, the actual facts included, sparse though they may be,
are true as far as I know; if you have evidence otherwise, please contact me
and *tell* me (a few people have contacted me and said "This is wrong!"
without actually saying *what* was wrong with it, which is of little
use... (Note: "Myths" are used to refer to stories involving gods or
other supernatural beings; "legends" refer to stories involving humans that
could be true.) The FAQ in each case should be considered to be "Who or what
is ____ and where can I get some (no wait.. umm..) why should I know this?
(yeah, that's it)". The miniFAQs mentioned are available by anon-ftp (as is
this FAQ) to cathouse.org, the awesome AFU archive, under /pub/cathouse/urban.
legends/net.legends, and are mostly composed of representative posts... they
--More--(0%)
```

Downloading files is covered in Chapter 10.

Be very careful about using wildcards with the rm command. Don't type **rm ***, for example, unless you want to delete every file in the current directory.

UNIX print command (lp or lpr), it will fail. Likewise for print commands in any programs you run.

Instead, to print a file, you have to send it back to your desktop computer. If it's short enough, simply cut the contents off the terminal window and paste them into a word processor or text editor on your desktop computer, and then print it. If it's longer, you'll need to *download* the file to your desktop computer.

Deleting Files

Every now and then you have to clear out the clutter in your directories, if only because some online services charge you for disk-space storage if you exceed a certain quota. It's like cleaning up your room, though; you should do it every now and then because it's good for the soul.

To delete a file, type **rm** *filename* and press Enter.

Copying Files

To copy a file, type **cp** *original-file copy-file* and press Enter. You can include a relative or absolute path to put the copy somewhere else.

Moving or Renaming Files

To move a file to a different directory, type **mv** *filename new-directory* and press Enter. You can use a relative path to indicate the new directory or an absolute one.

To rename a file, type **mv** *old-filename new-filename* and press Enter. For both moving and renaming, the **mv** command is equivalent to using a **cp** command to copy the file and then the **rm** command to delete the original.

UNIX won't warn you if you're about to copy a file over an existing file. Make sure the coast is clear before you do this.

You can use mv to rename a directory as well as a file. (This is something you can't do in DOS, so there!)

CHAPTER 10

Downloading Files back to Your Computer

Featuring

- Text files versus binary files
- Downloading and uploading
- Transferring files with kermit, xmodem, ymodem, and zmodem
- Sending and receiving text

If you get your access by dialing up a connection to a UNIX shell account, then you'll need to know how to download files back from your Internet account to your desktop computer, as well as how to upload files over the modem to your Internet account. Downloading just means bringing a file from a remote computer (such as the UNIX machine you log into) back to your desktop machine over the modem hookup. Similarly, uploading means sending a file over the modem from your desktop machine to a remote computer. They are essentially the same process in opposite directions.

If your computer is on a network connected to the Internet or you dial up with a SLIP or PPP account, then you don't need to take the extra step of downloading files from your Internet account to your desktop computer. You'll simply store your Internet files on your regular computer and manage your directories (or folders if it's a Mac) the normal way. See Chapters 11 and 12 for more on fetching files from the Net.

If you remember the difference between text files and binary files, then you can skip ahead.

The xmodem, ymodem, and zmodem protocols are all similar, as each is based on the previous one—ymodem on xmodem, zmodem on ymodem. zmodem is the fastest protocol, but not every program offers it.

Text Files and Binary Files

Text files (also sometimes called ASCII files) are files that just contain common text, words and numbers, punctuation marks and so on. They are easy to transport because they don't get corrupted easily.

Potential Problems Uploading Text Files

Because PCs and UNIX machines use different systems to indicate line endings (if you must know, PCs use two characters—carriage return and line feed—while UNIX machines use only one, carriage return), your text files might transmit with nonsense characters at the end of each line. This should not happen unless you mistakenly send a text file as a binary file. If your text file shows up on your UNIX machine with ^M at the end of each line, you should be able to convert the file with the dos2unix program. If it's not available, ask your system administrator.

Binary files are files containing data or compiled instructions. If you look inside a binary file, all you see is gibberish—computer talk, consisting of specially formatted information that computer programs know how to deal with. Pictures, data, and executable (runnable) programs are all stored in binary files. It is easier for binary files to get corrupted in the transportation process, so the *protocols* for transporting them, the special rules computers follow to avoid error, are more complicated. Binary files usually take longer than text files to transmit.

Downloading Protocols

In this chapter, I will explain how to use the four most popular downloading protocols—kermit, xmodem, ymodem, and zmodem. You'll most likely need to work with more than one, because different software accommodates different protocols. The computers at both ends of a transfer must be using the same protocols for the transfer to work.

I'll list the basic commands for each of these four protocols, using transfers between your Internet account and your desktop computer as examples.

Before we get into the details of the four protocols, let's get one confusing thing out of the way. Even when you're sending only a text file, you have to tell your communications program what kind of *binary* transfer you want to make. This is because from the point of view of your desktop machine, the file *is* a binary file (that happens to contain just text). The text transfer commands in your communications program deal with sending and receiving plain text. For more on this, see *Straight Text Transfers* at the end of this chapter.

File Transfers

Before transferring a file, you have to tell your communications (terminal) program which protocol you're using.

Downloading Files

To send a file back to your desktop computer:

1. Type the send command (see Table 10.1) and press Enter.
2. In your communications program, select the command for receiving a binary file.

While most of the time you'll be downloading from your Internet account to your desktop computer, you should be aware that other programs, such as gophers and World-Wide Web servers, also offer downloading capabilities and can send files directly to your desktop machine, using these same protocols.

Throughout this book, I've shown how you can access most Internet services even with a generic comm program such as Terminal, which comes for free with Windows. If you have a lot of downloading (or uploading) to do, however, I'd recommend investing in a comm program that can do ymodem and zmodem transfers.

TABLE 10.1
Downloading Commands

Protocol	Text Files	Binary Files
kermit	kermit –s *filename*	kermit –s *filename* –i
xmodem	sx *filename* –a	sx *filename*
ymodem	sb *filename* –a	sb *filename*
zmodem	sz *filename* –a	sz *filename*

> With ymodem or zmodem, you can send multiple files at once by listing them all on the command line or using wildcards.

Your communications program will show you the progress of the transfer (as a number of bytes and not as a percentage, because it doesn't know how long the incoming file is). When it's done, press Enter.

Uploading Files

To send a file *from* your desktop computer, first make sure the file you want to send is not in use by any of the programs on your desktop computer. Then:

1 Type the receive command (see Table 10.2) and press Enter.

2 In your communications program, select the command for sending a binary file.

You'll then be shown a dialog box in which you can select the file you want to send.

TABLE 10.2
Uploading Commands

Protocol	Text Files	Binary Files
kermit	kermit –r	kermit –r –i
xmodem	rx –a	rx
ymodem	rb –a	rb
zmodem	rz –a	rz

Your communications program will show you the progress of the transfer (as a running percentage or visual graphic). When it's done, press Enter. The file on your Internet account will have the same name as the original.

Straight Text Transfers

Your communications program should also provide you with commands for sending and receiving text over your modem. If you think about it, you'll realize that you are already sending and receiving text. When you type into the terminal window, the communications program is sending the characters you type over the modem to the computer at the other end of the connection. And when a UNIX program produces output, it appears on your screen because it is passing over the modem to your PC.

The text transfer commands differ only in that they allow you to send text directly from a text file (instead of from what you type at the keyboard) and they allow you to store the text appearing on the screen in a file.

Sending Text over Your Modem

Besides typing text into the terminal window, there are two other ways to send text over your modem. You can type the text in some other program on your computer, select and copy the text, and then paste it into the terminal window. This should work most of the time, although you can overload the buffer or otherwise cause the modem to cough and stop sending text.

The third way to send text is to send it from a text file. Again, create the file on your desktop computer, in a word processor or text editor. Save the text file and close it, so it's not in use by the program you created it in.

> If you create a text file in a word processor, be sure to save it as a text file, and make sure there are hard returns at the end of each line. You may have to save it as a text document with line breaks.

> Remember, if you're putting the text into a file with vi, to first type *i* to start inserting text, before sending the text file.

Don't use the more command to produce output if you're sending the text to a file on your PC. If you do, all the (xx%) MORE prompts will appear in the file, along with a bunch of weird characters such as ^] that are used to create reverse video on a vt100 screen.

Most communications programs have an "append" option for their receive text file command. This allows you to attach various pieces of text to a single file.

In your terminal window, run the text editor or other program you intend to dump the text into. When you are ready, select the command to send a text file. When prompted, type the name of the text file and press Enter. You'll see the text start spilling out across your screen until the entire file has been dumped. Then save the text file you've created.

Receiving Text over Your Modem

Although you can systematically cut text from your terminal window and then paste it into a text file (I do this a lot myself), it can get tiresome if you're transferring a great deal of text this way.

To save text output into a file on your desktop computer, first type whatever commands you need to create the output but *don't press Enter yet*. For example, to send the contents of a text file to a file on your PC, type cat *textfilename* but don't yet press Enter.

Select the command to receive a text file. When prompted, type a name for the text file and press Enter. Then press Enter in the terminal window. The text will scroll across the screen as normal but it will be captured in the text file you named.

CHAPTER 11

Fetching Files from Around the Net with ftp

Featuring

- Anonymous ftp
- Finding ftp sites
- Transferring files with ftp
- ftp with the Mac fetch program

You can send files attached to e-mail, but this is inefficient and wasteful of resources if the files are large. Instead, there's ftp (file transfer protocol), a method of retrieving files from (and sending files to) other computers on the Net.

ftp—Protocol or Program?

Both. It's a protocol *and* a program. Sure, ftp is the name of the file transfer protocol, the method for transferring files, but it's also the name of the most common UNIX program for doing this.

You'll also hear references to "anonymous ftp." Most of the time you'll do ftp, you'll do it anonymously, at public ftp sites. This means you log in as "anonymous" and give your e-mail address as a password. If you use ftp to transfer files from a machine that you are authorized to access, then you won't do it anonymously. You'll log in as yourself and give your password.

In some ways, ftp is similar to remote login, except that you don't log into the other machine, really. The ftp program negotiates with the other machine for you and enables you to transfer files. That's about it. Chapter 13 explains remote login.

How to Find ftp Sites

Say you're reading a Usenet newsgroup for a while (see Chapters 7 and 8) and then you wonder if the old posts you never got to see are archived anywhere. You post your question and someone e-mails you to tell you that, indeed, the archive is available by anonymous ftp at archive.big-u.edu. You cut the address and save it in a text file and then check out the ftp site with your ftp program. So that's one way to find out about sites.

There's an anonymous ftp FAQ and a huge, alphabetically organized, set of ftp site lists (11 in all) posted regularly to comp.answers, news.newusers.questions, and many other Usenet newsgroups.

To have any or all of these documents mailed to you, send an e-mail message (no subject) to mail-server@rtfm.mit.edu. Include in it any of the following lines: send usenet/news.answers/ftp-list/faq and/or send usenet/news.answers/ftp-list/sitelist/part1 *through* send usenet/news.answers/ftp-list/sitelist/part11.

Many ftp sites are also available via gopher programs and WorldWide Web browsers. See Chapter 14 for more on gophers and Chapter 15 for more on the Web.

If you know what you're looking for, you can also run a program called archie and search for the files you want. The archie program will tell you which sites have those files. I'll explain archie in detail in the next chapter.

One other way to hunt for ftp sites is to look for them on gopher menus. Chapter 14 explains gopher.

These same files are also available via (what else?) anonymous ftp to rtfm.mit.edu. Look in the /pub/usenet/news.answers/ftp-list/sitelist directory for the 11 site list files, and the /pub/usenet/news.answers/ftp-list/faq directory for the faq. We'll get to anonymous ftp in just a second.

Many of the largest, most popular ftp archives have *mirror sites*, other ftp sites that maintain the exact same files (updated regularly), in order to reduce the load on the primary site. Use mirror sites whenever you can.

How to Do ftp in General

The typical ftp session starts with you running the ftp program and connecting to an ftp site. This will put you at a login prompt.

Type **anonymous** and press Enter. Then type your e-mail address and press Enter. This will put you at an ftp prompt. (If you mistype *anonymous*, type **u** and press Enter and then correct your spelling.)

Now use the change directory command and the list-files command to hunt through the directory structure for the files you want. You might have connected to a UNIX machine or to any other type of computer on the Net. Fortunately, you won't have to know all the different commands they require. You only need to know the commands for your ftp program. It will then translate your requests into whatever format the host computer requires.

You'll notice that ftp programs are "verbose," meaning they give you a lot of feedback and updates on what they're doing.

If the files you want to transfer are not simple text files (if they're programs, for example), specify *binary* before doing the transfers. When you find the files you want, transfer them with the get command (or the multiple get command, to transfer many at once). Then quit the ftp program. You're done.

It's best to do your file transfers during off-peak hours, such as at night or on the weekends, to minimize the load on the ftp site.

When logging into an ftp site as anonymous, never enter your real password. This is a security breach, as your password will appear in a log file that many people can read. If you do this by mistake, immediately change your password (as explained in Chapter 3).

If you're not sure where to start looking at the ftp site, start off by looking for a pub directory. If there is one, change to it and then work your way through the subdirectories.

Recognizing Compressed Files by Their Extensions

Many files available by ftp have been compressed. This way they take less time to transfer and take up less storage space.

Files that have been squished down in size by the UNIX compress command end with .Z. To uncompress them, once you've got them in your home directory, type **uncompress filename.Z** at the UNIX prompt and press Enter. Files that end in .gz have been compressed by the gzip program. To uncompress them, type **gunzip filename.gz** at the UNIX prompt and press Enter.

If the files you've downloaded are ultimately destined for a DOS machine, then they might end in .zip, .arc, or .lhz, and you'll need the correct DOS decompression program to expand them. If you don't have the program you need, look for it around the ftp site where you got the compressed file. Likewise, compressed Mac files have extensions such as .hqx, .bin, or .sea.

Files that end in .tar contain several files all lumped together with the UNIX lumping program tar. To separate them, type **tar -xvf filename.tar** and press Enter. Files that end in .tar.Z have to be uncompressed and untarred.

To do this, type **gtar -tZvf filename.tar.Z** or **uncompress < filename.tar.Z | tar -tvf -**.

Once you get the files you've transferred, if you want to get them all the way to your desktop machine (assuming you don't have a direct connection to the Net), you'll need to download them. See Chapter 10 for how to download files.

Transferring Files with ftp

Every UNIX shell has the ftp program. If you've gotten the hang of working with directories and files in UNIX, then ftp should be a snap. To run the ftp program:

1 Type **ftp** *sitename* at the UNIX prompt and press Enter.

Transferring Files with ftp 143

2 Type **anonymous** and press Enter (or just press Enter if you mean to log in under your own name—you'll need a password to do that).

3 Type your full e-mail address and press Enter (or type your password if you're logging in under your real name). It won't show up as you type.

Figure 11.1 shows me ftp-ing to ftp.eff.org, the Electronic Frontier Foundation site.

4 Read whatever information floods across your screen, if any. You should now be at a prompt that looks like this: ftp>.

> You can also just type ftp and press Enter, and then at the ftp> prompt, type **open sitename** and press Enter.

Automating ftp Logins with a .netrc File

If there are a number of ftp sites that you visit regularly, you can create a .netrc file listing each one of them to make logging in easier. To create a .netrc file, type **vi .netrc** and press Enter. Each entry in the file starts with the word **machine** and looks like this:

machine sitename
login anonymous
password your-username@your-host.address

(Of course, you can list a real login and password for ftp sites for which you have them.)
Here's an entry from my .netrc:

machine rtfm.mit.edu
login anonymous
password xian@netcom.com

When I type **ftp rtfm.mit.edu** and press Enter, the ftp program looks for my .netrc file and finds an entry for that site. It looks for a login and password and then logs me in using them. You can have as many entries as you like.

> If your login fails (you'll know—the program will tell you), you'll still end up at an ftp> prompt, which can be confusing. Just try again by typing **user anonymous** and pressing Enter. Then continue with step 3.

FETCHING FILES FROM AROUND THE NET WITH FTP

5 Now use **ls** to list files and **cd** to change directories (does this sound familiar?). See Figure 11.2.

FIGURE 11.1

I've ftp-ed to ftp.eff.org, logged in as anonymous, and typed my e-mail address for a password.

```
{netcom10:2} ftp ftp.eff.org
Connected to ftp.eff.org.
220 ftp.eff.org FTP server (Version wu-2.4(2) Thu Apr 28 17:19:59 EDT 1994) read
Name (ftp.eff.org:xian): anonymous
331 Guest login ok, send your complete e-mail address as password.
Password:
```

I typed **cd pub** and pressed Enter, then **cd Net_info**, then **cd EFF_Net_Guide**, and then **ls**. This took me to the directory where EFF's Net Guide (netguide.eff) and accompanying FAQ file (netguide.faq) are located.

- Now, if you are planning to transfer binary files, type **binary** at the ftp prompt and press Enter. Otherwise, it is assumed that you are transferring text files. If you've transferred some binary files and *then* want to transfer some text files, type **ascii** at the ftp prompt and press Enter.

6 To transfer a file, type **get** *filename* and press Enter. To transfer multiple files, type **mget** *filename1 filename2 etc.* or use wildcards to get every file that matches a pattern. If you use mget, you'll have to type **y** for each file transferred (see Figure 11.3).

If you're transferring a big file, you can press Ctrl-Z to stop the job, and then type **bg** and press Enter to finish the transfer in the background.

Repeat steps 5 and 6 as often as you like.

If you plan to transfer several files and you don't want to be prompted about each one, type **prompt** at the ftp prompt and press Enter before getting the files.

7 When you are done, type **quit** at the ftp> prompt and press Enter. This should return you to the UNIX prompt.

Transferring Files with ftp

FIGURE 11.2

I used ls to list the files in the pub/Net_info/EFF_Net_Guide directory.

```
                  Terminal - NETCOM.TRM
 File  Edit  Settings  Phone  Transfers  Help
250-Please read the file README.zip-files
250-  it was last modified on Tue Jan 25 13:05:25 1994 - 184 days ago
250 CWD command successful.
ftp> cd EFF_Net_Guide
250-Please read the file README
250-  it was last modified on Tue Mar 22 16:25:10 1994 - 128 days ago
250 CWD command successful.
ftp> ls
200 PORT command successful.
150 Opening ASCII mode data connection for file list.
bdgtti.gif
netgd2_2.zip
README
netguide.eff
.cap
bigdummy.txt
netguide.faq
Updates
netguide_2.22.txt
Other_versions
00-INDEX.EFF_Net_Guide
226 Transfer complete.
150 bytes received in 0.029 seconds (5.1 Kbytes/s)
ftp>
```

*I typed **mget netguide.*** to get both netguide.eff and netguide.faq. They are text files, so I didn't have to enter binary first, and I didn't enter prompt, so ftp asks me before each transfer.*

FIGURE 11.3

I've just transferred the main netguide file and now I'm going to get the FAQ file that goes with it.

```
                  Terminal - NETCOM.TRM
 File  Edit  Settings  Phone  Transfers  Help
ftp> ls
200 PORT command successful.
150 Opening ASCII mode data connection for file list.
bdgtti.gif
netgd2_2.zip
README
netguide.eff
.cap
bigdummy.txt
netguide.faq
Updates
netguide_2.22.txt
Other_versions
00-INDEX.EFF_Net_Guide
226 Transfer complete.
150 bytes received in 0.029 seconds (5.1 Kbytes/s)
ftp> mget netguide.*
mget netguide.eff? y
200 PORT command successful.
150 Opening ASCII mode data connection for netguide.eff (394870 bytes).
226 Transfer complete.
local: netguide.eff remote: netguide.eff
403176 bytes received in 21 seconds (19 Kbytes/s)
mget netguide.faq?
```

Other ftp Commands

I've covered the basic drill, but there are some other commands and options you might want to know about.

- For a more complete directory listing, try typing **dir** instead of ls. (On some systems the result will be the same.)
- To go up one directory level, type **cdup**. To see what your working directory is on the remote machine, type **pwd**.
- To change the directory on your home machine, use **lcd**.
- To transfer a file *to* a site instead of from it, use the **put** or **mput** command.
- To transfer a file and give it a different name at the same time, use **get** *oldfilename newfilename*.
- To transfer a file and decompress it on the fly, leave off the .Z or whatever extension when you get it.
- To bail out in the middle of a transfer, press Ctrl-C or whatever keys normally kill a job.
- To close a connection without quitting the ftp program, type **close** and press Enter at the ftp> prompt.
- To open a new connection, type **open** *sitename* at the ftp> prompt and press Enter.

> If you're doing an ftp file transfer from an dial-up UNIX shell account, and you're transferring a large file, your modem might hang up if it doesn't pass along any characters for too long an interval. If this problem happens to you, type **hash** and press Enter before entering the get command. This will cause ftp to put a # symbol on the screen for every kilobyte transferred, which will in turn keep your modem awake.

> To get help, type **?** and press Enter to get a list of commands. Then type **help** **command** to get information about *command*. To get thorough help about the ftp program, type **man ftp** and press Enter at the UNIX prompt.

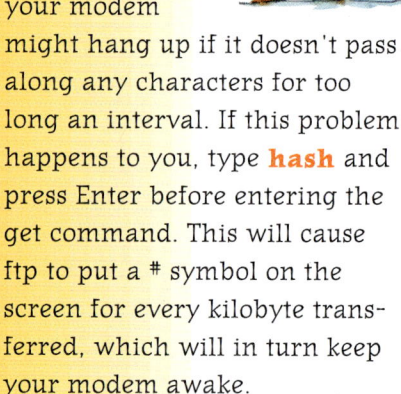

ftp Directly to Your PC

If you have the sort of Internet connection where your desktop computer is directly on the Net (such as a SLIP or PPP dial-up account, or a network connection to the Net) and your computer is not a UNIX box, then you should be able to run a windowed ftp program and transfer files directly to your computer with it.

On Macintoshes, the standard file-transfer program is called Fetch. When you double-click on the Fetch icon, it brings up

ftp Directly to Your PC **147**

the Open Connection dialog box (see Figure 11.4).

If you don't want the default host, type a new one. Enter your password in the password window and enter a directory if you know the one you're headed for. Then click OK.

Once you've connected to the host, you can navigate the directory structure by clicking on folder icons, just as with any Macintosh program. Click the Binary radio button to specify a binary file (or leave Automatic clicked to let the program figure it out automatically). Highlight the file or files you want and click the Get File button to get them (see Figure 11.5).

FIGURE 11.4

The Open Connection dialog box in Fetch.

When you are done, select File ➤ Exit, the usual Macintosh exit procedure.

FIGURE 11.5

The Macintosh interface makes fetching files simple.

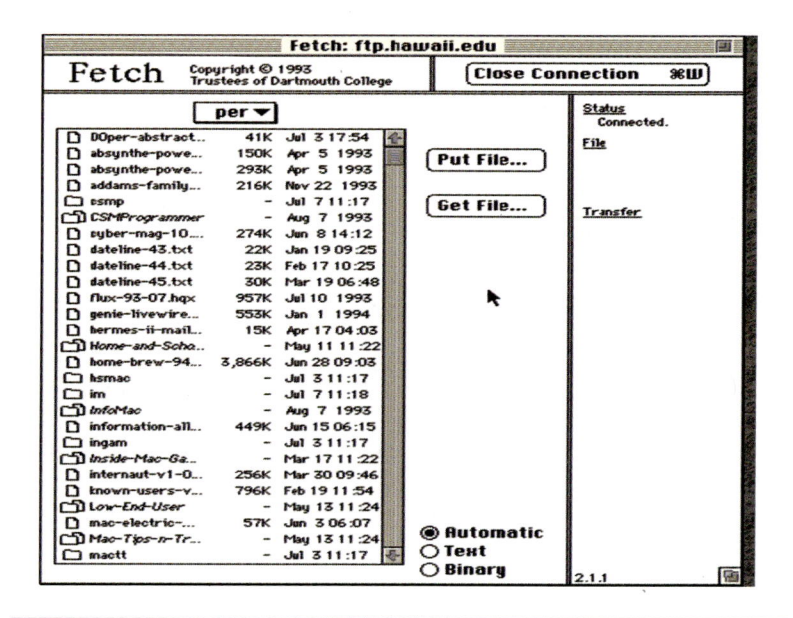

ncftp—A Better UNIX ftp

Some UNIX systems have a beefier version of ftp available, called ncftp. To run ncftp (if you've got it), type **ncftp** *ftp-sitename* at the UNIX prompt and press Enter. The main advantages of ncftp are:

- ncftp assumes you want to use anonymous ftp and saves you typing that word (start it with **ncftp -u** *ftp-sitename* to log in with your username).

- If you maintain a .netrc file of ftp sites, you can type just enough characters of the site name to distinguish it from others. So, for example, if you've got **rascal.ics.utexas.edu** and **rtfm.mit.edu**, you can type just **ftp rt**

Each entry in the .netrc file must start with the word machine. Type **man ncftp** and press Enter to see more about ncftp.

and press Enter to log into rtfm.mit.edu.

- ncftp automatically takes you to the last directory you went to at the site.

ftp by E-Mail If You Don't Have "Real" ftp

There are mail servers out there that will make ftp transfers for you and then mail you the resulting files. (It's a little like asking a third party to check out a book from the library and sent it through the mail to you.) This is more wasteful and less efficient than real ftp, but it will work in a pinch if you don't have ftp available.

To use ftpmail, send a message to either ftpmail@pa.dec.com or ftpmail@decwrl.dec.com.

Leave the subject line blank. Each line of the message should contain a single command, most of which are the same as the equivalent ftp command. Commands you need to know are

connect *sitename*	Tells the service to connect to the ftp site whose name you include.
chdir *directory*	Just like the cd command in real ftp, this tells the service to change to this directory.
ls	Sends you a listing of the current directory. You can then send another ftpmail message to get files.
binary	Just like the binary command in real ftp, this must precede a get command for a binary (nontext) file.
uuencode	Uuencodes binary files so they can be attached to your return e-mail message as regular text.

For more on setting up a .netrc file, see the *Automating ftp Logins with a .netrc* sidebar, earlier in this chapter. The only additional thing you need to know is that, since ncftp assumes you want to do an anonymous login, you can leave out the login and password lines unless you want to use a real login and password.

You'll find a thorough discussion of e-mail in Chapter 3.

get *filename*	Retrieves the specified file
quit	You must include this as the last command in the message.

So, for example, to have the EFF's net guide sent to you by e-mail, you'd send a message to one of the above addresses with no subject and the following contents:

```
connect ftp.eff.org
chdir pub
chdir Net_info
chdir EFF_Net_Guide
get netguide.eff
get netguide.faq
quit
```

Then check your mailbox in a few hours or the next day.

> Before you go get the EFF's net guide, I should warn you that it's long (longer than the amount of paper in a laser printer's paper tray, but shorter than the Sears catalog).

CHAPTER 12

Finding Files for ftp with archie

Featuring

- What is archie?
- Running an archie client
- archie by telnet
- archie by e-mail
- Anarchie for the Mac

In Chapter 11 we looked at ftp, which is fairly easy and straightforward to use. The only problem is finding out which ftp sites store the files and programs you want. Fortunately, there are huge database archives, called archie, on the Net. These archives keep track of every available file at every public ftp site.

There are also indexes of gopherspace out there, called veronica. Chapter 14 explains gophers and veronica. (gopher itself also provides another kind of organized access to ftp sites, with some gopher servers providing huge menus of sites.)

If you've got windowed Net access with a SLIP or PPP dial-up account, or access through a network at your work or school, then there's probably special archie client software available on your computer or network. Generally, such programs are easier to use than the UNIX archie program.

Whenever possible, make your archie searches during off-peak hours, generally nights and weekends, to help keep the loads manageable. This can also lead to faster results.

Instead of hunting through every ftp site there is, you just direct your search request to an archie server. Your request is called a *query* and it has to be phrased in a way the database (archie server) can understand.

General archie Procedures

There are three different ways to query archie servers. The easiest way is to run an archie client on your own system. This will only work if you have the archie program installed on your system.

Another way to query archie is to telnet to an archie server and submit your queries in an interactive session. The third way to query archie is to send mail to an archie server and include your queries in the body of the mail.

All queries include a *filename* for archie to match in its database. Generally, you want to allow matches that simply include the *filename* text, regardless of case.

The archie server will reply with a list of ftp sites that have files whose names include the *filename* text. Then you use anonymous ftp, as explained in Chapter 11, to get the files you want from the nearest site listed.

To see the manual pages for archie, type **man archie** at the UNIX prompt and press Enter.

Running an archie Client

If you're fortunate enough to have an archie client program available on your system, you can make your query by typing **archie −s** *filename* and pressing Enter at the UNIX prompt, using whatever text you want for *filename*. The archie client will tell you that it's searching and then will eventually list the sites (or "hosts") that have files whose names contain the text *filename*, along with information for each file found.

–s and Other Switches

The **–s** switch tells archie that the *filename* text can be any part of the filename found, and that different cases of the same letters should count as a match. If you want the search to be case sensitive and only match exact case matches, you can use the **–c** switch instead.

To have the files and sites listed in order of most recently changed files first, use the **–t** switch.

To limit the number of responses to some maximum (especially if the *filename* text is common and might yield a huge number of responses), use the **–m** *n* switch, and substitute the maximum number of responses you want for n. The default maximum if 95 (or whatever you changed it to last). One way to use this switch is to first submit your query with a small maximum number of responses (such as **–m 10**) to limit the turnaround time on the response. If you don't find what you're looking for the first time, repeat the request but up the maximum by some regular number (such as **–m 15**, an increase of 5). Lather, rinse, repeat.

You can set your query to have a lower priority than the default (which is the highest possible priority). To do so, use the switch **–N** *n*, and use a higher number for n to indicate a lower priority. The number for the lowest priority is 32767, but even the number 1 will put your query behind every query with the default (0) priority.

If you type just **archie** at the UNIX prompt and press Enter, you'll be given a list of switches and brief explanations of each.

If your system also hosts the archie server, the server will inform you about your request's "place in line" with all the other archie queries currently taking place, and about how long it should take.

FINDING FILES FOR FTP WITH ARCHIE

If the list is too long to fit on the screen, you can redo the query as *archie –s filename | more* and then page through the output that's returned.

Telnetting to archie

If you don't have an archie client on your system, you can either telnet or send e-mail to an archie host. Telnetting ties up more resources because it puts you into interactive communication with the server. This may be easier for you, as it's immediate (*synchronous* is the buzzword), but it's also wasteful, so use e-mail whenever possible.

To begin with, telnet to the (geographically) nearest archie site listed in Table 12.1.

> Sometimes searches fail or "time out." This probably means the server is too busy to handle your query just now. Try again later.

> Telnetting to the nearest site ties up the least amount of Net resources. All the archie servers have the same information, so there's no reason not to.

TABLE 12.1

archie Servers around the Globe

If You're Near	telnet To
United States	
Maryland	archie.sura.net
Nebraska	archie.unl.edu
New York	archie.ans.net *or* archie.internic.net
New Jersey	archie.rutgers.edu
Worldwide	
Australia	archie.au
Austria	archie.univie.ac.at *or* archie.edvz.uni-linz.ac.at
Canada	archie.mcgill.ca *or* archie.uqam.ca
Finland	archie.funet.fi

Telnetting to archie **155**

TABLE 12.1

archie Servers around the Globe (continued)

If You're Near	telnet To
France	archie.univ-rennes1.fr
Germany	archie.th-darmstadt.de
Israel	archie.ac.il
Italy	archie.unipi.it
Japan	archie.kuis.kyoto-u.ac.jp *or* archie.wide.ap.jp
Korea	archie.kr archie.hana.nm.kr *or* archie.sogang.ac.kr
New Zealand	archie.nz
Norway	archie.uninett.no
Spain	archie.rediris.es
Sweden	archie.luth.se
Switzerland	archie.switch.ch
Taiwan	archie.ncu.edu.tw *or* archie.nctuccca.edu.tw
United Kingdom	archie.doc.ic.ac.uk *or* archie.hensa.ac.uk

To do this, type **telnet archie.*sitename*** and press Enter. Then log in as **archie** and press Enter. If you are asked for a password, just press Enter. Figure 12.1 shows what happens when I telnet to the archie server at the University of Nebraska (the nearest one to me).

When you're connected to the server, you'll get a welcoming message on the screen and then the **archie>** prompt.

To make sure that whatever *filename* you specify will match even if it's only part of the file name found, type **set search sub** and press Enter.

Note that the UNL archie server automatically sets the search type to sub, so I don't need to set it to sub myself (not that it would hurt anything if I did).

FIGURE 12.1

The login procedure at the archie server at the University of Nebraska at Lincoln.

```
{netcom13:5} telnet archie.unl.edu
Trying...
Connected to crcnis2.unl.edu.
Escape character is '^]'.

SunOS UNIX (crcnis2)

login: archie
Password:
```

To get help (actually a list of commands), type **help** at the **archie>** prompt and press Enter.

If you expect to see a lot of responses to your query, you can type **set pager** and press Enter to have things come across one screenful at a time (just press spacebar to see each subsequent page).

If you're going to want to query results mailed to you, type **set mailto** *your-full-e-mail-address* and press Enter.

To actually search for programs, type **prog** *filename* at the archie> prompt and press Enter, using whatever text you want for *filename*. Figure 12.2 shows how I search for copies of the EFF Internet Guide.

archie will tell you about how long the search should take and then will go to work hunting for sites with those files. Figure 12.3 shows the first page of listed hosts that archie returned.

To have the output mailed to you (only if you used the set mailto command before submitting your query), type **mail** at the archie> prompt and press Enter.

FIGURE 12.2

I type **prog netguide** to search for any files with **netguide** in their file names.

```
unl-archie> set pager
unl-archie> set mailto xian@netcom.com
unl-archie> prog netguide
# Search type: sub.
# Your queue position: 2
# Estimated time for completion: 00:27
working... -
```

Telnetting to archie **157**

FIGURE 12.3

```
┌─────────────── Terminal - NETCOM.TRM ───────────────┐
│ File  Edit  Settings  Phone  Transfers  Help        │
│ Host mrcnext.cso.uiuc.edu    (128.174.201.12)       │
│ Last updated 09:54 25 Jul 1994                      │
│                                                      │
│     Location: /pub/linux/docs/linux-doc-project/network-guide │
│         FILE    -r--r--r--    5356 bytes  00:00 31 Aug 1993  netguide-0.4.README │
│                                                      │
│ Host dime.cs.umass.edu       (128.119.40.244)       │
│ Last updated 17:00 24 Jul 1994                      │
│                                                      │
│     Location: /pub/rcf/opine-dist/linux/docs/linux-doc-project/network-guide │
│         FILE    -rw-r--r--    5356 bytes  00:00 30 Aug 1993  netguide-0.4.README │
│                                                      │
│ Host ftp.engr.ucf.edu        (132.170.200.67)       │
│ Last updated 14:13 24 Jul 1994                      │
│                                                      │
│     Location: /pub/linux-mirrors/tsx11/docs/linux-doc-project │
│         FILE    -r--r--r--    5356 bytes  00:00  4 Sep 1993  netguide-0.4.README │
│                                                      │
│ Host ftp.germany.eu.net      (192.76.144.75)        │
│ db/tmp/AAAa12130                                    │
└─────────────────────────────────────────────────────┘
```

Just the first page (of many) of hosts with files containing the text netguide *in their file names.*

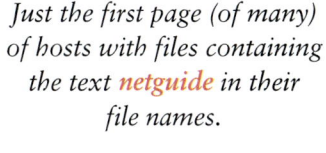

If you're paging through a long list, you can stop at any point by pressing an alphabetical key.

Searching for Files When You Don't Know Their Names

When you want to find programs related to a subject but you don't know any file names, you can use the whatis command to search for any files whose descriptions (also stored in the archie database) contain a key word. Type **whatis keyword** at the archie› prompt and press Enter.

If you see a file name that relates to the subject you were interested, type **prog filename** and press Enter at the archie prompt to see where you can get the program from.

FINDING FILES FOR FTP WITH ARCHIE

When you are finished with archie, type **quit** at the archie> prompt and press Enter.

> You can then retrieve the files you want by ftpmail. ftpmail is explained in Chapter 11.

archie by E-Mail

To submit an archie query by e-mail, send mail to **archie @quiche.cs.mcgill.ca** or to **archie @archie-server** (where *archie-server* is any of the sites listed in Table 12.1—preferably the one closest to you).

Leave the subject line blank. include the line **prog *filename*** in the text of the message. If you want to search for more than one file, you can also type **prog *filename1 filename2*** etc. If you want more information about archie by e-mail, include the word **help** on a line by itself in your message.

The archie server will mail you back a list of hosts and files.

Combined archie and ftp with Anarchie for the Mac

archie clients on windowed operating systems are generally much easier to use than character-based archie clients. There is an excellent program available for Macintoshes, called Anarchie, that combines archie and ftp. Why didn't someone think of this sooner?

To start Anarchie, you double-click the Anarchie icon. Anarchie first brings up a window called Bookmarks, with a very thorough, built-in list of ftp sites.

To make an archie query, press Command-T. This brings up the Archie dialog box (see Figure 12.4).

FIGURE 12.4

The Archie dialog box. Type the file you're looking for in the Find box and then click the Find button. I'm looking for the excellent Eudora e-mail program for the Mac.

The server in the Server box should be the nearest one to you. Choose the nearest one if it's not. Type the *filename* text into the Find box. Then click the Find button (bottom right). Anarchie will display a window with the *filename* text in the title bar and a guesstimate of how much longer it's going to take:

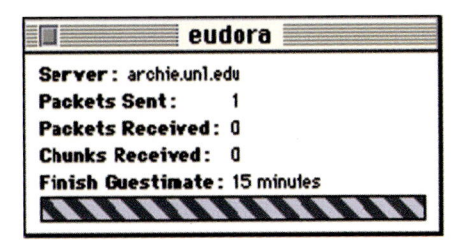

When it's done, Anarchie will display a window containing all the directories and files it's found with the *filename* search text, along with the host sites they're stored at (see Figure 12.5).

FIGURE 12.5

This window contains all the files and directories with eudora in their names, along with the ftp sites they're stored at.

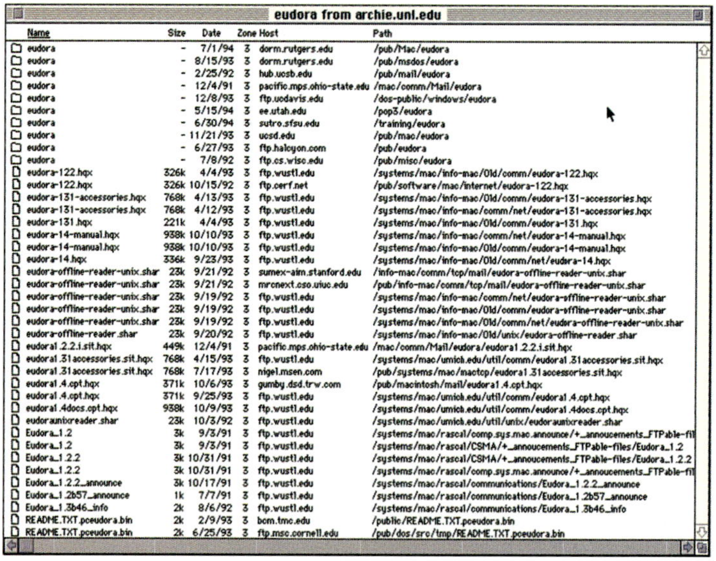

To retrieve the file you want, just double-click it.

CHAPTER 13

Remote Login with telnet and Other Programs

Featuring

- Remote login with telnet
- Getting help for telnet
- Guided telnet with Hytelnet
- A smattering of telnet sites

One aspect of the interconnectedness of the Net is that you can log into other machines on the Internet directly from your own computer. With telnet and other remote login programs, you can log into any computer or network for which you have a password, as well as thousands of public sites where passwords are not required.

Many Internet services, including archie, gopher, and lynx, are available by telnet even if your service provider does not offer client software for those services. See Chapter 12 to telnet to an archie client, Chapter 14 to a gopher client, and Chapter 15 to a lynx client.

You can even telnet to your own service provider and log into your own account, even if you're already logged in there! This is useful when you are borrowing someone else's access and want to log into your own account to, say, check your e-mail.

You can also run the telnet program by just typing **telnet** and pressing enter at the UNIX prompt. This will put you at a telnet› prompt. Then type **open host-sitename** and press Enter.

Many university libraries now make their catalogs available by telnet, as do countless other repositories of useful information. Of course, as with so many other Internet resources, you need to know where to go to take advantage of these public sites. Unfortunately, there's no overriding index or guide to available telnet sites. One remote login program, Hytelnet, does include an up-to-date index of university libraries, so that's a start. In general, though, you have to ask around and collect remote login sites just as you have to with ftp sites.

What Is telnet?

As with ftp, telnet is both a protocol (a prearranged form of communication) and the name of the most common UNIX program that executes that protocol. (It's also a client.) It's a generic enough name that if you have a windowed Internet interface, then you can most likely just open up a telnet window and make your connection that way.

Running telnet is a little like starting a new terminal session inside your current terminal window.

General telnet Procedure

Telnetting is easy. You type **telnet *host-sitename*** and press Enter. Sometimes you have to add a port number after the site name (there must be a space separating the site name and the port number). Then you have to log in.

Logging in with telnet

Logging in with telnet is the same as logging into any UNIX system. You type your username and press Enter. Then you type a password and press Enter.

General telnet Procedure 163

Figure 13.1 shows me telnetting to California State University's Advanced Technology Information Network to get information about California agriculture. The telnet site is caticsuf.cati.csufresno.edu, and the username that I'm supposed to log in with is public.

```
{netcom2:4} telnet caticsuf.cati.csufresno.edu
Trying...
Connected to caticsuf.cati.csufresno.edu.
Escape character is '^]'.

SunOS UNIX (caticsuf)

login: public
```

FIGURE 13.1

Logging into the Advanced Technology Information Network via telnet

I'm not asked for a password. Instead, a screen full of welcoming information appears.

From this point in, you're on your own. Depending on where you've telnetted to, you'll either be at a UNIX prompt or inside some information program. There are myriad such programs and each one works differently, but don't worry. They'll all prompt you and they're designed for lay people. Generally, you can press Enter to accept defaults until you're given a menu of information. Then you have to make some choices.

> For public sites, you might have to log in as some special name, and you'll either not be asked for a password or you'll be able to just press Enter when asked for a password.

Logging Out

Logging out from a telnet session is either a matter of typing **bye** or **exit** or **logout** at a UNIX prompt, or pressing **q** (for *quit*) or choosing the appropriate menu choice from within an information program. telnet will sign you off with Connection closed by foreign host.

> If you are left at a telnet> prompt after you log out, type **quit** and press Enter to quit the telnet program.

Getting Help with telnet

telnet is pretty easy to use, but there are nonetheless several way to get help with it. From your UNIX prompt, you can type **man telnet** and press Enter to see the manual pages for the telnet program.

Also, you can run the telnet program without specifying a host and then type **help** or **?** at the telnet> prompt and press Enter to get a short list of commands.

Logging In to Other UNIX Machines with rlogin

If you just want to log into another UNIX account (or even your own), the easiest way is with rlogin. Just type **rlogin sitename** at the UNIX prompt and press Enter. You won't be asked for your username or password. Log out as usual with **bye** or **exit** or **logout**.

Hytelnet—A Smart telnet Program

If you like telnet but would appreciate a little more guidance about which sites to log into, you should try Hytelnet. Hytelnet is a sort of meta-telnet program that works with menus and keeps up-to-date lists of library-catalog and other sites.

If Hytelnet is available on your system, just type **hytelnet** at the UNIX prompt and press Enter. This will bring up the Hytelnet main menu (see Figure 13.2).

Use the up and down arrows to move the highlight to the topic you want to see. Press Enter or the right arrow to jump to a highlighted topic. Press the left arrow to jump back to the previous topic.

If the Hytelnet client program is not available on your system, you can check out Hytelnet by (what else?) telnetting to the site where it resides. Type **telnet access.usask.ca** and press Enter. Log in as **hytelnet**. No password is required.

FIGURE 13.2

```
┌──────────────────── Terminal - NETCOM.TRM ────────────────────┐
│ File  Edit  Settings  Phone  Transfers  Help                  │
│                    Welcome to HYTELNET                        │
│                        version 6.3                            │
│                     ....................                      │
│                                                               │
│     What is HYTELNET?         <WHATIS>     .   Up/Down arrows MOVE
│     Library catalogs          <SITES1>     .   Left/Right arrows SELECT
│     Other resources           <SITES2>     .   ? for HELP anytime
│     Help files for catalogs   <OP000>      .
│     Catalog interfaces        <SYS000>     .   m returns here
│     Internet Glossary         <GLOSSARY>   .   q quits
│     Telnet tips               <TELNET>     .
│     Telnet/TN3270 escape keys <ESCAPE.KEY> .
│     Key-stroke commands       <HELP>       .
│                                                               │
│                     ....................                      │
│              HYTELNET 6.3 was written by Peter Scott,         │
│     U of Saskatchewan Libraries, Saskatoon, Sask, Canada. 1992│
│     Unix and VMS software by Earl Fogel, Computing Services, U of S 1992
└───────────────────────────────────────────────────────────────┘
```

Hytelnet—a smarter, menu-driven telnet

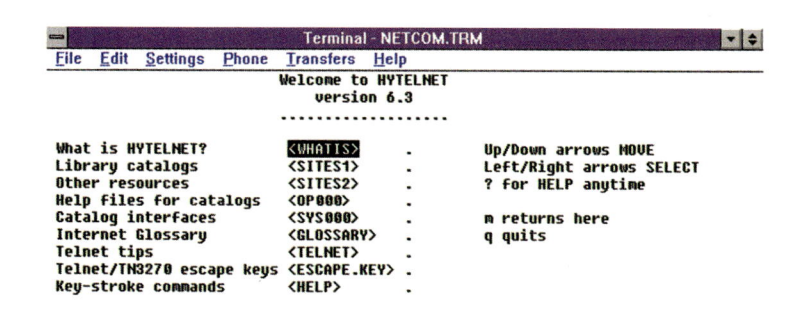

Press Enter with <WHATIS> highlighted for information about Hytelnet. To go to library catalogs, highlight <SITES1> and press Enter. To go to other information sources, highlight <SITES2> and press Enter.

When there is more than one screenful of information available, type **+** or press the spacebar to see the next page. Type **–** or **b** to see the previous page.

At any point, you can return to the main menu by typing **m**.

To get help from anywhere within Hytelnet, type **?**.

To quit Hytelnet, type **q**. If you have any problems with Hytelnet or it freezes up on you, press Ctrl-] to escape and then type **close** and press Enter.

Depending on your communications program, the arrow keys might not work for you in ytelnet. If so, use **j** to go up an item on a list, **k** to go down an item, **l** to jump to a topic, and **h** to jump back to a previous topic. (If you're in Windows, check your communications program's terminal preferences to see if you can assign arrow keys to your terminal emulation instead of to their normal Windows functions.)

telnet Sites to Check Out

As I mentioned, there's no unified source of telnet sites (though the Hytelnet program is a good start). In case you're interested in exploring, though, I'll list a smattering of telnet sites here for you to check out. Beyond that, you'll have to ask

To check out InterNIC's information on telnet sites, anonymous ftp to **ds.internic.net** and hunt around. To check out the CERFnet Archives, ftp to **ftp.cerf.net** and look in the cerfnet/cerfnet_info/library_catalog directory for the most recent file called internet catalogs.*date* (the most recent *date*), or gopher to **gopher.cerf.net**. Anonymous ftp is explained in Chapter 11. gopher is explained in Chapter 14.

around on mailing lists, newsgroups, and elsewhere for interesting telnet sites.

Weather Reports

telnet site: madlab.sprl.umich.edu 3000

The Exact Time

telnet site: india.colorado.edu

Geography Facts

telnet site: martini.eecs.umich.edu

Library of Congress

telnet site: locis.loc.gov

Government Documents

telnet site: fedworld.gov

login: new

CHAPTER 14

Looking for Things with a gopher

Featuring

- gopher basics
- Navigating gopher menus
- Getting to other gopher servers
- Leaving bookmarks in gopherspace
- ftp-ing with gopher
- Searching gopherspace with veronica and jughead

The Internet gopher is one of the most useful and seamless tools on the Net today. Technically, the gopher sits (or rides) on top of ftp, and performs telnet logins, archie searches, and other Internet services without requiring you to know (or type) the specific addresses and commands. The gopher does this by presenting everything to you in the form of menus. As long as you can highlight an item on a menu and select it, the gopher does the rest.

Another way to "surf" the Net is by browsing the WorldWide Web. A lot of what you can do with a gopher, you can also do on the Web. See Chapter 15 for more on this.

The gopher is so-called either because it can "go fer" stuff and bring it to you, or because the mascot of the University of Minnesota (where gopher was created) is a gopher; it is not named after the Love Boat character played by (now U.S. Representative) Fred Grandy.

Surfing the Net

You can start at any gopher server (site) and get to almost any other one, by choosing the Other Gopher Servers choice from the main menu. This brings the whole of "gopherspace" within your reach, no matter where you start.

The beauty of gopher is that everything is presented to you in the form of menus (or lists). The items on the menus can be directories, documents, searchable databases, other menus, and more. It doesn't matter if the source material is stored on a UNIX machine, nor VMS, DOS, Macintosh, or anything. With gopher, it's all the same to you. Another advantage is that the menu entries can be plain-English names, even when they point to a file, so you really know what you're getting or looking at.

For example, wouldn't you rather choose a menu item such as "Public Access to Government Information" rather than connect to gopher.well.sf.ca.us, port 70, directory path 1/Communications/, file name public-access?

You can start almost anywhere, follow any tangent that catches your fancy, and leave bookmarks in any part of gopherspace you might want to return to. When you find your way to a document, you can read it on screen, have it fetched (or mailed) to your Internet account, or even download it directly to your desktop machine (if you dial up your account on a different computer).

Don't worry if you get a "busy signal"—a message that you can't be connected right now because there are too many people using the server. Just try again a little later. As with other Internet resources, use the gopher whenever possible in the evenings and on weekends.

How to Use the gopher

Here's the general procedure for running a gopher client. First, start the program. You can specify a server when you start the program, but you don't have to. If you don't, the first menu you see will be for the default gopher server that your client starts you off with.

From this point on, it's all a matter of selecting from menus. No matter which server you start from, you can always choose to go to other gopher servers and keep searching from there.

When you find your way to documents, you can read them, one screenful at a time, search through them for key words, bring them back to your Internet account via ftp, have them mailed to your Internet address, or download them directly to your desktop computer.

Running a UNIX gopher

If there's a gopher client installed on your system, you can run it by typing *gopher* at the UNIX prompt and pressing Enter. To start the gopher client with a different server from its default, type *gopher server-sitename* and press Enter. This is called "pointing" your gopher client at the server.

Figure 14.1 shows the first-level menu that appears when I run my gopher client and point it at the University of Minnesota gopher.

You can also search through indexes of topics in gopherspace with veronica or through high-level gopher menus with jughead. (These two programs were obviously named after archie.) See the end of this chapter for how to use veronica and jughead.

FIGURE 14.1

The main menu from the University of Minnesota's Gopher server

```
                    Terminal - NETCOM.TRM
 File  Edit  Settings  Phone  Transfers  Help
               Internet Gopher Information Client 2.0 p15

                    Root gopher server: consultant.micro.umn.edu

     -->  1.  Information About Gopher/
          2.  Computer Information/
          3.  Internet file server (ftp) sites/
          4.  Fun & Games/
          5.  Libraries/
          6.  Mailing Lists/
          7.  News/
          8.  Other Gopher and Information Servers/
          9.  Phone Books/
         10.  Search Gopher Titles at the University of Minnesota <?>
         11.  Search lots of places at the U of M <?>
         12.  UofM Campus Information/



 Press ? for Help, Q to Quit, U to go up a menu          Page: 1/1
```

I pointed my gopher client at the U of M gopher by typing *gopher consultant.micro.umn.edu* and pressing Enter.

LOOKING FOR THINGS WITH A GOPHER

At any point you can return to the main menu by typing **m**. You can also connect to a new gopher server by typing **o** and then entering the host name.

> ### Telnet to a Gopher Server If You Haven't Got a Client
>
> If your system doesn't have a gopher client installed, you can still use gopher by telnetting to a server, preferably the one nearest to you. If you're asked for a password, just press Enter. Here are some gopher servers you can get to by telnet:
>
> | If You're Near | telnet To | Log In As |
> |---|---|---|
> | North America (Minnesota) | consultant.micro.umn.edu | gopher |
> | North America (Illinois) | ux1.cso.uiuc.edu | gopher |
> | North America (Iowa) | panda.uiowa.edu | panda |
> | Australia | info.anu.edu.au | info |
> | Sweden | gopher.chalmers.se | gopher |
> | Europe | gopher.ebone.net | gopher |
>
> You won't be able to save documents automatically to your home directory, but you will be able to mail them (use the **m** command) to your Internet address.

Getting Around the Menus

Browsing gopherspace is then just a matter of selecting menu choices and following them where they go. You can always just type the number of a menu item and then press Enter. Depending on your communications program, you may be able to use your arrow keys to get around the menus (↓ to go down an item, ↑ to go up one, → to select an item and follow it where it goes, ← to go back to the previous menu, if any).

The ability to always find your way back through previous menus (with **u**) is as useful as the proverbial trail of bread crumbs.

Otherwise, type **j** to go down an item and **k** to go up one. Press Enter to select and item and follow it where it goes, and type **u** to go back to the previous menu.

Running a UNIX gopher   **171**

If a menu is longer than one screen long, press the spacebar to go to the next screenful (or **>**, **+**, or PageDown). To go back to the previous screenful, press **b** (or **<**, **–**, or PageUp).

- Items that end in a forward slash (/) lead to new menus.
- Items that end in a period (.) or no punctuation lead to text documents.
- Items that end in <?> or <CSO> lead to searchable indexes.
- Items that end in <tel> activate telnet connections.

I pressed Enter to select *Information About Gopher/*. Because that item ends in a forward slash, it takes me to another menu (see Figure 14.2).

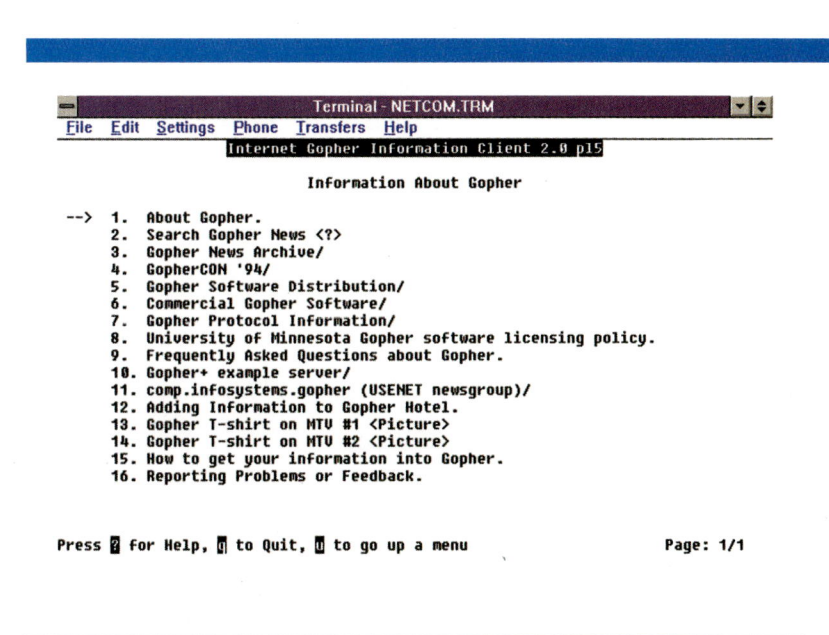

FIGURE 14.2

The Information About Gopher menu

```
                    Terminal - NETCOM.TRM
 File  Edit  Settings  Phone  Transfers  Help
             Internet Gopher Information Client 2.0 p15

                        Information About Gopher

 -->  1.  About Gopher.
      2.  Search Gopher News <?>
      3.  Gopher News Archive/
      4.  GopherCON '94/
      5.  Gopher Software Distribution/
      6.  Commercial Gopher Software/
      7.  Gopher Protocol Information/
      8.  University of Minnesota Gopher software licensing policy.
      9.  Frequently Asked Questions about Gopher.
     10.  Gopher+ example server/
     11.  comp.infosystems.gopher (USENET newsgroup)/
     12.  Adding Information to Gopher Hotel.
     13.  Gopher T-shirt on MTV #1 <Picture>
     14.  Gopher T-shirt on MTV #2 <Picture>
     15.  How to get your information into Gopher.
     16.  Reporting Problems or Feedback.


 Press ? for Help, q to Quit, u to go up a menu          Page: 1/1
```

Reading Documents in gopher

Eventually, your selections will lead you to a document. (You'll select an item that ends in a period or no punctuation.)

Actually, gopher documents might be piped through any paging program, not necessarily *more*, but the general rule is the same: Press the spacebar to advance another screenful.

Don't choose print if you're connected to a UNIX account by modem. gopher will attempt to print your document at the host computer, and it will probably fail.

The document will first appear on the screen. If you're not interested in reading it right away, type **q**.

Documents are piped through the UNIX paging program called more. To see the next page, press the spacebar. To go back one page, type **b**.

To search a document in gopher, type **/** and then type the text you'd like to search for and press Enter. To repeat a search with the same search text, just press **n**.

When you get to the end of a document, or quit reading it, you'll be given these options: **Press <RETURN> to continue, <m> to mail, <D> to download, <s> to save, or <p> to print:**. Press Enter to return to the previous menu. Type **m** to mail the document to yourself. You'll be prompted for the address:

```
+------------------------------------------------+
| Mail current document to:                      |
|                           [Cancel ^G] [Accept - Enter] |
+------------------------------------------------+
```

Type **D** to download the document (be sure to type an uppercase D). You'll be given a choice of download protocols (see Figure 14.3).

FIGURE 14.3

gopher prompts you for your preferred file-transfer (download) protocol.

See Chapter 10 for more on downloading files to your desktop computer.

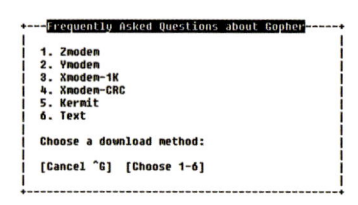

```
+--Frequently Asked Questions about Gopher--+
| 1. Zmodem                                 |
| 2. Ymodem                                 |
| 3. Xmodem-1K                              |
| 4. Xmodem-CRC                             |
| 5. Kermit                                 |
| 6. Text                                   |
| Choose a download method:                 |
| [Cancel ^G]  [Choose 1-6]                 |
+-------------------------------------------+
```

Choose whichever one you like to use with your communications program (by number). Then, in your communications program, choose to receive a binary file.

Type s to save a copy of the file in your home directory. gopher will prompt you for a file name. Press Enter or type a different file name and press Enter.

Getting to Another gopher Server

To get to a different gopher server from the one you started with, look for a menu item such as *Other Gopher and Information Servers/* (this is how it's worded on the U of M gopher main menu). Not all servers have this type of option, so if you're in a cul-de-sac, run your gopher client again but point it at a server such as consultant.micro.umn.edu to start with.

You'll be taken to a top-level menu from which you can select either a large alphabetical list of gopher servers or a general geographical area to start with.

If you know the name of the server you want, you can select the alphabetical option. Otherwise, start zeroing in with the correct region. I've found my way to the Electronic Frontier Foundation's gopher server in Austin (see Figure 14.4).

When a list is very long, such as a list of all the gopher servers in the world, you can save time paging through it by searching for a keyword. To start a search, type a forward slash (/). This will bring up a box into which you can type the text to search for. Then press Enter.

FIGURE 14.4

I searched for "electronic" and repeated the search twice.

```
                    Terminal - NETCOM.TRM
File  Edit  Settings  Phone  Transfers  Help
             Internet Gopher Information Client 2.0 p15

                     All the Gopher Servers in the World

       433.  Economic Democracy Information Network (EDIN)/
       434.  Economist, The (Magazine)/
       435.  Ecuador Gophers/
       436.  Ecuador Ministerio de Relaciones Exteriores/
       437.  Education Central project at Central Michigan University/
       438.  Education Gopher at Florida Tech/
       439.  Education Service Center, Region 20/
       440.  Educational Testing Center - Advanced Placement Program/
       441.  Eidgenoessische Technische Hochschule(ETH), Zuerich, (CH)/
       442.  Eindhoven University of Technology - Math & Computing Sci.,(NL)/
       443.  Eisenhower National Clearinghouse/
       444.  Eisenhower National Clearinghouse/
       445.  El Camino Community College District Gopher/
       446.  Electromagn. Wave Research Institute of NRC, Florence, (IT)/
       447.  Electronic Frontier Foundation/
  -->  448.  Electronic Frontier Foundation (EFF) Gopher/
       449.  Electronic Journal of Differential Equations/
       450.  Electronic Newsstand, The (tm)/

Press ? for Help, q to Quit, u to go up a menu           Page: 25/103
```

To get the EFF's Internet Guide from here, first select *Net Info (EFF's Guide to the Internet, FAQs, etc.)/*, then select *EFF's Guide to the Internet (ex-Big Dummy's Guide)/*, then choose the format you want and save it to your home directory.

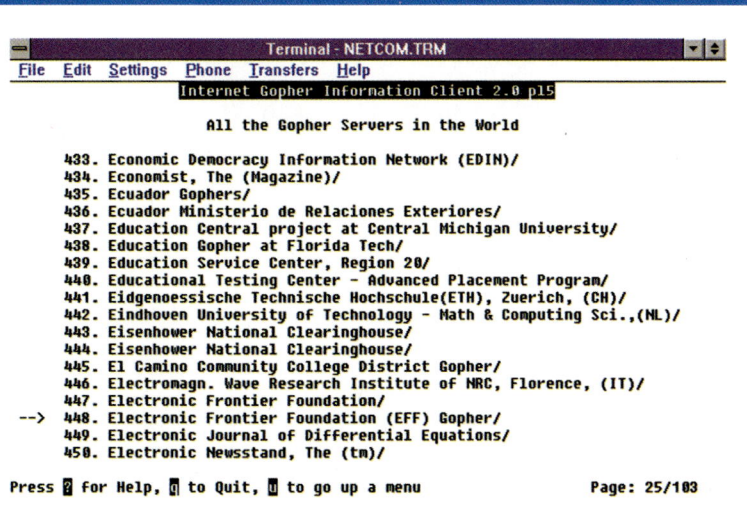

Bookmarks in gopherspace

If you find your way to or stumble upon an interesting gopher site or stash of documents, you might want to create a bookmark there so that you can find your way back more easily.

To add a menu item to your bookmark list, type **a**. To add the current menu to your bookmark list, type **A**. gopher will prompt you for a name for the bookmark (suggesting the name of the item or menu):

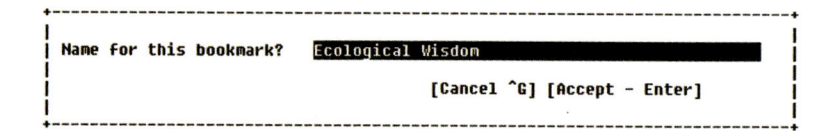

```
Name for this bookmark?   Ecological Wisdom
                                    [Cancel ^G] [Accept - Enter]
```

Press Enter to accept the suggested name or type a different name and press Enter. You can view your bookmark list at any time by typing **v**. (The bookmark list will appear as a gopher menu, just like any other, with the heading Bookmarks.) To delete a bookmark from your bookmark list, type **d**.

To start your gopher client with your bookmark list as the first menu, type **gopher –b** at the UNIX prompt and press Enter.

Info from Behind the Scenes

Though gopher shields you from having to know the exact name or Internet address of the menu or menu item you're looking at, you can always see the reference for the current menu item by typing **=**. The reference will look something like this:

```
#
Type=0
Name="Literary Ecology"
Path=R0-41927-//journals/pmc/v2/WHITE-1.991
Host=una.hh.lib.umich.edu
Port=70
```

And you can mail it, download it, or save it just like any other document.

Quitting gopher

You can quit gopher at any time by typing q or pressing Ctrl-C. gopher will ask you if you're sure: Really quit (y/n) ? y. Press Enter to quit. To quit without being prompted, type Q.

Getting Help for gopher

You can get a quick reference of gopher commands by typing ? at any time. The help document can be saved, downloaded, or mailed just like any other document.

You can see the manual pages for gopher by typing man gopher at the UNIX prompt and pressing Enter.

You can also ask questions about and discuss gopher in the Usenet newsgroup comp.infosystems.gopher. *See Chapters 7 and 8 for more on Usenet newsgroups.*

ftp via gopher

As I mentioned before, gopher uses ftp to bring documents to your screen, though you don't need to think about that or even notice it, but you can also use your gopher client to perform your own ftp file transfers. Look for a menu item similar to *Internet file server (ftp) sites/* on the U of M gopher's main menu. This should take you to a menu like the one shown in Figure 14.5.

From such a menu, you can get information about ftp, perform file transfers, use archie or even a special gopher version

Chapters 11 and 12 discuss ftp.

FIGURE 14.5

The gopher menu of Internet file server (ftp) sites

```
                  Terminal - NETCOM.TRM
File  Edit  Settings  Phone  Transfers  Help
           Internet Gopher Information Client 2.0 p15

                   Internet file server (ftp) sites

  -->  1.  About FTP Searches.
       2.  InterNIC: Internet Network Information Center/
       3.  Popular FTP Sites via Gopher/
       4.  Query a specific ftp host <?>
       5.  Search FTP sites with Archie (gopher+ version)/
       6.  Search FTP sites with Archie (non-gopher+ version)/
       7.  UnStuffIt.hqx <HQX>
```

LOOKING FOR THINGS WITH A GOPHER

There's an excellent gopher program for the Macintosh called TurboGopher. Each menu is displayed in its own window. Documents are shown with a document icon. Menus are shown with a folder icon. For the Mac user, browsing gopherspace feels just like opening files on your own hard drive: You click on folders and they open into windows; you click on documents and they open for you to read.

The WorldWide Web is another system that allows the participation of users on any type of computer platform and with any level of connectivity. Chapter 15 explains the Web.

of archie, or get a listing of ftp sites organized by subject. This can make ftp a lot easier to use.

Running a Windowed gopher Client

gopher is a sophisticated Internet client-server system that allows seamless integration of different data types and protocols without regard to the type of computer the client (you, more or less) is running on. If you run gopher from a character-based UNIX account, you see things as lists, consisting of text entries. If you run a gopher client on another platform, the menus and items will look appropriate to that type of computer.

To run a gopher client directly in Windows or on the Mac, you need either dial-up SLIP or PPP access, or a network connection to the Internet. Netcom's NetCruiser for Windows runs with a SLIP connection and includes a gopher application.

To run the NetCruiser gopher, you just click the gopher icon (shown here). This starts you off at NetCruiser's site chooser, where you can accept the default gopher site (gopher.netcom.com), type in the name of another site, or click on the map to get lists of sites by geographical region. Clicking OK takes you to the Netcom gopher's main menu. Items that lead to further menus appear as folders. Items that are documents appear with document icons (see Figure 14.6).

Navigate the gopher by double-clicking items you want to pursue. At any point, you can type in the site address of any gopher server in the box at the top of the window. Figure 14.7 shows the dWELLers' choice menu at the Well's gopher server, which lists items that Well users have selected as their favorites.

Scroll through documents the way you would with any Windows program, by clicking the scroll bar or dragging the scroll box. To search for key words, just click the search button (it shows a magnifying glass and the letters SE), type the text you want to search for, and press Enter.

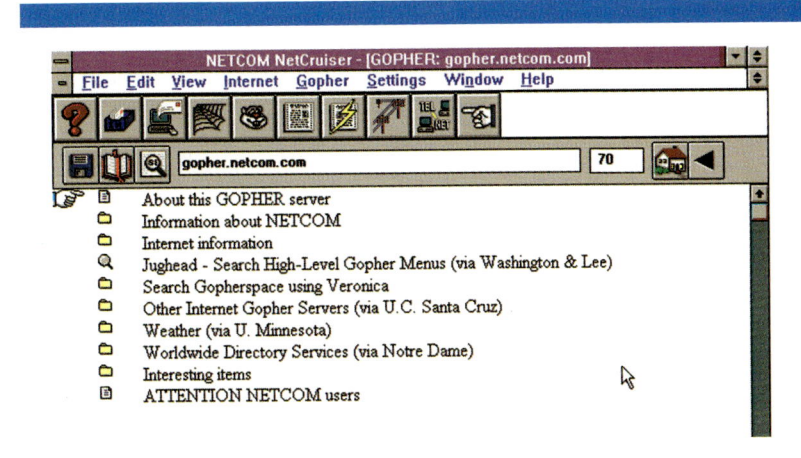

FIGURE 14.6

The NetCruiser gopher's main menu

FIGURE 14.7

The dWELLer's choice menu, which can be reached from the Internet Outbound (Links we think are cool) item on the Well gopher's main menu.

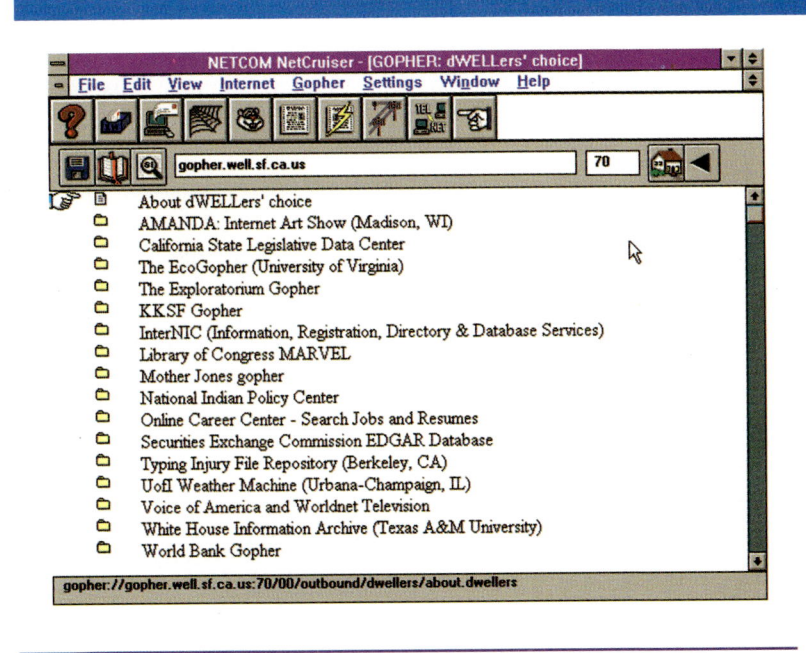

Sifting through gopherspace with veronica

gopher's biggest advantage is its comprehensiveness. It can take you almost anywhere. This is also its biggest disadvantage, one that's endemic to the Internet. With so many resources available at your fingertips, how do you find something specific? Fortunately, there's a gopher facility called veronica that enables you to search for keywords in titles (menu items) throughout gopherspace.

veronica searches don't include the contents of documents, which is just as well, as they'd probably take forever if they did. veronica databases have every menu item (or title or heading, if you will) from just about every gopher server on the Internet. The only limitation is the delay in keeping up to date.

> They say veronica stands for "very easy rodent-oriented netwide index to computerized archives," but I'm sure the acronym preceded the full name. (Veronica is one of the main characters in Archie comics, so it's a sort of pun or allusion.)

Getting to veronica

To get to a veronica server, run your gopher client and select the *Other Gopher and Information Servers/* or similar option. Then select *Search titles in Gopherspace using veronica/*. (The veronica option might also be on your main menu.) This will take you to a gopher menu like the one shown in Figure 14.8.

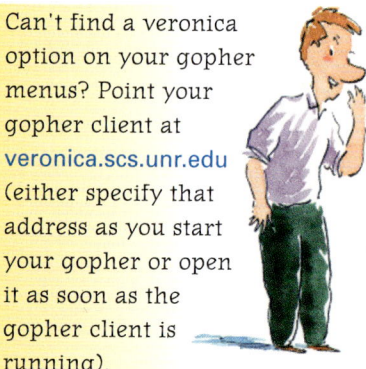

> Can't find a veronica option on your gopher menus? Point your gopher client at veronica.scs.unr.edu (either specify that address as you start your gopher or open it as soon as the gopher client is running).

Selecting a Search Type

If your menu looks like the one in Figure 14.8, then you have a choice of veronica servers. Your menu might not include so many options, in which case a veronica server will be chosen for you (possibly by default). This doesn't matter much.

Another choice you can make is to search directory titles only (so that your search results will lead to menus, not menu items), or to search titles of menus and documents. Why would you want to search only menus? Mainly to limit your search and lead you to the general sources of information, so that you can sift through the document titles yourself.

> Once you get to a veronica menu, you can make a bookmark for it to make it easier to get to. In the UNIX gopher program, just type **a** when the menu is on the screen (and press **v** to view your bookmarks and choose one).

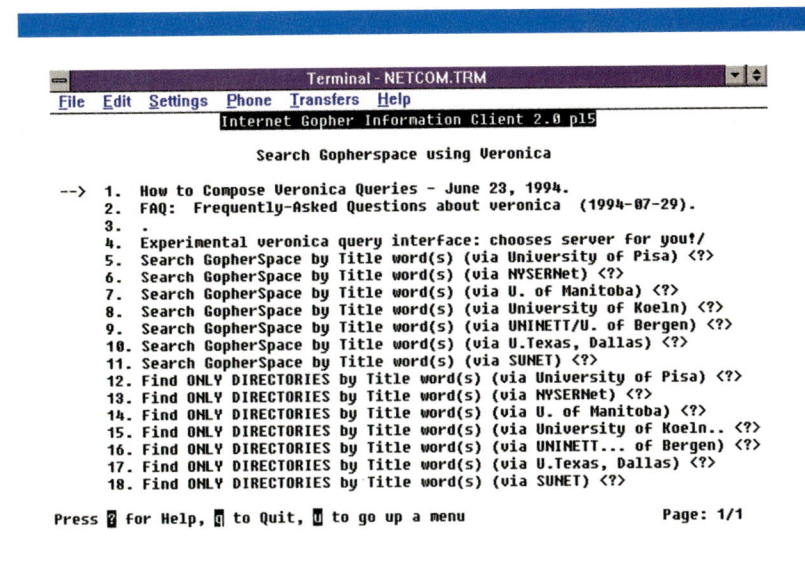

FIGURE 14.8

A typical veronica gopher menu

> If you have to choose a veronica server, choose one close to you geographically. This helps to conserve resources and make the Net run better for everyone.

When you select a type of search, you'll be presented with a box to type your search words into.

Entering the Search Text

You can search for a single word or for a combination of words. veronica searches are not case-sensitive. The more specific you make your search, the fewer results you'll have to peruse to find what you're looking for.

To search for titles that contain more than one word, just type the words, separated by spaces (the order makes no difference). For example, a search for **television violence** will find all titles with both of those words in them. You can put **or** between words to find titles with either of the two words in them. Be careful, though—this makes it easier to find a match.

Use **not** to look for titles not containing the word that comes after *not*. Use parentheses, if necessary, to group elements of a search together. For example, to search for any title with the word *television* or *TV*, and *violence*, enter **(television or tv) violence**.

> Include an asterisk (*) at the end of a string of characters to find all words that start with those characters. A search for **improvi*** will match both *improvise* and *improvisation*, but not *improve*.

LOOKING FOR THINGS WITH A GOPHER

> Some veronica servers have a different default maximum from 200.

Limiting the Number of Matches

Normally, veronica will show you the first 200 titles that matched your entry. You can change the number of titles it should show by including −m *number* as a separate word in the search box, substituting the maximum number of titles you want to see for *number*. Without a number, −m means show an unlimited number of titles.

The Results of a veronica Search

veronica creates a customized gopher menu with all the titles that matched your request as menu items. It's a normal gopher menu and you follow up any interesting items in it the normal way.

Searching gopher Menus with jughead

Another search facility now available through gopher is called jughead (yet another Archie comics character). jughead is less common than veronica (so far), and its database entries don't go as deep into gopherspace as the veronica databases do. It's great for finding starting points for likely searches, though. To try jughead, start with *Other Gopher and Information Servers/* and look for a menu item such as *Jughead - Search High-Level Gopher Menus (via Washington & Lee) <?>*.

> You can save the customized menu by putting it in your bookmark list. To do this in the UNIX gopher program, type **a**.

If you don't seem to have that option available, point your gopher client at liberty.uc.wlu.edu and select *Finding Gopher Resources/* and then *Search High-Level Gopher Menus by JUGHEAD at W&L <?>*. When you select that item, you'll be shown a search box. Enter the words to search for in it and press Enter. jughead creates a gopher menu from the results, just as veronica does.

CHAPTER 15

Surfing the WorldWide Web

Featuring

- What is the WorldWide Web?
- Browsing the Web with lynx and www
- Browsing the Web with Mosaic and NetCruiser
- Getting help and information on the Web
- Doing gopher, ftp, telnet, and Usenet with your browser
- Some interesting Web destinations

One of the newest media available over the Internet is the WorldWide Web. The Web (or sometimes W^3) is a huge collection of interconnected hypertext documents. Hypertext documents can contain links to other documents, or to ftp sites, gopher sites, telnet sites, etc. With a Web browser, you can jump from one link to the next, following the trail of links in any direction that interests you. Not everything on the Internet is available via the Web, but more and more of it is getting linked up.

What Is Hypertext?

On the Web, hypertext is simply text with links. Links are just elements of the hypertext documents that you can select. Select a link and you'll be transported to the document it's linked to (or to a different part of the current document). If you use Windows, then you've got hypertext right in front of you, in the form of Windows help files. Whenever you select options from the Help menu of a Windows program, you are shown a hypertext help document with definitions and links available at the click of a mouse. (Mac users also have a form of hypertext available, with the built-in Hypercard program.)

In addition to taking you to other documents, links can take you to gopher servers, ftp sites, telnet sites, Usenet news groups, and other Internet facilities. Links can also take you to programs, pictures, sounds, movies, and other binary files.

Once we start expanding the idea to include other media besides text, the rubric of hypertext is replaced by the word hypermedia. But the idea is the same: links. An advantage of hypertext (or hypermedia) is that it allows you to navigate through all kinds of related documents (and other kinds of files), using one simple procedure—selecting a link.

A drawback is that, for now, you generally must follow links that other people have created, so the medium is not yet fully interactive. Also, there's a lot more text out there than hypertext. A Web browser can lead you to a plain text document as easily as to a hypertext document. You won't be able to jump anywhere else from there, so it's a sort of cul-de-sac, but you can always come back the way you came.

The beauty of the Web is that the browser programs with which you "read" the Web are incredibly easy to use. This gives you access to all kinds of data, programs, news, pictures, and so on, without having to master the syntax of difficult protocols (such as the ones explained in earlier chapters of this book).

What's on the Web?

New Internet media, protocols, and files are created all the time, so I can't give you a comprehensive list of what's available via the WorldWide Web, but I can remind you of the Internet services already covered in this book, all of which are reachable through the Web:

- Items on Gopher menus
- Files at ftp sites
- Usenet newsgroups
- Anything available through telnet
- Anything available in hytelnet
- Manual pages
- Hypertext documents

As they say on Madison Avenue, "and much, much, more!"

Different Types of Web Browsers

If you have a character-based UNIX shell account, then you'll run a Web browser such as lynx or www. They won't be able to show you pictures and won't allow you to click your mouse to select links, but they can take you anywhere and you can always fetch or download binary files that the character-based readers aren't able to display.

> In some ways the idea of the Web is similar to that of the gopher. The gopher also presents all information in one form (as menus). But the menu model is not nearly as flexible as the hypertext medium. And for that matter, you can get access to gophers via the Web. Chapter 14 explains gophers.

> telnet won't work for you if you're reading the Web with a public access browser. More on that later.

While graphical browsers such as Mosaic are certainly a pleasure to use and a great way to skim through the material of the Net, reading the Web with lynx or www can be just as fascinating.

The Web is growing more popular all the time, and you may sometimes experience delays connecting to new addresses. Attempts to follow links may even result in timing-out and failure. If this happens, just try again later, ideally in off-hours.

If you've used the UNIX gopher client program, then you'll notice that several of the lynx commands are the same (for example, the bookmark commands).

If you have a SLIP or PPP dial-up account or a network account running in a Macintosh, Windows, or other windowed environment, then you can run full-screen graphical-interface Web browsers, such as the original one, Mosaic. Then you'll be able to see image files and navigate the Web with clicks of your mouse.

Using Web Browsers

Generally, when you start a browser, you begin at a *home page* (hypertext documents on the Web are called *pages*). This will either be the default home page for your browser or a custom home page that you have selected. You can usually also start a browser by pointing it at a Web address (also called a *URL*—a uniform resource locator).

Then you just follow the links that interest you. At any point you can retrace your steps so far, or bring up a complete history of everywhere you've been this session and jump immediately back to one of those pages.

You can insert bookmarks that enable you to jump back to an interesting page without having to find it again by the original process. You can always view the hidden URL (Web address) that a given link points to.

You can customize your home page so that you always start at a page with links that interest you, rather than having to start at a generic home page.

You can also save, mail, or download interesting documents and files.

Browse the Web with lynx

If you've got a character-based UNIX account, then the best Web browser for you is lynx. lynx is a full-screen program that is very easy to use.

Start lynx

You start lynx by typing **lynx** at the UNIX prompt and pressing Enter. This will start you off at the default lynx home page (see Figure 15.1).

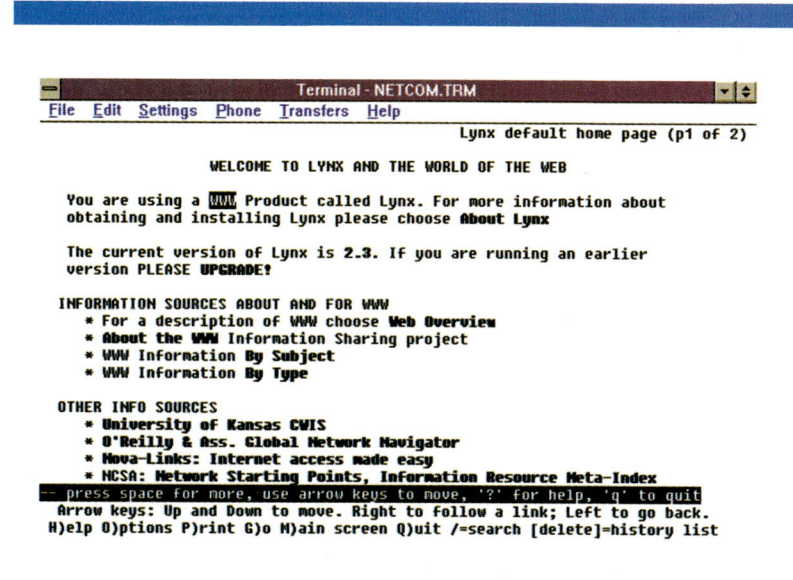

FIGURE 15.1

The default lynx home page. There are lots of excellent links available directly from this page.

As you can see, there's pretty good help information across the bottom of the lynx screen.

If you have a specific URL in mind, you can also start lynx by pointing it at that address. Type **lynx** *url* and press Enter, substituting the actual URL for *url*, of course.

You can get help at any time in lynx by typing **?**.

If you don't have lynx installed on your system, UNIX will tell you **lynx: Command not found**. You can still run lynx by telnetting to a public-access browser. Type **telnet ukanaix.cc.ukans.edu** and press Enter, and log in as **www** (no password required).

How to Read a Page in lynx

Most of a Web page will be regular text and headings. In lynx, hypertext links are shown in boldface, and the current link is shown in reverse video. The first link on the page is the current link when you first arrive at a page.

186   SURFING THE WORLDWIDE WEB

For more ways to get help for and information about the Web, see *Web Help and Information*, later in this chapter.

If the arrow keys don't work for you and you have a numeric keypad, try turning NumLock on and then using the number keys on the numeric keypad. Your communications program might be reserving the arrow keys (along with some Control keys and scrolling commands) for their standard uses in your operating environment. Check the terminal-emulation settings to see if you can change this.

HTTP, HTML, and URLs

Don't get thrown by the alphabet soup of acronyms you're confronted with when you start looking into the Web. URL, as I mentioned before, stands for uniform resource locator. It's a form of address that all Web browsers can understand. URLs always take this form: **protocol://host:port/dir/filename**. So the URL **gopher://dixie.aiss.uiuc.edu:6969/11/urban.legends** tells a browser "use the gopher protocol to connect to the host machine called **dixie.aiss.uiuc.edu**, connect to port **6969** there, look in directory **/11**, and get the file called **urban.legends**."

The protocol generally used to connect to hypertext documents is called HTTP. HTTP stands for HyperText Transport Protocol, because browsers use it to "transport" you to hypertext documents. If that protocol is called for, the URL will begin with **http:**. (As you can imagine, other protocols are ftp:, telnet:, and so on—the file: protocol is equivalent to ftp:.)

The other confusing acronym you might come across is HTML. HTML stands for HyperText Markup Language, and it is the code used to mark up text documents to make them into hypertext documents. Hypertext documents on the web end in the extension .html, generally.

Often a page won't fit on the screen all at once. To see the next screenful of a page, press the spacebar or type **+** (or PageDown or **3** on your numeric keypad if NumLock is on).

To go back up a page, type **b** or **–** (or PageUp or **9** on the numeric keypad with NumLock on).

To move down to the next link, press Tab, ↓, or **2** on the numeric keypad (with NumLock on). To move up to the previous link, press ↑ or **8** on the numeric keypad (NumLock).

To search for specific text, type **s** or **/**. Then type the text you want to search for and press Enter. Type **n** to repeat a search.

Follow a Link in lynx

To select the current link (and jump to the address it refers to), press Enter (or → or **6**, numeric keypad, NumLock on). To return to the previous link, press ← or **4** (numeric keypad, NumLock).

Though you can always retrace your steps, by pressing ← or **4** (NumLock) repeatedly, you can also jump back to any previous point in just two steps. To see your history page (a list of all the links you've followed in this session), press Delete. (Try Backspace if Delete doesn't work.) Figure 15.2 shows a history page.

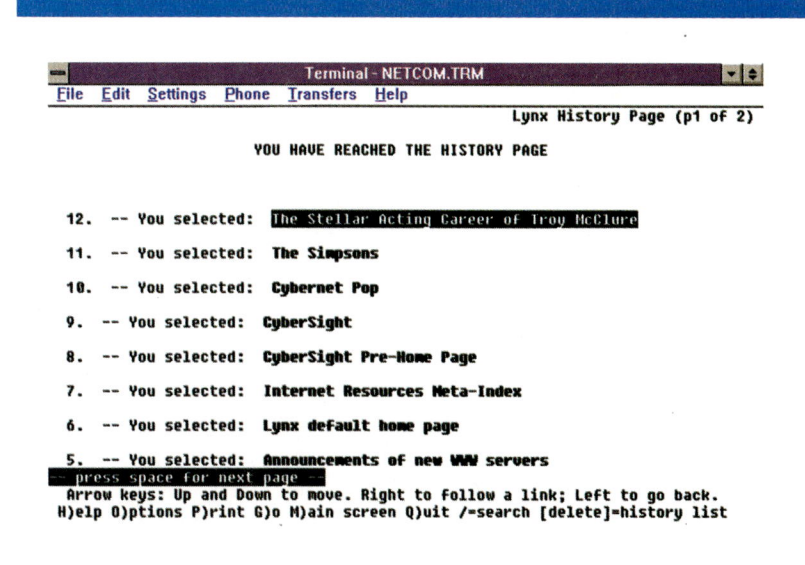

> If the screen gets messed up (say, if reverse video is left all over the screen), press Ctrl-W to redraw it.

FIGURE 15.2

The history page shows all the links I've followed this time around. You can select any link on the page to go back to it directly.

How to Know Where to Go

It's hard to get oriented in the Web, since there's no real starting point on "top" of it. Your default home page should provide some pretty useful jumping-off points. I recommend surfing around for a while to see where these points lead.

In lynx, at any point you can type *i* to go to the Internet Resources Meta-Index, which includes many more starting points for you to try. Figure 15.3 shows the first screenful of the Meta-Index page.

FIGURE 15.3

Not sure how to get started? Check out the Meta-Index.

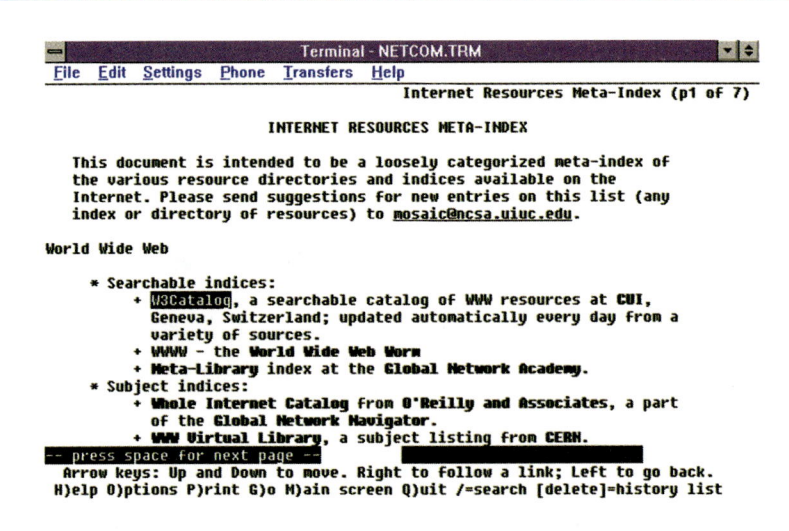

Go Directly to a URL in lynx

At any point lynx, you can type *g* to enter a URL directly. (Say someone has posted an interesting URL to a newsgroup you read. You can copy it and save it somewhere. Then run lynx and go to it.) lynx will prompt you with URL to open:.

Type (or paste in) the URL and press Enter.

> If you've done this once already, the previous URL will already be there. Delete it (press Ctrl-U) before typing in the new one.

Return to Your Home Page

Also at any time, you can return to the default home page by typing **m**.

Leave a Bookmark in lynx

Much like with the gopher, you can save interesting Web destinations by adding bookmarks to your bookmark page. (lynx will create one for you if you don't have one.) To add a bookmark link to the current page, type **a**.

You can view your bookmark page at any time by typing **v**.

Copy a Document in lynx

If you want to save a copy of a document you're reading on the Web, type **p**. This will bring up the Printing Options page. Press Enter to save the document to a file. lynx will prompt you Please enter a file name: and suggest a file name. Press Enter or type a different name and press Enter.

To mail the document to yourself, press Tab to go to the next link (Mail the file to yourself) and then press Enter. lynx will prompt you with Please enter a valid internet mail address:. If you've told lynx your address (see *Customize lynx* below), it will appear there. If not, type your address. Then press Enter.

> To send mail to the owner of the page you're on, type **c**. (The owner just means the person who created and who maintains the page.)

Peek Behind the Scenes

To see the URL associated with the current link, type **=**. Type **=** again to go back to the normal view. To see the actual HTML text of the current page, type ****. Type **** again to go back to the normal view.

Quit lynx

Quit lynx at any time by typing **q**. Then press Enter. To quit without being prompted, type **Q**.

Customize lynx

To change some of the lynx settings, type **O**. This brings up the Options Menu. Type **e** to change the default editor (for sending e-mail to mailto URLs). Type **b** to change your bookmark file. Type **p** to enter or change your e-mail address. When you are done, type **>**. To return to where you left off without saving the changes, type **r**.

Change Your Home Page

To make a different document your default home page, put the line **setenv WWW_HOME** *url* (using the correct URL for the page you want) in your startup file (usually .login, .profile, or .cshrc).

Browse the Web with www

If you don't have lynx installed on your system, you can telnet to a public-access lynx server (see *Start lynx* earlier in the chapter), or you can see if you have www available. www is the original character-based Web browser. It doesn't let you move around the screen the way lynx does, but it's just about as easy to use.

Start www

To start www, type **www** at the UNIX prompt and press Enter. This will bring up the default home page (see Figure 15.4).

You can also start www at a specific page by typing **www** *url* (and using the correct URL for *url*, of course).

Don't have www either? You can use a public-access www. Type **telnet info.cern.ch** at the UNIX prompt and press Enter. (You won't be able to go to telnet URLs.) Also, note that this address is in Switzerland. Use resources wisely.

FIGURE 15.4

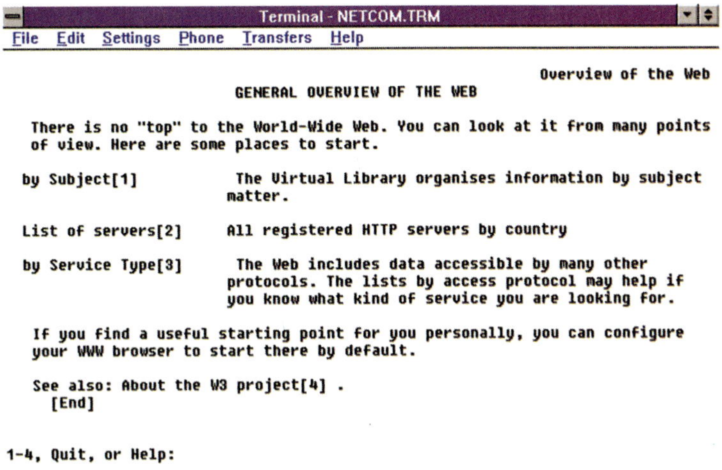

The www default home page.

```
                    Terminal - NETCOM.TRM
 File  Edit  Settings  Phone  Transfers  Help
                                            Overview of the Web
                GENERAL OVERVIEW OF THE WEB
   There is no "top" to the World-Wide Web. You can look at it from many points
   of view. Here are some places to start.

   by Subject[1]          The Virtual Library organises information by subject
                          matter.

   List of servers[2]     All registered HTTP servers by country

   by Service Type[3]     The Web includes data accessible by many other
                          protocols. The lists by access protocol may help if
                          you know what kind of service you are looking for.

   If you find a useful starting point for you personally, you can configure
   your WWW browser to start there by default.

   See also: About the W3 project[4] .
     [End]

   1-4, Quit, or Help:
```

See HTTP, HTML, and URLs (earlier in this chapter) for more on URLs and other Web jargon.

To get help in www, type **h** and press Enter. To see an online www reference manual, type **m** and press Enter.

How to Read a Page in www

In www, links are shown followed by bracketed numbers. If a page is longer than one screenful, you can see the next screen by pressing Enter. To go back a screenful, type **u** and press Enter. To go to the top of a page, type **t** and press Enter. To go to the bottom of a page, type **bo** and press Enter.

Follow a Link in www

To follow a link in www, type the number of the link and press Enter. To go back, type **b** and press Enter. To see a list of all the documents you have visited, type **r** and press Enter.

Go Directly to a URL in www

To go directly to a URL, type **go** *url* and press Enter. (Replace *url* with the complete URL you want to go to.) To go to the Internet Resources Meta-Index, then, type **go http://www.ncsa.uiuc.edu/SDG/Software/Mosaic/MetaIndex.html** and press Enter.

Copy a Document in www

To save a copy of the document you're currently reading in www, type **>***filename* and press Enter. To add the current document to the end of an existing file, type **>>***filename* and press Enter.

> You can get Mosaic via anonymous ftp from **ftp.ncsa.uiuc.edu** in the /Web/Mosaic-binaries directory. See Chapter 11 for more on ftp.

Peek Behind the Scenes

To see a list of all the URLs in the current document, type **l** and press Enter.

Quit www

To quit www, type **q** and press Enter.

Browse the Web with Mosaic

Mosaic is the original graphical Web browser, and there now exist versions of it for just about every graphical user interface. Of course, you need a SLIP or PPP dial-up account or a network account with a graphical environment to run Mosaic.

On a Macintosh, you start Mosaic by clicking the Mosaic icon. Mosaic will start at a default home page or your own home page if you've selected (or created) a different one. To

> Pictures take a while to load up. To browse faster, select the Turn Off Pictures option. You can always turn pictures back on when you want to see them.

Browse the Web with Mosaic **193**

move through a page, just scroll as you would in any Mac document. To follow a link, simply click it.

To go directly to an address, select the Load URL command. This will bring up a dialog box. Type or paste in the URL you want and press Enter.

Mosaic shows you more of the potential of the Web. Go to the URL http://http.ucar.edu/metapage.html to see the pictures shown in Figure 15.5 for yourself.

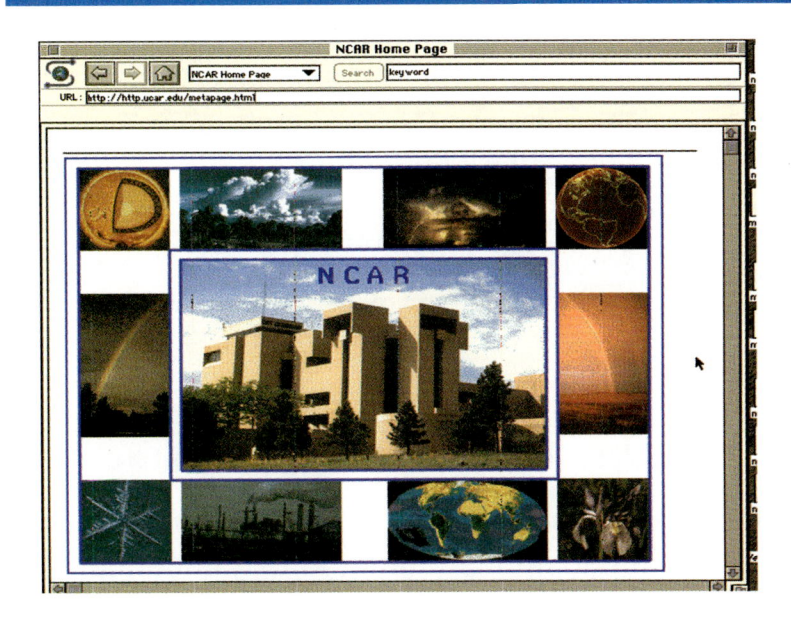

FIGURE 15.5

The NCAR home page displays some very attractive images.

Then go to http://www-swiss.ai.mit.edu/samantha/travels-with-samantha.html to see the award-winning *Travels with Samantha* hypermedia document, part of which is shown in Figure 15.6.

FIGURE 15.6

Part of the cover page of Travels with Samantha.

Browse the Web with NetCruiser

NetCruiser for Windows includes a Mosaic clone for browsing the Web. To run it, click the Web icon. This takes you to the Netcom home page, a pretty good jumping-off point.

Scroll through a page with the scroll bars. Follow links by clicking them. Enter a new URL directly in the URL box at the top of the window. Figure 15.7 shows an interesting destination, a gallery of solar images.

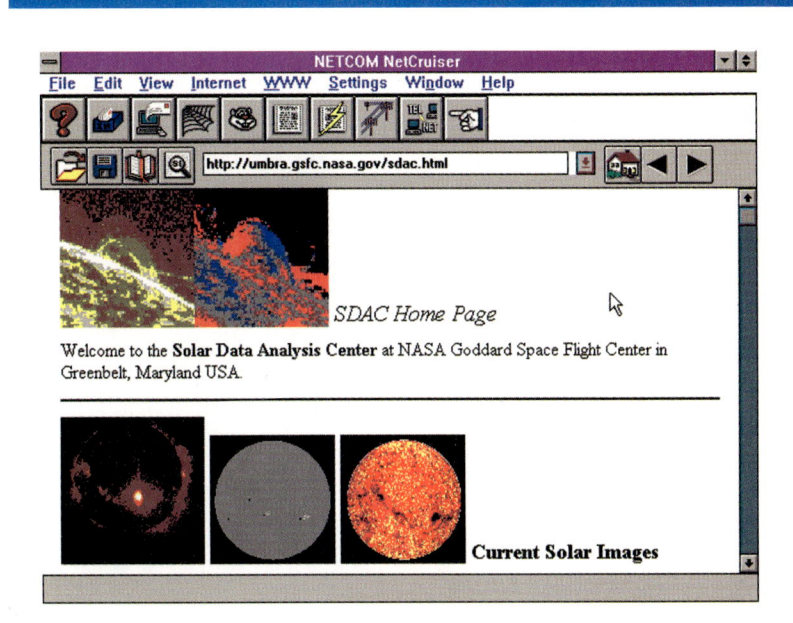

FIGURE 15.7

Solar images from the NASA Solar Data Analysis Center

Web Help and Info

There are a number of helpful resources for the Web, both hypertext and plain text documents. Try the WWW FAQ, an excellent document. Its URL is http://sunsite.unc.edu/boutell/faq/www_faq.html. If you're not sure where to get started, go to the WWW Virtual Library: http://info.cern.ch/hypertext/DataSources/bySubject/Overview.html or the Internet Resource Meta-Index (just type *i* in lynx): http://www.ncsa.uiuc.edu/SDG/Software/Mosaic/MetaIndex.html.

You'll also find information about the Web and browsers in the Usenet newsgroups comp.infosystems.announce, comp.infosystems.www.users, comp.infosystems.www.misc, and alt.hypertext.

Get EFF's Internet Guide as Hypertext on the Web

The Electronic Frontier Foundation has published a hypertext version of its Internet Guide on the World-Wide Web. You could hunt around for it by looking in one of the many indexes or other jumping-off pages on the Web, but why don't I just tell you the URL? Point your browser at **http://www.eff.org/papers/bdgtti/bdg_toc.html** to go to the table-of-contents page for the Guide.

Keep Up with What's New

If you want to keep up-to-date on the latest interesting home pages, visit the NCSA What's New Page (the unofficial newspaper of the Web): **http://www.ncsa.uiuc.edu/SDG/Software/Mosaic/Docs/whats-new.html**.

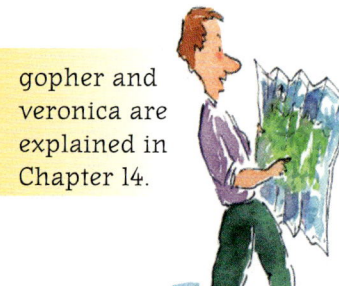

Using Other Internet Resources via the Web

gopher and veronica are explained in Chapter 14.

I've mentioned that you can use the gopher, ftp, telnet, and so on via the Web. Now I'll quickly run through some examples, using lynx, so you'll see what I meant. (The links I'll point to are not nearly the only ones around that might get you to the resources you want to use, but they're as good as any others.)

gopher with Your Web Browser

Start your browser. (If you know the gopher site you want to go to, point your browser at it. In lynx, do this by typing **lynx gopher://host-site** and pressing Enter, or by running lynx and then typing **g** and entering the gopher address URL.)

To look for Gopher sites, go to the Internet Resources Meta-Index (http://www.ncsa.uiuc.edu/SDG/Software/Mosaic/MetaIndex.html). If you're using lynx, you can just type *i* to go there.

Page down to the Gopher section of the Meta-Index. If you want to start with a veronica search, select the Veronica link. (There's also a Jughead link.) Other links include many Subject trees, a Gopherspace overview, and assorted other indices and listings.

*If you find a gopher site you like, make a bookmark for it (in lynx, type **a**).*

ftp with Your Web Browser

Start your browser. (If you know the ftp site you want to go to, point your browser at it. In lynx, do this by typing **lynx ftp://*host-site*** and pressing Enter, or by running lynx and then typing **g** and entering the ftp address URL.)

To look for ftp sites, go to the Resources Classified by Type of Service page (http://info.cern.ch/hypertext/DataSources/ByAccess.html). If you're using lynx, you can just select the *By Type* link on the lynx default home page. Page down to the *Anonymous FTP* link. Then either select that link (http://hoohoo.ncsa.uiuc.edu/ftp-interface.html) to go to the FTP Interface page or select one of the other two in that paragraph—*full hypertext archie gateways* (http://web.nexor.co.uk/archie.html) or telnet to *ARCHIE* (http://info.cern.ch:8002/arc/arc000).

ftp and archie are explained in Chapters 11 and 12.

telnet with Your Web Browser

Start your browser. (If you know the site you want to telnet to, point your browser at it. In lynx, do this by typing **lynx telnet://*host-site*** and pressing Enter, or by running lynx and then typing **g** and entering the telnet address URL.)

To look for telnet sites, try selecting the *Hytelnet database: Telnet information resources* link (http://www.cc.ukans.edu/hytelnet_html/START.TXT.html) on the lynx default home page

*If you find an ftp site you plan to return to, make a bookmark for it (in lynx, type **a**).*

telnet is explained in Chapter 13. If you are browsing the Web with a public-access browser, then you will not be able to use the browser to go to telnet sites.

Usenet is explained in Chapters 7 and 8.

If you get an error when you start trying to read the newsgroup, it may be because your news host is not defined. Ask your system administrator about this.

(http://www.cc.ukans.edu/about_lynx/www_start.html). If you find a telnet site you plan to return to, make a bookmark for it (in lynx, type **a**).

Read Usenet News with your Web Browser

Start your browser and point it at http://info.cern.ch/hypertext/DataSources/News/Groups/Overview.html. In lynx, do this by typing **lynx http://info.cern.ch/hypertext/DataSources/News/Groups/Overview.html** and pressing Enter, or by running lynx and then typing **g** and entering the URL. You can also get there from the lynx default home page by selecting the *By Type* link and then the *Network News* link.

The links on this page are all top-level Usenet hierarchy categories. Select a link to read newsgroups in that hierarchy. The page you get to will list all the newsgroups in the hierarchy you selected (too bad you can't keep working your way through subcategories). In lynx, type **/** and then the newsgroup name you want to save skipping through the screens to get to it.

Then select the newsgroup you want and start reading it. Threads are linked so you can move easily back and forth through related posts. For now, you cannot follow-up or reply to posts, and your Web browser will not keep track of which articles you have read.

You may have noticed HTML codes in Usenet posts before (or maybe you didn't know what you were looking at). If a post contains an HTML code, such as the code for a link: **<a href="URL">**. Then the codes will be interpreted correctly when the post is viewed with a Web browser.

If you're interested in the FAQs that Usenet newsgroup participants have compiled, check out the Usenet FAQs page (http://www.cis.ohio-state.edu/hypertext/faq/usenet/top.html).

Some Interesting URLs

I believe I've given you more than enough jumping-off points in this chapter and that you'll be able to spend (or waste) many hours playing around on the Web, but I'll finish up here with a quick listing of some additional interesting Web pages. Read what you like into my interests from this highly subjective and entirely arbitrary listing.

Music and Arts

The Jack Kerouac page:

file://ftp.netcom.com/pub/brooklyn/WWW/People/JackKerouac.html

The "Bringing It All Back Home Page" (Bob Dylan):

ftp://ftp.netcom.com/pub/howells/dylan.html.

The Grateful Dead home page:

http://www.cs.cmu.edu:8001/afs/cs.cmu.edu/user/mleone/web/dead.html

The R.E.M. home page:

http://www.halcyon.com/rem

The MeTaVerse home page (music industry gossip):

http://metaverse.com

Empty.tv.com's parody of the MeTaVerse home page:

http://www.galcit.caltech.edu/~a/mtv/main.html

The Enterzone home page (Enterzone is my hypermedia magazine):

http://enterzone.berkeley.edu/enterzine.html

Here are a few of my favorite home pages related to writing and music. The Kerouac page, maintained by Levi Asher, contains links for other Beat figures and related topics. The musician pages contain archival information related to their respective rec.music newsgroups.

The Net has been around long enough to grow its own culture. When you start poking around on Usenet, you'll notice a lot of jokes about people you've never heard of. Some are net.kooks and others are net.gods. Here are some pointers to more information about these personalities, as well as some more serious sources of information about the Net itself.

Net Personalities and Culture

The (somewhat controversial) Net Legends FAQ:

gopher://dixie.aiss.uiuc.edu:6969/11/urban.legends/net.legends

The alt.usenet.kooks FAQ and other archival information:

ftp://netcom.com/pub/crd

Kibo, a Kilroy for the wired age:

http://rescomp.stanford.edu/~asuter/kibo/kibo.html

The Electronic Frontier Foundation:

http://www.eff.org

Wired Magazine:

http://www.wired.com

Miscellaneous

> Here's a smattering of other Web pages that I find interesting or amusing.

The Whole Internet Catalog's Top 50:

http://nearnet.gnn.com/gnn/wic/top.toc.html

The Encyclopedia Britannica's Britannica Online:

http://www.eb.com

The Well:

http://www.well.com

Hypernews (a potential alternative to Usenet):

http://ginko.cecer.army.mil:8000/hypernews/hypernews.html

Comics:

http://nearnet.gnn.com/arcade/comix/

Urban legends, pursued, revealed, and debunked:

gopher://dixie.aiss.uiuc.edu:6969/11/urban.legends

APPENDIX A

Getting Connected

Featuring

- Types of connections
- Hardware you'll need
- Software you'll need
- Shopping for a service provider
- A huge list of service providers
- How to get updated lists

This appendix is here to help you out if you're looking for an Internet service provider, if you need to get the equipment together for a dial-up account, or if you've already got an Internet account or access to Internet e-mail but you'd like to shop around for better services.

Different Types of Connections

To start with, we need to go over the different types of Internet connections. First, there are *direct connections* and *modem connections*. A direct connection is a computer attached to a network that itself is connected to the Internet. Many university accounts work this way, as do some work-related Internet connections. There are also direct connections to Internet gateways that allow the sending and receiving of Internet e-mail but not much more.

There are also several types of modem connections:

- Relatively full-access SLIP or PPP accounts
- Client-access accounts
- Host-machine accounts (including Free-nets)
- Online services
- BBSs (Bulletin Boards)

A SLIP or PPP account is a dial-up account that puts your desktop computer, when you're connected, directly on the Internet. The modem connection makes your computer part of the a network attached to the Net. This type of access is growing in popularity.

A client-access account makes a temporary connection to a server and downloads your e-mail, Usenet news articles, and what-have-you and then logs off, allowing you to read and respond to your messages offline.

A bulletin board allows you to log on, and then select options from menus. They can provide UNIX command-line access to the Internet, but they do not necessarily do so.

An account with an online service may offer anything from partial to complete Internet access through the proprietary interface of the service. So far, only America Online and Delphi offer complete Internet access. Most others, such as CompuServe and

---

A host-machine account allows you to log on, using your desktop computer as a dumb terminal, to a host computer on the Internet. This usually entails working in a UNIX environment on the host machine, although there are many offline mailers and newsreaders available to help minimize your connect time and insulate you from the cryptic UNIX commands. For now, this is the most common type of dial-up access.

Prodigy, offer Internet e-mail (for an extra charge per message) and possibly access to Usenet newsgroups.

So you can see that, depending on your type of access, you may be running programs in your desktop computer's native environment (SLIP, PPP, client access, host-machine account with offline readers), you may be working in a UNIX environment (host-machine account), or you may be working in the interface provided by your online service or BBS. Of these possibilities, the native environment and the online service are generally the easiest to use, although the UNIX accounts are still the vast majority on the Net.

> Looking for software with archie is covered in Chapter 12.

This book covers the general procedures for using Internet services no matter what type of access you have, but it goes into great detail explaining the cryptic UNIX programs you might have to use.

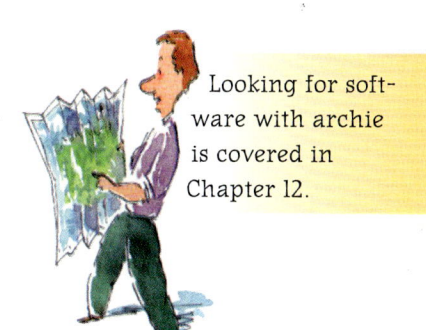

Equipment You'll Need

If your computer is directly connected to the Net, then you need no special equipment. You run the client software installed on your computer for reading e-mail. If you don't have the client programs needed to use other Internet services, such as ftp, gopher, and so on, you should be able to use an archie program to hunt for them on the Net.

Hardware

For every other type of connection, you'll need a modem. More and more often, PCs and Macs are sold with a modem pre-installed. If you were not so lucky, then you'll have to make a few decisions in figuring out what type of modem to buy.

> If at all possible, get a Hayes-compatible modem. This should not be difficult, as most modems on the market are at least somewhat Hayes compatible.

You have to decide first of all if you want an *internal* modem or an *external* modem. An internal modem is a circuit board with a modem chip on it that you have to install into a vacant slot inside your computer (or pay or cajole someone else to

> You may want to consider getting a fax/modem as well. A fax/modem can send electronic information to fax machines and receive faxes as graphic images (though some can just receive and not send). Some are finicky, though, and you have to decide how much to burden your phone line with.

install). An external modem is a flat box that plugs into a port on the outside of your computer.

Internal modems cost a little less than external modems and take up less space, but they're a real pain to mess with if a problem comes up. Internal modems draw their power from the computer's power supply, while external modems require a separate power supply. Expect to pay from eighty to a couple hundred bucks for your modem.

The next thing you need to consider is speed. The speed of your modem is the limiting factor in the speed of operations when you're connected. Like all things computerish, this year's standard model is next year's dud, this year's supercomputer is next year's idler. But from where I stand right now, I can suggest that you get at least a 9600-bps modem (bps stands for bits per second, but who cares?). If you're forward thinking, invest in a 14.4-kps (kilobits per second) modem, as they'll be the standard before you know it. If you economize on something like a 2400 bps modem, your operations will be annoyingly slooooow.

It goes without saying that once you install your modem, you must plug your phone into one of its jacks, and plug another cord into the other jack and into the wall jack.

Software

> Online services such as America Online and CompuServe will provide you with software designed for their services (though you can access CompuServe with regular communications software just as well).

If you'll be dialing up a connection with your modem, then you'll need to run some kind of communications software to communicate with the modem and to produce the terminal emulation so you can interact with the host computer. (If you'll be dialing up a SLIP or PPP connection, then you'll only need the client software for the Internet programs you want to run, not a communications program.)

Windows comes with a basic communications program called Terminal. The Macintosh likewise comes with a straightforward Mac Terminal program. Such free programs are perfectly adequate for this type of connection. Commercial communications programs such as ProComm and QModem Pro are a little easier to work with and better integrated, especially when it comes to downloading or uploading files, but I'd recommend not buying one until you're sure you need it.

No matter what kind of software you're running, you'll need to set it up the first time you run it, telling it some crucial things about your modem and the type of connection it should make. These things you only have to tell it once include:

- Which COM port the modem is connected to
- What type of "parity," "data bits," and "stop bits" to use. Your provider will tell you information you need. You don't need to know what it's about.
- What kind of terminal emulation to use (for communication programs)—most likely vt100.

You can also choose a transfer protocol, but you're not stuck with the choice you make at that point.

You might also want to get an offline mail reader or newsreader so that you can make your connection, collect your messages, and then read and reply to them while offline. You should be able to find such programs (like Eudora for the Macintosh) on the Internet once you've connected. Client accounts offer this kind of service with their proprietary software.

Finding a Service Provider

Once you have all the equipment you need, you've got to find a service provider. The greatest consideration for most people is cost. One of the biggest factors in cost can be the telephone charges for connect time.

If you can find a service with a dial-up number local to you, then you can reduce this charge to virtually nothing. If not, investigate several other options to see which will be cheapest for you. Look into services that provide 800 numbers or access via public data networks. You'll have to compare total costs, including both phone charges and charges from the service. If you can't avoid phone charges, try to do as many of your activities offline as possible, to minimize phone charges.

The next biggest charge issue is whether you are charged by the service based on how long you're connected (as opposed

800 numbers are free to call, but your service will charge you extra to cover their cost, so choose carefully.

Another type of free service that some people are able to finagle is free university accounts. If you know a system administrator who's so inclined, she can create an account for you, adding little overhead to her system (unless you fill up your directories). But you didn't hear it from me.

There are thousands of BBSs out there, untold numbers of other service providers, and more popping up like mushrooms each day. There's no way I could promise to list them all. But I've given you a good start here.

to paying a flat rate). The other cost issues are the monthly charge and a first-time connection charge, if any.

Throughout the U.S., there are networks called Free-nets that charge nothing for an account or for connect time (although their public accounts may not always be available). You'll still need to pay phone charges unless the number to call is local for you.

I've included in this appendix a reference to various commercial and free Internet access providers. The information is compiled from various sources found on the Internet. Because this type of information gets out of date quickly, I've also included where to find this information yourself, once you're online.

Providers Available on Public Data Networks

As I've mentioned, some Internet access providers are available over public data networks (PDNs). These are high-speed phone linkups that allow you to connect to the network from a local access number. I can tell you (thanks to Peter Kaminski) how to get local access numbers from some of the PDNs, but not all of them.

I've listed some services with public-data-network–access (what a mouthful!) in Table A.1 without specifying the PDN, because I don't know what it is. For these services, and for those with the SprintNet PDN, you'll have to contact the service directly (by phone or e-mail) for help getting a local access number.

Compuserve Packet Network   Call (800) 848-8199.

PSINet   Call (800) 82PSI82 or (703) 620-6651, or send e-mail to numbers-info@psi.com.

Tymnet   Call (800) 937-2862 or (215) 666-1770.

Finding a Service Provider

The services are organized first by area code, so that you can find your own local area and see what services are available. Table A.1 lists service providers by area code. Services with 800 numbers and public data network access are listed at the end.

TABLE A.1

Area codes and Available Service Providers

Area Code	Local Access Providers
201	The Connection; JvNCnet; Planet Access Networks
202	Capon Connect; ClarkNet; Express Access; Michnet; Netcom Online Communications; TMN
203	CPBI—Free-Net; Danbury Area Free-Net; JvNCnet; Netcom Online Communications
205	Mobile Free-Net; Nuance Network Services; Tennessee Valley Free-Net; Tuscaloosa Free-Net
206	Clark County Free-Net; Eskimo North; GLAIDS; Halcyon; Kitsap Free-Net; Netcom Online Communications; NorthWestNet; Northwest Nexus; OPEN; Olympus; Seattle Community Network; Seattle Online
207	Maine Free-Net; MAINE.NET Internet Connectivity Services
208	Sandpoint Free-Net
210	San Antonio Free-Net
212	EchoNYC; Interport Communications; Maestro; MindVox; Netcom Online Communications; Panix Public Access Unix; Pipeline
213	CERFnet; CRL; EarthLink Network; KAIWAN; Netcom Online Communications
214	Netcom Online Communications; North Texas Free-Net; Texas Metronet
215	Chester County Free-Net; JvNCnet; Netcom Online Communication; Philadelphia Free-Net; PREPnet
216	APK—Public Access UNI* Site ; Akron Regional Free-Net; Canton Regional Free-Net; Cleveland Free-Net; Learning Village Cleveland; Lorain County Free-Net; Medina County Free-Net; OARnet; Youngstown Free-Net
217	Prairienet
219	Michiana Free-Net Society

GETTING CONNECTED

TABLE A.1

Area codes and Available Service Providers

Area Code	Local Access Providers
301	Capon Connect; ClarkNet; Garrett Communiversity Central; Express Access; Michnet; TMN
302	Systems Solutions
303	Community News Service; CSN; Denver Free-Net; Netcom Online Communications; Nyx, the Spirit of the Night
304	WVnet
305	CyberGate; Miami Free-Net; Naples Free-Net; Palm Beach Free-Net; SatelNET Communications; SEFLIN Free-Net
310	CERFnet; CLASS; CRL; Express Access; KAIWAN; Netcom Online Communications
312	InterAccess; MCSNet; Netcom Online Communications; Public Telecomputing Network; Tezcatlipoca; Xnet Information Systems
313	Almont Expression; Greater Detroit Free-Net; Huron Valley Free-Net; MichNet; MSEN
314	COIN; Organizing Committees
315	NYSERnet
318	Acadiana Free-Net
319	CedarNet
401	Anomaly; IDS Network; JvNCnet; NEARnet; Ocean State Free-Net; RIScnet
403	PUCnet; UUNET-Canada
404	404 Free-Net; CRL; MindSpring Enterprises; Netcom Online Communications
405	Oklahoma Public Information Network; Ponca City/Pioneer Free-Net
406	Big Sky Telegraph; Omaha Free-Net
407	CyberGate; MCNet; Orlando Free-Net
408	a21 communications; DASNET; Portal Communications; Netcom Online Communications
410	Capon Connect; ClarkNet; Community Service Network; Express Access; Free State Free-Net

TABLE A.1 *Area codes and Available Service Providers*

Area Code	Local Access Providers
412	Pittsburgh Free-Net; PREPnet; Telerama
414	Milwaukee Internet X
415	a2i communications; Anterior Technology; BARRNet; CLASS; CERFnet; CRL; Institute for Global Communications; Netcom Online Communications; Portal Communications; Silicon Valley Public Access Link; The Well
416	HookUp Communication; UUNET-Canada; UUnorth
417	ORION
419	Lima Free-Net; Richland Free-Net; Toledo Free-Net; OARnet
501	Greater Pulaski County Free-Net; Sibylline
502	Owensboro Bluegrass Free-Net; Pennyrile Area Free-Net
503	RainDrop Laboratories; Netcom Online Communications; Teleport
504	Baton Rouge Free-Net; Greater New Orleans Free-Net; Sugar Land Unix
505	New Mexico Free-Net; New Mexico Technet; Santa Fe Metaverse
507	Northfield Free-Net; Twin Cities Free-Net
508	Anomaly; The Granite State Oracle; NEARnet; North Shore Access; NovaLink
509	Inland Northwest Community Network; Internet On-Ramp; Tri-Cities Free-Net
510	CLASS; Community ConneXion; CRL; CERFnet; HoloNet; Netcom Online Communications
512	Austin Free-Net; Illuminati Online; Real/Time Communications; THEnet
513	Dayton Free-Net; Freelance Systems Programming; Internet Access Cincinnati; OARnet; Tristate Online
514	Communications Accessibles Montreal; UUNET-Canada
515	Fairfield Free-Net; Iowa Knowledge Exchange
516	JvNCnet; Long Island Information; Network-USA

GETTING CONNECTED

TABLE A.1

Area codes and Available Service Providers

Area Code	Local Access Providers
517	Capitol City Free-Net; Michnet
518	Capital Region Information Service; Wizvax Communication
519	HookUp Communication; UUNET-Canada; UUnorth
601	Meridian Area Free-Net
602	AzTeC Computing; CRL; Data Basix; Evergreen Communications; Internet Direct
603	EZ-E-Mail; MV Communications; NEARnet
604	UUNET-Canada
607	Rochester Free-Net; Southern Tier Free-Net
609	JvNCnet; New Jersey Computer Connection
610	FishNet; Lehigh Valley Free-Net
612	InforMNs; StarNet Communications
613	UUNET-Canada; UUnorth
614	Greater Columbus Free-Net; OARnet; SEORF
615	Greater Knoxville Community Network; Edge
616	Grand Rapids Free-Net; Great Lakes Free-Net; MichNet
617	Bix; Delphi; NEARnet; Netcom Online Communications; North Shore Access; NovaLink; Pioneer Neighborhood; Village of Cambridge; The World
618	Shawnee Free-Net; SWIF-NET
619	CERFnet; CLASS; CTSNET; The Cyberspace Station; E&S Systems Public Access *Nix; Netcom Online Communications
703	Capon Connect; ClarkNet; Express Access; Michnet; Netcom Online Communications; Performance Systems International; TMN; UUNET Technologies
701	SENDIT
703	Blue Ridge Free-Net
704	Charlotte's Web; CONCERT; FXNET; Vnet Internet Access
707	CRL

TABLE A.1
Area codes and Available Service Providers

Area Code	Local Access Providers
708	InterAccess; MCSNet; WorldWide Access; Xnet Information Systems
713	The Black Box; Houston Civnet; SESQUINET; South Coast Computing Services; Sugar Land Unix
714	CLASS; CERFnet; Express Access; KAIWAN; Netcom Online Communications; Orange County Free-Net
715	Chippewa Valley Free-Net
716	Buffalo Free-Net
717	PREPnet
718	Maestro; MindVox; Netcom Online Communications; Panix Publix Access Unix; Pipeline
719	Community News Service; CSN; Old Colorado City Communications
802	Lamoille Net
803	GreenCo-NET; Greenet; MidNet
804	Central Virginia's Free-Net; VaPEN; Wyvern Technologies; VERnet
808	Aloha Free-Net Project; Maui Free-Net
810	Genesee; Michnet; MSEN
813	SMART; Suncoast Free-Net
814	PREPnet
815	InterAccess; MCSNet; Xnet Information Systems
816	KC Free-Net
817	Texas Metronet; Tarrant County Free-Net
818	CLASS; CERFnet; Lightside, Inc.; Los Angeles Free-Net; Netcom Online Communications
901	Jackson Area Free-Net
904	Tallahassee Free-Net; Alachua Free-Net
905	UUNET-Canada
906	MichNet

TABLE A.1

Area codes and Available Service Providers

Area Code	Local Access Providers
907	Anchornet; FairNet; University Of Alaska Southeast, Tundra Services
908	Express Access; JvNCnet
910	CONCERT
912	Worth County-Sylverster Ga. Free-Net
914	TZ-Link; Cloud 9 Internet
915	Big Country Free-Net; Rio Grande Free-Net; West Texas Free-Net
916	CONCERT; Davis Community Network; Netcom Online Communications; Northern California Regional Computing Network; Sacramento Free-Net; Vnet Internet Access
919	Forsyth County Free-Net; Triangle Free-Net
800	AlterNet; America Online; CERFnet; CLASS; Community News Service; CompuServe; CRIS; CRL; CSN; Delphi; Express Access Service; HookUp Communication; IDS Network; IGC; IgLou Internet Services; InfiNet; JvNCet; MCI Mail; Neosoft; Oarnet; PCNet; PSI; Prometheus Information Network Group; The Rabbit Network; Savvy; UUNET Technologies

Public data networks (most area codes)

> CERFnet; HookUp Communication; JvNCnet; MichNet; Millennium Online; OARnet

CompuServe Packet Network (most area codes)

> The Well; The World

PSINet (most area codes)

> Holonet; PSI

SprintNet (most area codes)

> America Online; IGC; MichNet; NovaLink; Portal; TMN

Tymnet (most area codes)

> America Online; Delphi; HoloNet; Portal

Table A.2 gives the pertinent information about each of the providers I've mentioned. Some are networks, some are Free-nets, some are BBSs. Some started off as university networks and some still are.

TABLE A.2

Service Providers and Their Vital Statistics

Service Name	Phone Number	E-mail
a2i communications	(408) 293-8078	info@rahul.net
Acadiana Free-Net	(318) 837-9374	bobbrant@delphi.com
Akron Regional Free-Net	(216) 972-6352	r1asm@vm1.cc.uakron.edu
Alachua Free-Net	(904) 372-8401	76314.352@compuserve.com
Almont Expression	(313) 798-8171	gpratt@aol.com
The Aloha Free-Net Project	(808) 533-3969	mathews@gold.chem.hawaii.edu
AlterNet	(800) 488-6383	
America Online, Inc.	(800) 827-6364	info@aol.com
AnchorNet	(907) 261-2891	pegt@muskox.alaska.edu
Anomaly—Rhode Island's Gateway To The Internet	(401) 273-4669	info@anomaly.sbs.risc.net
Anterior Technology	(415) 328-5615	info@radiomail.net
APK—Public Access UNI* Site	(216) 481-9436	zbig@wariat.org
Austin Free-Net	(512) 288-5691	jeff_evans@capmac.org
AzTeC Computing	(602) 965-5985	joe.askins@asu.edu

TABLE A.2

Service Providers and Their Vital Statistics

Service Name	Phone Number	E-mail
BARRNet	(415) 723-7520	info@nic.barrnet.net
Baton Rouge Free-Net	(504) 346-0707	anniemac@acm.org
Big Country Free-Net	(915) 674-6964	davidb@alcon.acu.edu
Big Sky Telegraph	(800) 982-6668 (Montana only), (406) 683-7338	jrobin@CSN.org
BIX	(800) 695-4775 (617) 354-4137	TJL@mhis.bix.com
The Black Box	(713) 480-2684	info@blkbox.com, mknewman@blkbox.com
Blue Ridge Free-Net	(703) 981-1424	obrist@leo.vsla.edu
Buffalo Free-Net	(716) 877-8800 ext. 451	finamore@ubvms.cc.buffalo.edu
California On-line Resources for Education	(800) 272-8743	kvogt@eis.calstate.edu
Canton Regional Free-Net	(216) 499-9600 ext. 322	mkilcullen@ksuvxm.kent.edu
Cape Girardeau Free-Net	(314) 334-9322	LLoos@delphi.com
Capital Region Information Service	(518) 442-3728	nkurland@albnyvms.bitnet
Capitol City Free-Net	(517) 321-4972	whit@jcn.com
Capon Connect	(202) 466-7057	jhagermn@capcon.net
CedarNet	(319) 273-6282	muffoletto@uni.edu
Central Virginia's Free-Net	(804) 828-6650	kguyre@cabell.vcu.edu

TABLE A.2

Service Providers and Their Vital Statistics

Service Name	Phone Number	E-mail
CERFnet (DIAL n' CERF)	(800) 876-2373 (619) 455-3900	help@cerf.net
Channel 1	(617) 864-0100	whitehrn@channel1.com
Charlotte's Web	(704) 358-5245	shsnow@vnet.net
Chester County Free-Net	(215) 430-6621	jseidel@locke.ccil.org
Chippewa Valley Free-Net	(715) 836-3715	smarquar@uwec.edu
Clark County Free-Net	(206) 696-6846	tryan@netcom.com
ClarkNet (Clark Internet Services, Inc.)	(800) 735-2258 then dial (410) 730-9764 (MD Relay Service)	info@clark.net
CLASS (Cooperative Library Agency for Systems and Services)	(800) 488-4559	class@class.org
Cleveland Free-Net	(216) 368-2982	jag@po.cwru.edu
Cloud 9 Internet	(914) 682-0626	info@cloud9.net
COIN (Columbia Online Information Network)	(314) 443-3161 (ext. 350 for voice mail)	ebarrett@bigcat.missouri.edu
Communications Accessibles Montreal	514-931-0749	info@CAM.ORG
Community News Service (CNS)	(800) 748-1200 (719) 592-1240	info@cscns.com
Community Service Network	(410) 822-4132	david_boan@martha.washcoll.edu

TABLE A.2

Service Providers and Their Vital Statistics

Service Name	Phone Number	E-mail
CompuServe Information System	(800) 848-8990 (614) 457-0802	postmaster@csi.compuserve.com
The Connecticut Internet Exchange		info@connix.com
The Connection	(201) 435-4414	info@cnct.com
CONCERT	(919) 248-1404 (919) 248-1999	info@concert.net, jrr@concert.net
CPBI—Free-Net	(203) 278-5310 ext. 1230	steela@csusys.ctstateu.edu
CRIS	(800) 877-5045	
CRL (CR Laboratories Dialup Internet Access)	(415) 381-2800	info@crl.com
CSN (Colorado SuperNet)	(303) 273-3471	info@csn.org
CTSNET (CTS Network Services)	(619) 637-3637	info@crash.cts.com (server), support@crash.cts.com (human)
CyberGate, Inc.	(305) 428-GATE	info@gate.net or sales@gate.net
The Cyberspace Station	(619) 944-9498 ext. 626	help@cyber.net
Danbury Area Free-Net	(203) 797-4512	waldgreen@bix.com
DASNET	(408) 559-7434	postmaster@das.net
Data Basix	(602) 721-1988	info@Data.Basix.com (automated), sales@Data.Basix.com (human)
Davis Community Network	(916) 752-7764	acmansker@ucdavis.edu
Dayton Free-Net	(513) 873-4035	pvendt@desire.wright.edu

TABLE A.2

Service Providers and Their Vital Statistics

Service Name	Phone Number	E-mail
Delphi	(800) 544-4005 (800) 695-4005 (617) 491-3393	walthowe@delphi.com
Denver Free-Net	(303) 270-4300	drew@freenet.hsc.colorado.edu
E&S Systems Public Access *Nix	(619) 278-4641	steve@cg57.esnet.com
EarthLink Network	(213) 644-9500	info@earthlink.net
Echo Communications	(212) 255-3839	horn@echonyc.com
Edge	(615) 726-8700	edge.ercnet.com
Education Central	(517) 774-3975	374cylb@cmuvm.csu.cmich.edu
Eskimo North	(206) 367-7457	nanook@eskimo.com
Evergreen Communications	(602) 955-8315	evergreen@libre.com
Express Access Online Communications Service	(800) 969-9090 (301) 220-2020	info@digex.com
EZ-E-Mail	(603) 672-0736	info@lemuria.sai.com
Fairfield Free-Net	(515) 472-7494	sterry@ins.infonet.net
FairNet	(907) 474-5089	ffmob@aurora.alaska.edu
FishNet	(610) 337-9994	
Forsyth County Free-Net	(919) 727-2597 ext. 3023	annen@ledger.mis.co.forsyth.nc.us
404 Free-Net	(404) 892-0943	mike_bernath@solinet.net
Free State Free-Net	(410) 313-9259	aduggan@well.sf.ca.us

TABLE A.2

Service Providers and Their Vital Statistics

Service Name	Phone Number	E-mail
Freelance Systems Programming	fsp@dayton.fsp.com	(513) 254-7246
FXNET	(704) 338-4670	info@fx.net
Garrett Community-niversity Central	(301) 387-3035	71072.2304@compuserve.com
Genesee Free-Net	(810) 762-3309	dcheslow@umich.edu
GLAIDS NET	(206) 323-7483	tomh@glaids.wa.com
Grand Rapids Free-Net	(616) 459-6273	andyb@bethany.org
The Granite State Oracle	(508) 442-0279	quentin.lewis@sun.com
Great Lakes Free-Net	(616) 961-4166	merritt_tumanis@fc1.glfn.org
Greater Columbus Free-Net	(614) 292-4132	sgordon@freenet.columbus.oh.us
Greater Detroit Free-Net	(313) 825-5293	raine@gdls.com
Greater Knoxville Community Network	(615) 974-2908	gcole@solar.rtd.utk.edu
Greater New Orleans Free-Net	(504) 286-7187	nrrmc@uno.edu
Greater Pulaski County Free-Net	(501) 666-2222	john.eichler@grapevine.lrk.ar.us
GreenCo-NET	(803) 223-8331	oukmddn@cluster1.clemson.edu
Greenet	(803) 242-5000 ext. 231	sgr002@sol1.solinet.net
Halcyon	(206) 955-1050 (206) 426-9298	info@halcyon.com
HoloNet	(510) 704-0160	info@holonet.net

TABLE A.2

Service Providers and Their Vital Statistics

Service Name	Phone Number	E-mail
HookUp Communication Corporation	(519) 747-4110	info@hookup.net
Houston Civnet	(713) 869-0521	paul@sugar.neosoft.com
Huron Valley Free-Net	(313) 662-8374	michael.todd.glazier@umich.edu
The IDS World Network	(401) 884-7856	sysadmin@ids.net
IGC (Institute for Global Communications)	(415) 442-0220	support@igc.apc.org
IgLou Internet Services	(800) 436-IGLOU	info@iglou.com
Illuminati Online	(512) 447-7866	info@io.com
InfiNet, L.C	(800) 849-7214	
InforMNs	(612) 638-8786	howe@informns.k12.mn.us
Inland Northwest Community Network	(509) 359-6567	kmichaelson@ewu.edu
INTAC Access Corporation		info@intac.com
InteleCom Data Systems	(800) IDS-1680	info@ids.net
InterAccess	(800) 967-1580	info@interaccess.com
Internet Access Cincinnati	(513) 887-8877	
Internet Direct, Inc.	(602) 274-0100 (Phoenix), (602) 324-0100 (Tucson)	info@indirect.com (automated), support@indirect.com (human)
Internet On-Ramp, Inc.	(509) 927-7267	info@on-ramp.ior.com

TABLE A.2

Service Providers and Their Vital Statistics

Service Name	Phone Number	E-mail
Interport Communications	(212) 989-1128	info@interport.net
Iowa Knowledge Exchange	(515) 242-3556	garyb@ins.infonet.net
Jackson Area Free-Net	(901) 425-2640	dlewis@jscc.cc.tn.us
JvNCnet (The John von Neumann Computer Network—Dialin' Tiger)	(800) 358-4437 (609) 897-7300 (609) 258-2400	info@jvnc.net, market@jvnc.net
KAIWAN Public Access Internet Online Services	(714) 638-2139	info@kaiwan.com
KC Free-Net	(816) 340-4228	josbourn@tyrell.net
Kitsap Free-Net	(206) 377-7601	michael@kitsap.lib.wa.us
Lamoille Net	(802) 888-2606	braman@world.std.com
Learning Village Cleveland	(216) 247-5800	jmk@nptn.org
Lehigh Valley Free-Net	(610) 758-4998	tpl2@lehigh.edu
Lightside, Inc.	(818) 858-9261	
Lima Free-Net	(419) 226-1218	monus@clipo1.usachem.msnet.bp.com
Long Island Information, Inc.	(516) 248-5381	info@liii.com
Lorain County Free-Net	(800) 227-7113 ext. 2451 (216) 277-2451	aa003@freenet.lorain.oberlin.edu
Los Angeles Free-Net	(818) 954-0080	aa101@lafn.org

TABLE A.2

Service Providers and Their Vital Statistics

Service Name	Phone Number	E-mail
Maestro	(212) 240-9600	info@maestro.com (autoreply), staff@maestro.com, rkelly@maestro.com, ksingh@maestro.com
Maine Free-Net	(207) 287-6615	efrey@mmp.org
MAINE.NET Internet Connectivity Services	(207) 780-6381	sales@maine.net
Maui Free-Net	(808) 572-0510	don.regal@tdp.org
MCI Mail	(800) 444-6245 (202) 833-8484	2671163@mcimail.com, 3248333@mcimail.com
MCNet	(407) 221-1410	hammerg@firnvx.firn.edu
MCSNet	(312) 248-8649	info@mcs.net, info@genesis.mcs.com
Medina County Free-Net	(216) 725-1000 ext. 2550	gfl@freenet.medina.edu
Meridian Area Free-Net	(601) 482-2000	ric4aardvark@delphi.com
Miami Free-Net	(305) 357-7318	currye@mail.seflin.lib.fl.us
Michiana Free-Net Society	(219) 282-1574	dmclaugh@darwin.cc.nd.edu
MichNet (Merit Network, Inc.—MichNet project)	(313) 764-9430	info@merit.edu, jogden@merit.edu
MIDnet		info@mid.net
MidNet—Columbia	(803) 777-4825	bajjaly@univscvm.csd.scarolina.edu
Millennium Online	(800) 736-0122	jjablow@mill.com
Milwaukee Internet X	(414) 962-8172	sysop@mixcom.com
MindSpring Enterprises, Inc.	(404) 888-0725	

TABLE A.2

Service Providers and Their Vital Statistics

Service Name	Phone Number	E-mail
MindVox	(212) 989-2418 (212) 989-4141	info@phantom.com
Mobile Free-Net	(205) 344-7243	geoffp@netcom.com
Mordor—Public Access Unix		info@ritz.mordor.com
MSEN, Inc.	(313) 998-4562	info@msen.com
MV Communications	(603) 429-2223	info@ mv.com
Naples Free-Net	(800) 466-8017	hainswm@firnvx.firn.edu
NEARnet	(617) 873-8730	nearnet-join@nic.near.net
Neosoft, Inc.	(800) GET-NEOS	info@neosoft.com
Netcom Online Communication Services	(408) 554-8649 (800) 501-8649	info@netcom.com
Network-USA	(516) 543-0234	all-info@netusa.net
NevadaNet	(702) 784-6133	zitter@nevada.edu
New Jersey Computer Connection	(609) 896-2799	info@pluto.njcc.com
New Mexico Free-Net	(505) 277-8148	lnewby@unm.edu
New Mexico Technet	(505) 345-6555	reynolds@technet.nm.org
NIC		info@nic.com
North Shore Access	(617) 593-3110	info@northshore.ecosoft.com
North Texas Free-Net	(214) 320-8915	kenlc@tenet.edu
Northern California Regional Computing Network	(916) 891-1211	pblythe@aol.com

Finding a Service Provider

TABLE A.2

Service Providers and Their Vital Statistics

Service Name	Phone Number	E-mail
Northfield Free-Net	(507) 645-9301	andreacris@aol.com
Northwest Nexus Inc.	(206) 455-3505	info@nwnexus.wa.com
NovaLink	(800) 274-2814	info@novalink.com
Nuance Network Services	(205) 533-4296	staff@nuance.com
NYSERnet	(315) 443-4120	info@nysernet.org
Nyx, the Spirit of the Night		aburt@nyx.cs.du.edu
OARnet	(614) 292-8100	nic@oar.net
Ocean State Free-Net	(401) 277-2726	howardbm@dsl.rhilinet.gov
Oklahoma Public Information Network	(405) 947-8868	fn-mail@okcforum.osrhe.edu
Old Colorado City Communications	(719) 632-4848 (719) 593-7575 (719) 636-2040	dave@oldcolo.com, thefox@oldcolo.com
Olympus—The Olympic Peninsula's Gateway To The Internet	(206) 385-0464	info@pt.olympus.net
Omaha Free-Net	(402) 554-2516	lowe@unomaha.edu
OPEN (Olympic Public Electronic Network)	(206) 417-9302	lhaas@aol.com
Orange County Free-Net	(714) 762-8551	palmer@world.std.com
ORION	(417) 837-5050 ext. 15	annie@ozarks.sgcl.lib.mo.us
Orlando Free-Net	(407) 833-9777	bruce@goliath.pbac.edu

TABLE A.2

Service Providers and Their Vital Statistics

Service Name	Phone Number	E-mail
Owensboro Bluegrass Free-Net	(502) 686-4530	donna@ndlc.occ.uky.edu
Palm Beach Free-Net	(305) 357-7318	currye@mail.seflin.lib.fl.us
Panix Public Access Unix	(212) 877-4854 (212) 691-1526 (718) 965-3768	alexis@panix.com, jsb@panix.com
PCNet	(800) 664-INET	
Pennyrile Area Free-Net	(502) 886-2913	mroseberry@delphi.com
Philadelphia Free-Net	(215) 688-2694	torgj@delphi.com
Pioneer Neighborhood (Pioneer Global)	(617) 646-4800	info@pn.com
The Pipeline	(212) 267-3636	info@pipeline.com, staff@pipeline.com
Pittsburgh Free-Net	(412) 622-6502	iddings@clp2.clpgh.org
Planet Access Networks	(201) 691-4704	info@planet.net
Ponca City/Pioneer Free-Net	(405) 767-3461	philber106@aol.com
Portal Communications, Inc.	(408) 973-9111	cs@cup.portal.com, info@portal.com
Prairienet Freenet	(217) 244-1962 (217) 244-3299	abishop@uiuc.edu, jayg@uiuc.edu
PREPnet	(412) 268-7870	prepnet@cmu.edu
Prometheus Information Network Group, Inc.	(800) PING-TEL	info@ping.com

TABLE A.2

Service Providers and Their Vital Statistics

Service Name	Phone Number	E-mail
PSI (PSILink/ Performance Systems International, Inc.)	(800) 827-7482 (703) 620-6651	info@psi.com, all-info@psi.com, psilink-info@psi.com
Public Telecomputing Network	(312) 464-5138	pionke@interaccess.com
PUCnet Computer Connections	(403) 448-1901	info@PUCnet.com, pwilson@PUCnet.com
The Rabbit Network Inc.	(800) 456-0094	info@rabbit.net
RainDrop Laboratories		info@agora.rain.com
Real/Time Communications	(512) 451-0046	info@realtime.net, hosts@wixer.bga.com
Richland Free-Net	(419) 521-3111 (419) 521-3110	earmrcpl@class.org
Rio Grande Free-Net	(915) 775-6077	donf@laguna.epcc.edu
RISCnet	(401) 885-6855	info@nic.risc.net
Rochester Free-Net	(716) 594-0943	jerry@rochgte.fidonet.org
Sacramento Free-Net	(916) 484-6789	sacrapar@class.org
San Antonio Free-Net	(210) 561-9815	mlotas@espsun.space.swri.edu
Sandpoint Free-Net	(208) 263-6105	mcmun911@crow.csru.uidaho.edu
Santa Barbara RAIN	(805) 967-7246	rain1.018558e312ngrhub@hub.ucsb.edu
Santa Fe Metaverse	(505) 989-7117	

TABLE A.2

Service Providers and Their Vital Statistics

Service Name	Phone Number	E-mail
SatelNET Communications	(305) 434-8738	admin@satelnet.org
Savvy	(800) 275-7455	info@savvy.com
Seattle Community Network	(206) 865-3424	randy@cpsr.org
Seattle Online	(206) 328-2412	bruceki@online.com
SEFLIN Free-Net	(305) 357-7318	currye@mail.seflin.lib.fl.us
SENDIT	(701) 237-8109	sackman@sendit.nodak.edu
SEORF	(614) 662-3211	bawn@oucsace.cs.ohiou.edu
SESQUINET	(713) 527-4988	farrell@rice.edu
Shawnee Free-Net	(618) 549-1139	ad592@freenet.hsc.colorado.edu
Sibylline, Inc.	(501) 521-4660	info@sibylline.com
Silicon Valley Public Access Link	(415) 968-2598	msiegel@svpal.org
SLONET	(805) 544-7328	pwagner@oboe.calpoly.edu
SMART	(813) 951-5502	
South Coast Computing Services, Inc.	(713) 661-3301	info@sccsi.com
Southern Tier Free-Net	(607) 752-1201	cubicsr@vnet.ibm.com
StarNet Communications, Inc.	(612) 941-9177	info@winternet.com
Suncoast Free-Net	(813) 273-3714	mullam@firnvx.firn.edu
Sugar Land Unix	(713) 438-4964	info@NeoSoft.com
SWIF-NET	(618) 397-0968	gulery@minuet.siue.edu
Systems Solutions	(302) 378-1386 (800) 331-1386	sharris@marlin.ssnet.com

TABLE A.2

Service Providers and Their Vital Statistics

Service Name	Phone Number	E-mail
Tallahassee Free-Net	(904) 644-1796	levitz@cs.fsu.edu
Tarrant County Free-Net	(817) 763-8437	jcoles@pubcon.com
Teleport	(503) 223-4245	info@teleport.com
Telerama Public Access Internet	(412) 481-3505	info@telerama.lm.com, info@telerama.pgh.pa.us
Tennessee Valley Free-Net	(205) 544-3849	
Texas Metronet	(214) 705-2900 (817) 543-8756	info@metronet.com
Tezcatlipoca Inc	(312) 850-0181	
THEnet	(512) 471-2444	info@nic.the.net
TMN (The Meta Network)	(703) 243-6622	info@tmn.com
Toledo Free-Net	(419) 537-3686	rad@uoft02.utoledo.edu
Triangle Free-Net	(919) 962-9107	hallman@gibbs.oit.unc.edu
Tri-Cities Free-Net	(509) 586-6481	tcfn@delphi.com
Tristate Online	(513) 397-1396	sysadmin@cbos.uc.edu
Tuscaloosa Free-Net	(205) 348-2398	rdoctor@ua1vm.ua.edu
Twin Cities Free-Net	(507) 646-3407	fritchie@stolaf.edu
TZ-Link	(914) 353-5443	info@j51.com
University Of Alaska Southeast, Tundra Services	(907) 465-6453	JNJMB@acad1.alaska.edu
UUNET Canada, Inc.	(416) 368-6621	info@uunet.ca

TABLE A.2

Service Providers and Their Vital Statistics

Service Name	Phone Number	E-mail
UUNET Technologies, Inc.	(800) 488-6383 (703) 204-8000	info@uunet.uu.net
UUnorth	(416) 225-8649	uunorth@uunorth.north.net
VaPEN—Richmond	(804) 225-2921	hcothern@vdoe386.vak12ed.edu
VERnet	(804) 924-0616	jaj@virginia.edu
Village of Cambridge	(617) 494-5226	service@village.com
Vnet Internet Access Internet Access, Inc.	(704) 374-0779	info@char.vnet.net
The WELL (Whole Earth 'Lectronic Link)	(415) 332-4335	info@well.sf.ca.us
West Texas Free-Net	(915) 655-7161	timelwell@delphi.com
Wizvax Communication	(518) 271-0049	info@wizvax.com
The World—Public Access UNIX	(617) 739-0202	office@world.std.com
WorldWide Access	(708) 367-1870	info@wwa.com
Worth County-Sylvester Ga. Free-Net	(912) 776-8625	guske@freenet.fsu.edu
WVNET	(304) 293-5192	cc011041@wvnvms.wvnet.edu
Wyvern Technologies, Inc.	(804) 622-4289	system@wyvern.com
XNet Information Systems	(708) 983-6064	info@xnet.com
Youngstown Free-Net	(216) 742-3075	lou@yfn.ysu.edu

The Chicken or the Egg

Here's how to get updated service-provider information once you're already online.

For InterNIC's thorough lists of access providers organized by U.S. states, non-U.S. countries, and listed alphabetically, ftp to nis.nsf.net, go to the internet/providers/ directory and get the following three files (you'll find them in this order):

>   internet-access-providers-alphabetical.txt
>   internet-access-providers-non-us.txt
>   internet-access-providers-us.txt

Peter Kaminski maintains an excellent list of access-providers, called pdial. He posts it regularly to the Usenet newsgroups alt.internet.access.wanted, alt.bbs.lists, and ba.internet. You can get the current list via anonymous ftp to rtfm.mit.edu. Go to the /pub/usenet/news.answers directory and get the file called pdial.

Anonymous ftp is explained in Chapter 11.

You can also get the most recent pdial by sending mail to info-deli-server@netcom.com. For your subject line, put Send PDIAL. The message can be anything.

Ritesh Patel maintains another list of access providers, available as a WorldWide Web page. To see the current list, point your Web browser at http://www.umd.umich.edu/~clp/i-access.html.

A commercial service on the Web is making an effort to assemble the various lists of providers out there on a single Web page, allowing users to look for providers by region. To see the current state of this effort, point your Web browser at http://www.tagsys.com/Providers/index.html.

The WorldWide Web is explained in Chapter 15.

Another list of providers is FSLIST, the Forgotten Site List. It is posted to the Usenet newsgroup alt.internet.access.wanted and available via anonymous ftp from freedom.nmsu.edu, in the /pub/docs/fslist/ directory or from login.qc.ca in the /pub/fslist/ directory.

Finally, there is a list of public-access UNIX providers called nixpub, posted to the Usenet newsgroups comp.bbs.mis and alt.bbs. It's available via anonymous ftp at vfl.paramax.com in the /pub/pubnetc directory. And you can get it by sending e-mail to mail-server@bts.com, with any subject, and the line get PUB nixpub.long in the body of the message.

Good luck.

APPENDIX B

Quick Reference to All Them Nasty UNIX Commands

Featuring

- Sending e-mail
- Looking for people on the Net
- Reading Usenet news
- Transferring and managing files
- Hunting around with a gopher
- Browsing the Web

I hate UNIX as much as you probably do, so I don't expect you to remember any of the UNIX commands explained in this book (at least not right away). That's why I've included this quick reference. All commands are to be typed at the UNIX prompt unless otherwise specified.

Since you may not even remember the UNIX command you want to use, I'm listing the Internet (and UNIX) activities covered in this book, and then the relevant UNIX commands needed to get things done. Oh, and did I mention UNIX is case sensitive?

Getting Started in UNIX

Tell UNIX you're emulating a vt100 terminal
setenv TERM vt100

Cancel the command you're typing   Ctrl-U (don't press Enter)

Retype the command you're typing   Ctrl-R (don't press Enter)

Kill a process   Ctrl-C (don't press Enter)

Kill a process and make a core dump   Ctrl-\ (don't press Enter)

Delete a core dump   rm core

Stop a job   Ctrl-Z (don't press Enter)

Continue a stopped job in the background   bg

Kill a stopped job   kill %1 *or* kill %*n* (if it is job *n* and not job 1)

See manual pages for a UNIX command   man *command*

Log out   logout *or* bye *or* exit

Run a Mail Program

Start elm   elm

Start pine   pine

Start mail   mail

Set up a vacation message   vacation

Look for People on the Net

finger your own network   finger

finger a domain   finger *host.sudomain.domain*

finger a single user   finger *username@address.domain*

Make a .plan file readable to others   chmod a+x $HOME *then* chmod a+r $HOME/.plan%

Look people up with Whois   whois '*lastname, firstname*'

For each of these commands, press Enter after typing them (unless otherwise specified).

If Ctrl-C doesn't kill the process, try Ctrl-Shift-C.

Obviously, this is not a UNIX book. If you're interested in learning more about UNIX (and I doubt you are), consider looking for a friendly book specifically about UNIX, such as **Understanding UNIX** *or the upcoming* **es.sen'.tial ac.ces'.si.ble Unix Dictionary**, *both from SYBEX.*

Chat with People in Realtime

Send a talk request   talk *username*

Start irc   irc

Compose E-Mail

Change your default e-mail editor (except for elm)
setenv EDITOR */full-path/filename*

Start vi   vi *or* vi *filename*

Start pico   pico *or* pico *filename*

Uuencode a file   uuencode *old.file.name new.file.name > text.file.name*

Uudecode a file   uudecode *filename*

> Include the full Internet address if the user you want to talk to is not on your network (does not have the same e-mail @ address). Use **talk *username*** to agree to a talk request as well as to send a talk request.

Read Usenet News

Create a .newsrc file   vi .newsrc

Start trn   trn *or* trn *newsgroup*

Start tin   tin *or* tin *newsgroup*

Start nn   nn *or* nn *newsgroup*

Start rn   rn *or* rn *newsgroup*

Change your "real name"   chfn

Manage Your Files and Directories

Find out where you are   pwd

Change to a different directory   cd *directory-name*

Change to your home directory   cd

Change to the parent of the current directory   cd ..

Make a new directory **mkdir** *new-directory-name*

Remove a directory **rmdir** *directory-name*

List the files in the current directory **ls**

List all the files, including those that start with . **ls –a**

List the files in any directory **ls** *directory-path*

List files one screenful at a time **ls | more**

List full information for each file **ls –l**

List files with directories marked by a trailing / **ls –F**

Direct the output of a UNIX command to a file
command **>** *filename*

View the contents of a file **more** *filename*

Delete a file **rm** *filename*

Copy a file **cp** *original-file copy-file*

Move or rename a file **mv** *filename new-directory*
or **mv** *old-filename new-filename*

Make a file readable by others **chmod o+r** *filename*

You can mix and match these ls options.

Download and Upload Files

Download a text file with kermit **kermit –s** *filename*

Upload a text file with kermit **kermit –r**

Download a binary file with kermit **kermit –s** *filename* **-i**

Upload a binary file with kermit **kermit –r –i**

Download a text file with xmodem **sx** *filename* **-a**

Upload a text file with xmodem **rx –a**

Download a binary file with xmodem **sx** *filename*

Upload a binary file with xmodem **rx**

Download a text file with ymodem **sb** *filename* **-a**

Upload a text file with ymodem **rb –a**

Download a binary file with ymodem sb *filename*

Upload a binary file with ymodem rb

Download a text file with zmodem sz *filename* –a

Upload a text file with zmodem rz –a

Download a binary file with zmodem sz *filename*

Upload a binary file with zmodem rz

Convert a DOS text file to UNIX format dos2unix

Convert a UNIX text file to DOS format unix2dos

ftp Commands

Start ftp ftp *ftp-sitename*

Start ncftp ncftp *ftp-sitename*

List files with ftp ls

Change directories with ftp cd *directory*

Change to the parent directory of the current directory with ftp cdup

Prepare to get a binary file binary

Tell ftp to put a # on the screen for every kilobyte transferred hash

Get a file with ftp get *filename*

Turn off prompting before getting several files prompt

Get several files mget *filename1 filename2 etc.*

Find out the current directory at the ftp site pwd

Change the directory on your home machine lcd *directory*

Put a file at the ftp site put *filename*

Put several files at the ftp site mput *filename1 filename2 etc.*

Change a file's name as you get it
get *oldfilename newfilename*

Aside from the command to start the ftp (and ncftp) programs, the rest of these are not strictly speaking UNIX commands. You don't type them at the UNIX prompt, rather at the ftp prompt.

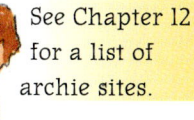

See Chapter 12 for a list of archie sites.

If the Hytelnet client program is not available on your system, telnet to access.usask.ca and log in as **hytelnet**

Telnet to the gopher server earest to you. They're listed in Chapter 14.

If you don't have lynx installed on your system, you can still run lynx by telnetting to ukanaix.cc.ukans.edu. Log in as **www**. If you don't have www either? You can telnet to **telnet nfo.cern.ch** or telnet to a public lynx site (as described above).

Close the connection   close

Open a new connection   open *ftp-sitename*

Finding Files for ftp with archie

Start an archie client   archie –s *filename*

Telnet to an archie client   telnet archie.*sitename*

Log In to Other Computers and Networks

Log in to a site via telnet   telnet *host-sitename*

Log in to other UNIX machines with rlogin
rlogin host-*sitename*

Start Hytelnet   hytelnet

Look for Things with a gopher

Start your gopher client   gopher *or* gopher server-sitename

Telnet to a gopher server   telnet *gopher-sitename*

Browse the Web

Start lynx   lynx

Point lynx at a URL   lynx *url*

Start www   www

Point www at a URL   www *url*

APPENDIX C

Glossary of Internet Jargon and Related Terms

Featuring

- Usenet terminology
- Definitions of technical terms
- Names of Internet programs
- Slang expressions used on the Net

If you've run into some jargon in this book that you don't understand, you should find an explanation here. The Internet is a community unto itself, and has therefore quite naturally evolved its own vocabulary. Much of that vocabulary is drawn from the world of computers and networking, as you might expect. Many other terms have been coined or borrowed from other disciplines to describe new concepts and situations. Still other terms are simply the sort of slang that always arises when a group of people share experiences and need to talk about them.

You could fill a book with Internet terms, but this glossary should cover anything unfamiliar in this book as well as a large handful of the words you'll encounter as you explore the Net.

$0.02 Appended to the end of a Usenet post, this means "my two cents."

:-) The basic smiley symbol, this is often used to mean "just kidding," "don't flame me," or "I'm being sarcastic," but it can also mean "I'm happy."

^] This garbage symbol may appear on your screen, or in text-transferred files, from time to time. It's an uninterpreted Esc character. Ignore it.

^H In the standard VT100 terminal emulation, Delete is used to erase characters, and Backspace either backs up over the previous character (without deleting it) or produces this character on the screen. It's a sign that a clueless newbie has tried to erase something and failed.

^M In text files transfered from DOS to UNIX as binary files, this character will sometimes appear at the end of each line. Get rid of it with the dos2unix program.

acceptable use Internet service providers require that all their users agree to some guidelines of acceptable use of Internet and Usenet resources. Acceptable use guidelines vary from provider to provider.

address On the Net, this means a fully specified Internet address of the form *username@host.subdomain.domain.*

administrivia Information regarding the administering of an mailing list or moderated newsgroup, posted to the list or group.

alias An abbreviation for an e-mail address.

alt. A quasi-Usenet hierarchy devoted to "alternative" topics. It is easier to create alt. groups than to create standard Usenet groups, and it's effectively impossible to remove them.

alt.fan groups Newsgroups devoted to a real-world or Net celebrity or villain.

Amiga A line of desktop PCs, famous for their handling of graphics and the evangelical zeal of their users. Many Amiga users include an ASCII-graphic double checkmark in their .sigs.

anon.penet.fi The best-known anonymous remailer service.

anonymous ftp The most common use of ftp, the Internet file transfer protocol. ftp sites that allow anonymous ftp don't require a password for access—you only have to log in as anonymous and enter your e-mail address as a password (for their records).

anonymous remailers A service that provides anonymity to users on the Net by allowing them to send mail and Usenet posts through the remailer.

*****.answers** Moderated newsgroups dedicated to the posting of FAQs.

application A program (or piece of software) that isn't a shell, environment, or operating system.

> The * in *.answers stands for anything. *.answers newsgroups include news.answers, alt.answers, rec.answers, misc.answers, and so on.

Glossary of Internet Jargon and Related Terms

archie A client-server application that gives users access to databases that keep track of the contents of anonymous ftp archives (hence the name). Your *archie client* gets information from an *archie server* running at an *archie site*.

ARPAnet The legendary predecessor to the Internet.

article A Usenet post.

ASCII American standard code for information exchange. ASCII is a standard character set that's been adopted by most computer systems around the world (usually extended for foreign alphabets and diacriticals).

ASCII file A file containing only straight text. ASCII files are easier and quicker to transfer.

asynchronous Not happening at the same time. E-mail is an asynchronous form of communication.

autoselect In Usenet killfiles, the opposite of killing. A killfile comprises instructions to search for certain key words and then either kill or autoselect the articles containing those words.

back The command in paging programs to go back one page (screenful).

backbone A large, fast network connection.

bandwidth The amount of information that can pass through the wires in a certain amount of time. Also, a more general term for what everyone is encouraged not to waste on the Net.

baud Usually conflated with bps, baud is technically the number of times per second that your modem changes the signal it sends through the phone lines.

BBS A bulletin board system. Many BBSs are connected to the Internet.

B1FF A legendary persona from the early days of BBSs, B1FF liked to talk about what was *k00l*, specifically *warez*, pirated computer games.

Big Dummy's Guide to the Internet The former name of EFF's excellent free Internet guide.

binary file As opposed to a text file, a file that contains more than simple text. It must be copied literally, bit for bit, or it will be corrupted. Also called an image file.

binary transfer A file transfer in which every bit of the file is copied (as opposed to a text transfer, in which the text is transferred to whatever format the receiving machine prefers).

BinHex A form of file compression native to the Macintosh.

bitnet A huge network, distinct from the Internet, but fully connected to it, used largely for e-mail and listserv mailing lists.

bitnet. A newsgroup hierarchy in the Usenet mold, comprising newsgroups that correspond to bitnet mailing lists.

To get a copy of EFF's Guide to the Internet (formerly Big Dummy's Guide to the Internet), see Chapter 11, 14, or 15.

biz. A newsgroup hierarchy in the Usenet mold that expressly permits advertising (biz stands for *business*).

bookmark In gopherspace or on the Web, a bookmark is a record of a destination that allows you to get back there immediately at any time.

'bot A robotic entity on the Net that automatically performs some function that people usually do.

bounce When e-mail fails to reach its destination and returns to you, it is said to have bounced.

bozo filter A killfile that allows you to filter out the bozos whose Usenet posts you don't wish to see.

bps Bits per second, a measurement of modem speed.

browse To skim an information resource on the Net, such as Usenet, gopherspace, or the Web.

browser The program you use to read the Web.

bulletin board system A set of computers and modems running bulletin board software that allow users to dial in, send mail, participate in forums, and (sometimes) access the Internet.

cancel an article On Usenet, to delete an article after you've posted it. It takes a while for the article to vanish everywhere, as the cancel message has to catch up with the propagating article.

cascade A nonsensical series of follow-up posts designed to create a huge triangle of >'s on the screen.

CFV Call for votes. A step in the creating of a Usenet newsgroup that comes after the RFD (request for discussion).

chat Synchronous, line by line communication over a network.

client An application that communicates with a server to get you information.

client-server application On networks, client-server applications are efficient because the server does much of the work for the users, while the users need only have the client running on their own machines.

clueless newbie A derogatory term for a beginner who POSTS IN ALL CAPS or betrays some ignorance of the Net. We were all clueless newbies once.

.com An Internet domain, it stands for *commercial*.

COM port A communication port in your PC. Your modem plugs into one.

comp. A Usenet hierarchy devoted to computers.

compress To squish a file. A UNIX program that squishes files.

compression The method of squishing a file or the amount of squishing.

copyright People debate how standing copyright law applies to articles posted to Usenet. Some people attach copyright notices to their posts.

cracker A hacker who breaks into computers.

Craig Shergold If you get the chain mail telling you to send this poor kid a get-well card, don't!

crosspost To post a Usenet article to several newsgroups at once. This takes up less disk space than posting it separately and repeatedly.

cyberspace A term, coined by author William Gibson, for the shared imaginary reality of computer networks.

daemon In UNIX, a program that runs all the time, in the background, waiting for things to do (possibly from Maxwell's Demon).

data bits One of the things you have to set to use your modem. Usually set to 7 or 8, it depends on the modem you're calling.

decrypt To remove the encryption from a file or e-mail message and make it readable.

delurk To post to a list or newsgroup for the first time.

dial-up account An Internet account on a host machine which you must dial up with your modem to use.

digest A collection of mailing list posts, sent out as one message.

digestified Turned into a digest. Not all mailing lists are available in a digestified form.

domain The generalized category that an Internet network or computer belongs to, such as .com, .org, .edu, .mil, and so on.

download To transfer a file over a modem from a remote computer to your desktop computer.

e-mail Electronic mail, but you knew that already, didn't you?

.edu An Internet domain, it stands for educational.

EFF See *Electronic Frontier Foundation*.

EFF's Guide to the Internet Formerly *Big Dummy's Guide to the Internet*, EFF's excellent free Internet guide, available via ftp, gopher, and the Web.

Electronic Frontier Foundation Founded by Mitch Kapor and John Barlow, the EFF lobbies for the preservation of freedom on the cyberspace frontier.

elm A popular UNIX mail program.

.elmrc A setup file for elm.

emacs A UNIX operating environment that doubles as a text editor.

emoticons Those little smiley faces people use to indicate emotions.

> Some people use cyberspace as a synonym for the Internet. Others hold out for the more complete physical-seeming consensual reality of Gibson's novels.

> To get a copy of *EFF's Guide to the Internet*, see Chapter 11, 14, or 15.

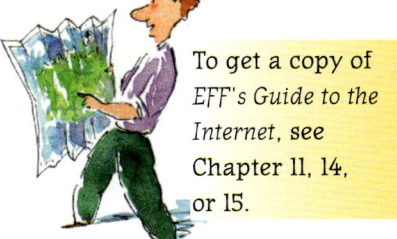

GLOSSARY OF INTERNET JARGON AND RELATED TERMS

To find FAQs, look in the *.answers newsgroups or the ftp archive at rtfm.mit.edu.

Flamebait can be recognized by the fact that it goes beyond the premises of the list or newsgroup. Nobody objects to provocative or even argumentative posts, but posts to the alt.fan.frank-zappa newsgroup saying that "zappa was a no-talent potty-mouthed dweeb" betray a lack of legitimate interest in the subject at hand.

Always check the follow-up line before posting. Pranksters sometimes direct follow-ups to *.test groups, resulting in thousands of automated replies stuffing the inbox of anyone hapless enough to follow up without editing the follow-up line.

encrypt To scramble the contents of a file or e-mail message so that only those with the key can unscramble and read them.

encryption A process of rendering a file or e-mail message unreadable to anyone lacking the encryption key.

Eudora An e-mail program for the Macintosh that can work as an offline mail reader.

fair use The legal doctrine that allows limited quotation of other people's work if the use of their work does not undercut its market value.

FAQ Frequently asked questions. Also a file containing frequently asked questions and their answers, also sometimes called a FAQL (frequently asked question list).

fetch The common Macintosh term for transfering files via ftp.

FidoNet A network of BBS's with Internet e-mail access.

file transfer To copy a file from one computer to another.

film at 11 A common tag in Usenet follow-up posts mocking the timeliness of the news. Often follows "imminent death of the Net predicted."

finger A UNIX command that reports back on the status of a user or a network.

flame An ill-considered, insulting e-mail or Usenet retort. An insulting post.

flamebait A list or newsgroup post designed to elicit flames.

flamer One who flames or likes to flame others (from "a flaming asshole").

flamewar An out-of-control series of flames and counterflames that fills up a list or newsgroup with noise. Traditionally, flamewars end when Nazis are mentioned.

follow-up A post that replies to and possibly quotes an earlier post.

follow-up line In Usenet articles, if there is a follow-up line, follow-up articles will be posted to the newsgroups listed there, and not necessarily the original newsgroups.

FQDN Fully Qualified Domain Name; the full *hostname.subdomatin.domain* address of an Internet site.

free-net A free public network.

freeware Software available for downloading on the Net for free.

ftp File transfer protocol, the standard Internet way to transfer files from one computer to another and the name of the common UNIX program that executes the protocol.

ftp site A computer on the Net containing archives and set up for ftp.

ftpmail A way to use ftp by e-mail if you don't have an ftp application.

full name Your full name as it appears in e-mail messages and Usenet posts.

<g> Indicates the author is grinning, similar to **:-)**.

gate Short for gateway, a computer that transfers files or e-mail from one network to another, or from a newsgroup to a list, and vice versa.

gated A newsgroup or mailing list that is connected to a mailing list or newsgroup, respectively.

gateway A computer that connects one network to another, for transferring files or e-mail, when the two networks use different protocols; or a computer that transfers posts from a newsgroup to a list, and vice versa.

GIF A compressed graphics (image) file format (GIF stands for graphics interchange format) invented by CompuServe, or a file in that format (with the extension .gif).

gnu. A hierarchy in the Usenet mold devoted to the Free Software Foundation and to emacs.

gopher A client-server application that performs ftp transfers, remote logins, archie searches, and so on, presenting everything to you in the form of menus. This saves you from having to know (or type in) the addresses of the Internet resources being tapped. You run a *gopher client* program you run to get information from a *gopher server* running at a *gopher site*.

gopherspace A collective name for all the gopher servers on the Net, so called because all the servers can connect to each other, creating a unified "space" of gopher menus.

.gov An internet domain, it stands for government.

green-card lawyer A derogatory term for people who spam the net with unwanted advertisements, and then go on TV to defend their actions.

<grin> Equivalent to the :-) emoticon.

group A newsgroup.

gunzip The uncompression program for gzipped files.

gzip A file compression program.

hack To dig into some computer activity, going beneath the surface and reinventing things when necessary.

hacker A computer adept.

Hayes compatible Modems that understand the Hayes AT instruction set are said to be Hayes compatible.

hierarchy In file storage, the arrangement of directories into a tree of parents and children. In Usenet, the organization of newsgroups into general areas, topics, and subtopics.

history A record of your last so many actions.

$HOME In UNIX, a variable that means your home directory.

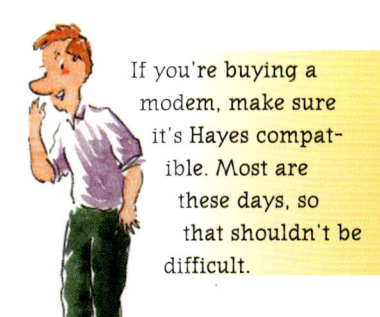

> If you're buying a modem, make sure it's Hayes compatible. Most are these days, so that shouldn't be difficult.

home directory The directory you start off in when you log into your UNIX account.

home page On the Web, the page you begin with when you start your browser.

host A computer on the Internet.

HTML Hypertext markup language, the hypertext language used in Web pages. It consists of regular text and "tags" that tell the browser what to do when a link is activated.

HTTP Hypertext transport protocol. The Web protocol for linking one Web page with another.

hypermedia Linked documents that consist of other media in addition to plain text, such as pictures, sounds, movies, and so on.

hypertext Text that contains links to other text documents.

hypertext link A link from one text document to another.

Hytelnet A telnet shell that helps you find the telnet site you want and then runs the telnet session for you. It contains a huge list of university and public library catalogs.

image file A binary file.

imminent death of the Net predicted A parody of the perennial warnings that traffic on the Net has gotten to be too much. Often followed by "film at 11."

inbox A file containing your incoming e-mail.

info Many Internet providers have an info address in the form (info@*host.subdomain.domain*).

Internet A network of networks. It's not a place, it's a way to go through.

InterNIC A repository of Internet information.

IP Internet protocol, the protocol that allows computers and networks on the Internet to communicate with each other.

irc Internet relay chat. A protocol and a client-server program that allows you to "chat" with people all over the Internet, in "channels" devoted to different topics.

JPEG A compressed file format for images (extension .jpg).

jughead An index of high-level gopher menus.

k12. A hierarchy in the Usenet mold devoted to kindergarten through 12th grade education.

kermit A protocol for download and upload file transfers.

key In encryption, a code that allows you to decrypt encrypted text.

key encryption A form of encryption that relies on keys.

Macintosh users with Hypercard should already be familiar with concept of hypertext.

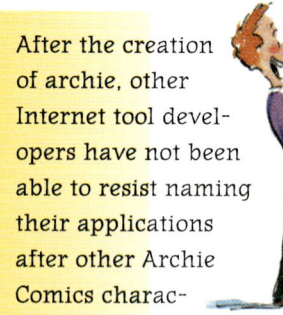

After the creation of archie, other Internet tool developers have not been able to resist naming their applications after other Archie Comics characters. Besides jughead, there is also veronica. Can reggie be long in following?

Glossary of Internet Jargon and Related Terms

Kibo Some say he is the first deity of the Internet. Also known as "he who greps," Kibo reportedly notes every mention of his name on Usenet and replies to worthy posts.

kibology The religion (or is it a science?) of Kibo. Its main doctrine is that You're Allowed. Only Spot, Kibo's dog, is Not Allowed.

killfile A file containing search instructions for automatically killing or autoselecting Usenet posts.

Knowbot An information service on the Net that, mong other things, helps find e-mail addresses.

kps Kilobits per second, a measurement of modem speed.

LAN A local-area network. A computer network usually confined to a single office or building.

lharc A file-compression program for DOS

library catalogs Most university and public library catalogs are available via telnet (and some via gopher). Hytelnet has an excellent index of library catalogs.

link On Web pages, a button or highlighted bit of text that, when selected, jumps the reader to another page.

list A mailing list.

listserv A type of mailing list software that runs on bitnet computers.

log in To start a session on your Internet account.

log out To end a session on your Internet account.

login A username, the name you log in with.

lurk To read a mailing list or newsgroup without posting to it. You should lurk for a while before posting.

lurker One who lurks.

lynx An excellent, text-based, UNIX browser for the Web.

mail On the Internet, synonymous with e-mail.

mail reader A program that allows you to read and reply to e-mail, and to send out new mail of your own.

mail reflector A computer than sends copies of mail to a list of addresses.

mailing list A list of people with a common interest, all of whom receive all the mail sent, or posted, to the list.

.mailrc A resource file for mail programs, other than elm.

majordomo A type of mailing list software.

MAKE.MONEY.FAST A chain letter still making its rounds on the Net. A classic Ponzi/pyramid scheme.

> There is also an evil anti-Kibo named Xibo, whose legions are much fewer than the trolling readers of alt.religion.kibology.

> As someone replied last time I saw this garbage reposted, "Don't make your first act of fraud one that includes your name and address at the top!"

message An item of e-mail.

.mil An Internet domain; it stands for military.

MIME Multipurpose Internet Mail Extensions, a protocol that allows e-mail to contain more than simple text.

misc. A Usenet hierarchy devoted to whatever doesn't fit in the other hierarchies.

modem A device that connects your computer to a phone jack and, through the phone lines, to another modem and computer. (It stands for *mo*dulator/*dem*odulator.)

moderated Lists and newsgroups whose posts must pass muster before appearing are said to be moderated.

moderator The volunteer who decides which submissions to a moderated list or newsgroup will be posted.

more The most common UNIX pager program.

Mosaic A Web browser, developed by NCSA, for graphical user interfaces.

motto! A follow-up post on Usenet proposing the previous post as a motto for the group.

MPEG A compressed file format for movies (extension .mpg).

MU* Any one of a series of acronyms for multiuser role-playing game environments.

MUD A multiuser domain/dimension/dungeon. A role-playing game environment that allows people all over the Net to play together.

MUSE A multiuser simulation environment (for role-playing games).

my two cents A tag appended to Usenet or list posts, indicating "this is just my opinion," or "I just wanted to get my two cents in."

ncftp A more sophisticated ftp program (than ftp).

NCSA The National Center for Supercomputing Applications, founded by the NSF in 1985; inventor of Mosaic.

the Net Often used as an abbreviation for the Internet or for Usenet, the Net is really a more general term for the lump sum of interconnected computers on the planet.

.net An Internet domain; it stands for network.

net.celebrity A celebrity on the Net.

net.cop Someone accused of trying to control others' posts in mailing lists or in Usenet newsgroups.

net.god An apparently powerful being on the Net.

net.personality A somewhat well known person on the Net.

Netfind An Internet resource for finding e-mail addresses.

nethead A Deadhead on the Net.

netiquette Accepted proper behavior on the Net, especially in regard to e-mail and Usenet.

netizen A citizen of the Net.

.netrc A resource file for ftp.

newbie A beginner, not as derogatory as "clueless newbie."

newsfeed The packet of news articles passed along from one computer to the next on Usenet.

newsgroup A Usenet discussion group.

.newsrc A resource file that keeps track of which Usenet newsgroups you are subscribed to and which articles you have read.

newsreader A program used to read Usenet articles.

NFS Not to be confused with NSF, NFS is the Network File System protocol, developed by Sun Microsystems, for transferring files over a network.

NIC A network information center.

node Any computer on the Internet, a host.

nn A UNIX newsreader.

NSF The National Science Foundation, maintainers of the NSFnet.

NSFnet A high-speed backbone, crucial (but not essential) to the Internet, maintained by the NSF.

Ob A prefix added to an obligatory addendum to a Usenet or list post.

offline Not currently connected to the Net.

offline mail reader A mail program that connects to the Net, downloads your e-mail, and then disconnects, allowing you to read, reply to, and send mail without being charged for connect time.

offline newsreader A newsreader that connects to the Net, downloads all unread articles in all subscribed newsgroups, and then disconnects, allowing you to read, reply to, and post articles without being charged for connect time.

online Currently connected to the Net.

.org An Internet domain, it stands for (non-profit) organization.

page A hypertext document available on the WorldWide Web.

pager A program that presents text one screenful at a time.

parent directory The parent for which the current directory is a subdirectory.

parity One of the things you have to set to use your modem. Usually set to None or Even, parity depends on the modem you're calling.

Violate netiquette at your peril. Although the Internet and Usenet are effectively anarchies, they still have strong social cultures, and most of the rules and regulations of the Net are enforced by peer pressure.

The most popular offline mail reader is Eudora for the Macintosh. If you've got a Mac, you want this program.

pgp   A shareware encryption program (it stands for pretty good privacy).

pico   A UNIX text editor based on the text editor built into the pino mail reader.

pine   A popular UNIX mail program.

ping   A somewhat obsolete UNIX command that checks on the status of another network.

pkunzip   The uncompression program for pkzipped files.

pkzip   A DOS file compression program

.plan   A text file that is displayed when someone fingers your e-mail address. Your plan can be anything.

plonk   I just put you in my killfile.

point at   For gopher clients or Web browsers, to start them up with a specific address to begin at.

POP   Point of presence, a local access number for a service provider, or post-office protocol, a standard way to download and upload e-mail.

post   To send a message to a mailing list or an article to a newsgroup.

PPP   Point-to-point protocol, a protocol for an Internet connection over a modem.

private key   In key encryption, the key that allows you to encrypt your signature and read messages encrypted with your public key.

.project   A text file that might be displayed when someone fingers your e-mail address. Not all fingers check for a .project file. You can describe the project you're working on in it.

propagation   The process of dissemination for Usenet posts, as they are passed from computer to computer. propagation delays sometimes

protocol   Any agreed-upon method for two computers to communicate.

/pub   A UNIX directory often found on ftp hosts.

public data network   A public data network allows you to make a local call to connect to a national network.

public key   In key encryption, the key someone else uses to encrypt private mail to you; you give it out to anyone who asks.

query   A search request submitted to a database, such as an archie query.

real name   Your full name as it appears on e-mail messages and Usenet posts.

realtime   The time it takes real people to communicate, as on a telephone.

rec.   A Usenet hierarchy devoted to recreation.

remote login   Logging into another computer over a network.

The word "post" comes from the bulletin-board metaphor, in which scraps of paper are posted to the board, to be read by anyone who comes by.

Propagation delays are responsible for the sometimes confusing situation that occurs when you read a follow-up to a post that hasn't yet appeared at your site.

reply An e-mail message or Usenet post responding to, and possibly quoting, the original.

repost To post again. A subsequent post of the same information.

-request Human-administered mailing lists have an address for sending administrative requests (such as subscriptions), with -request appended to the username for the list.

RFC Literally, request for comments. RFCs are founding documents of the Internet.

RFD Request for discussion, a stage in the creation of a new Usenet newsgroup, preceding the CFV.

RINGO An experimental service out of ringo@media.mit.edu that allows you to rate a list of musicians and bands and receive back some suggestions about other music you might like.

rlogin A UNIX program that allows you to log onto another UNIX machine without having to give your password.

rn A nonthreaded newsreader for UNIX.

roboposter An automatic process, disguised as a person, automatically posting and reposting huge amounts of articles to Usenet. Roboposters have rendered some newsgroups unreadable (without a killfile).

root The directory with no parent. An Internet address at a network usually monitored by a system administrator.

RTFM "Read the fucking manual!"—a dismissive response to a request for help.

sci. A Usenet hierarchy devoted to science.

select articles In newsreaders, to choose ahead of time (by their titles or authors) which articles you want to read

server A network application providing information to client programs that connect to it.

service provider A company that provides access to the Internet.

shareware Software available for a free trial that must be registered and paid for if you decide to use it.

shell A computer operating environment.

shell account An Internet account that gives you access to a UNIX shell.

.sig A signature file.

signal-to-noise ratio An engineering term adapted as a metaphor for the proportion of useful information to junk on a list or in a newsgroup.

signature file A text file that is automatically attached to the end of your e-mail messges or Usenet posts, usually containing your name and other pertinent information about you.

So the administrative address for the imaginary list epictetus@netcom.com would be epictetus-request@netcom.com.

A reputed roboposter, using the human name of Serdar Argic, single-handedly rendered soc.history (and a number of other newsgroups) unreadable for those without killfiles. His howling through the wires (ranting holocaust revisionism about the Turks and the "x-Soviet" Armenians) came to an unexpected halt in the spring of 1994.

GLOSSARY OF INTERNET JARGON AND RELATED TERMS

The signature file for elm is called signature, *without the dot.*

.signature A signature file.

site An Internet host that allows some kind of remote access—telnet, ftp, gopher, and so on.

SLIP Serial Line Internet Protocol, a protocol for an Internet connection over a modem.

smileys Sideways smiley faces such as :-), ;^), and %$, used to indicate emotions.

SMTP Simple Mail Transport Protocol. This protocol is what enables Internet e-mail to flow so freely.

snail mail Internet slang for "surface" mail.

soc. A Usenet hierarchy devoted to society (and usually sectarian groups in it).

spam To post (or robopost) huge amounts of material to Usenet, or to post one article to huge numbers of inappropriate groups.

spew To post excessively.

stop bits One of the things you have to set to use your modem. Usually set to 1 or 2, it depends on the modem you're calling.

subdirectory A directory that is the child of another directory.

subdomain A named portion of an Internet domain, usually a network, university, or company.

In my e-mail address, xian@netcom.com, *netcom is the subdomain.*

subscribe To join a mailing list or start reading a newsgroup.

surf To browse, following tangents.

synchronous Happening at the same time. Chat is a synchronous form of communication.

sysadmin A system administrator. Someone who runs or maintains a network.

sysop A system operator, a type of sysadmin.

system administrator Someone who runs or maintains a network.

system operator A type of sysadmin.

You can surf Usenet or gopherspace, but the Web is best for surfing.

talk One-to-one synchronous chatting over the Net.

talk. A Usenet hierarchy devoted to discussion, argument, and debate.

tar To lump together a bunch of files in an archive. The UNIX program that does said lumping.

TCP Transmission Control Protocol. A protocol that transmits information over the Internet, one small piece at a time.

TCP/IP The Internet protocol using TCP.

telnet A protocol for remote login, and the UNIX program that uses that protocol.

Glossary of Internet Jargon and Related Terms

*.test Usenet newsgroups, such as misc.test, alt.test, etc. used for posting test messages to see if they propagate properly.

text editor A program for editing text files; less fully featured than a word processor.

text file A file containing text only.

text transfer A transfer of straight text over the modem, between the remote computer and a text file.

thread A series of posts and follow-ups in a newsgroup.

threaded newsreader A newsreader that organizes posts according to thread and allows you to read your way up or down a thread.

time out To fail, as a network process, because the remote server or computer has not responded in time.

tin A threaded newsreader for UNIX.

trn A threaded newsreader for UNIX, similar to rn.

troll To deliberately post egregiously false information to a newsgroup, in hopes of tricking dense know-it-alls into correcting you. Also, such a post itself.

UL An urban legend. The Internet is a perfect medium of communication for tracking down and verifying or debunking urban legends.

uncompress To unsquish a compressed file. A UNIX uncompression program.

uncompression The process of unsquishing a file.

uniform resource locator A Web address. It consists of a protocol, a hostname, a port (optional), a directory, and a file name.

UNIX An operating system common to workstations and still dominant on the Internet.

unmoderated Said of a newsgroup or list whose articles are not vetted by a moderator.

unselect articles To remove the selection tag from Usenet articles selected for reading.

unsubscribe To remove yourself from a mailing list or stop reading a Usenet newsgroup.

untar To separate a tarred file into its component parts.

upload To transfer a file over a modem from your desktop computer to a remote computer.

urban legends Stories passed around and always attributed to a friend of a friend (a FOAF), frequently (but not always) based on a kernel of falsehood.

URL Uniform resource locator, a protocol of the WorldWide Web that enables browsers to address many different types of resources.

If you post something to a *.test newsgroup, be prepared for a mailbox full of confirming replies to your post, sent back by daemons as your post propagates around the world.

If you follow up a bizarre post to point out that Grover Cleveland Alexander was never president of the U.S., you may see an even more confusing reply to your post saying just "YHBT. YHL. HAND." This stands for "You have been trolled. You have lost. Have a nice day."

> The Usenet newsgroup alt.folklore.urban (and its less noisy cousing alt.folklore.suburban) is the home of UL debunkers.

> Choose your user-name well. In many ways it is more important (on the Net) than your real name. It's the name people see most often.

> If you lack access to a Web server but have access to an ftp site, then you can store your home page there and make sure that URLs pointing to it use the ftp protocol instead of the http protocol..

Usenet The collection of computers and networks that share news articles. The hierarchy of newsgroups. Usenet is not the Internet (though it overlaps pretty good).

username Login. The first part of your e-mail address (up to the @).

UUCP Unix to Unix Copy. A protocol and a program for intermittent network connections and file and mail transfers.

uudecode To turn a uuencoded file back into its normal form. The UNIX program that does this.

uuencode To convert a binary file into a text form that can be sent as part of an e-mail message. The UNIX program that does this.

vacation A UNIX program that sets up a return message to be sent to anyone who sends you mail, telling them you're on vacation.

veronica An index of gopher menus that you search. The results are presented to you as a gopher menu.

vi A common UNIX text editor.

virus A program that deliberately does damage to the computer its on.

VT100 A terminal type, originated by DEC, that has become the standard terminal. If you dial up a UNIX shell, then your communications program probably emulates a VT100.

w^3 An abbreviation for the WorldWide Web.

WAN A wide-area network. A computer network spanning a wide geographical area.

warlording Reposting a Usenet article to alt.fan.warlord and mocking its signature for being too large, ugly, or stupid.

Web The WorldWide Web.

Web address A URL.

Web browser A Web client program that allows you to view hypertext pages and follow links.

Web page A hypertext document on the Web. Surfing the Web consists of following links from page to page.

Web server A Web application that allows you to store home pages and make them available via the hypertext transport protocol.

Whois An Internet resource for identifying e-mail addresses.

wizard An expert, usually one willing to help newbies.

working directory The current directory. The directory you're "in" right now.

WorldWide Web A collection of hypertext pages, linked together, that spans the Internet (and hence, the globe).

worm   A program that duplicates itself, potentially worming its way through an entire network.

www   The original text-based UNIX browser for the Web.

xmodem   A protocol for download and upload file transfers.

xwindows   A graphical user interface for UNIX.

ymodem   A protocol for download and upload file transfers.

zip file   A compressed file.

zmodem   A protocol for download and upload file transfers.

Index

Note to the Reader: Throughout this index **boldfaced** page numbers indicate primary discussions of a topic. *Italic* page numbers indicate illustrations.

Numbers and Symbols

800 numbers. *See also* telephone numbers
   for service providers, 205, 206, 212

<> (angle brackets), in signature files, 102
* (asterisk)
   in tin newsreader, 111
   in veronica searches, 179
   as wildcard in UNIX commands, 128, 130
(number sign), in irc conversation names, 54
% (percent sign), restarting and canceling stopped processes with, 11
. (period)
   double period (..) for parent directory, 126–127, 233
   listing files beginning with, 127
| (pipe symbol), in ls command, 127–128, 234
+ (plus sign), in tin newsreader, 110
? (question mark)
   ? command, 12
   as wildcard in UNIX commands, **128**, 130
> (redirection symbol), in UNIX commands, 129

/ (slash)
   in irc commands, 54
   for root directory, 124

A

accessing. *See also* connecting to Internet
   via e-mail
      archie searches, 158
      ftp, 149–150, 158
      InterNIC, 14
      Usenet newsgroups, 92
   gopher servers, 173
   via telnet
      archie searches, 154–158, *156–157*, 236
      chat programs, 53
      gopher servers, 170, 236
      lynx Web browser, 185
      www Web browser, 190
   veronica, 178, *179*
   via WorldWide Web
      ftp, 197
      gopher servers, 196–197
      telnet, 197–198
      Usenet newsgroups, 102, 198
acronyms, in Usenet newsgroups, 86–87

address books, in pine e-mail program, 34–35
addresses (e-mail)
  collecting, 46
  finding, 46–52
    with finger command, 47–48, 49, 232, 242
    with Knowbot, 52, 52, 245
    with Netfind program, 49–52, 51
    with postmaster@ addresses, 46–47
    real names associated with addresses, 47
    with whois command, 48–49, 232
addresses (Internet)
  defined, 238
  viewing in gopherspace, 174
addresses (mailing), for InterNIC, 14
addresses (WorldWide Web). See URLs
aliases
  creating in elm e-mail program, 27–28, 28
  defined, 238
alt Usenet hierarchy, 81
America Online
  connecting to Internet via, 3, 202–204, 212–213
  e-mail on, 38, 39
  Internet addresses on, 20
  reading Usenet newsgroups on, 120
Anarchie program, 158–160, 159–160
angle brackets (<>), in signature files, 102
anonymity, on Usenet newsgroups, 67–68, 84
anonymous ftp, 140, 238. See also ftp
anonymous remailing services, 68, 238
appending
  results of UNIX commands to files, 129, 234
  text to a file, 138
.arc files, 142
archie searches, 151–160
  Anarchie program, 158–160, 159–160
  defined, 239
  e-mail access to, 158
  finding
    ftp sites, 140
    PGP program, 68
  general procedures, 152
  locations of archie servers, 154–155
  overview of, 151–152
  starting archie clients, 152–154, 236
  switches, 153
  telnetting to, 154–158, 156–157, 236
  whatis command in, 157
archives. See archie searches; ftp
articles (Usenet). See also files; home pages
  autoselecting in newsreaders
    in nn newsreader, 117–118
    overview of, 101, 239
    in tin newsreader, 113–114, 114
    in trn newsreader, 108
  canceling, 82, 240
  canceling deletion of in trn newsreader, 107
  crossposting to multiple newsgroups. See also posting
    in nn newsreader, 117
    overview of, 100–101, 241
    in tin newsreader, 113
    in trn newsreader, 107
  defined, 82, 239
  marking as unread
    in tin newsreader, 111
    in trn newsreader, 106
  posting to newsgroups. See also crossposting
    with nn newsreader, 116
    overview of, 98–99
    threads and, 98–99
    with tin newsreader, 112
    with trn newsreader, 106
  reading
    from filtering services, 93
    from mailing lists, 78, 92–93
    with nn newsreader, 114–115
    from online services, 120
    overview of, 96–97, 97
    with tin newsreader, 111
    with trn newsreader, 97, 102, 105
    on WorldWide Web, 102
  replying to via e-mail
    with nn newsreader, 116
    overview of, 83, 98
    with tin newsreader, 112
    with trn newsreader, 106
  saving
    in nn newsreader, 116
    overview of, 97
    in tin newsreader, 111
    in trn newsreader, 106
  selecting
    in nn newsreader, 115
    overview of, 96
    in tin newsreader, 110–111, 110

in trn newsreader, 104–105, *104*
testing propagation of, **101**, 248, 251
arts Web pages, 199
ASCII files. *See* text files
asterisk (*)
in tin newsreader, 111
in veronica searches, 179
as wildcard in UNIX commands, 128, 130
asynchronous communications
defined, **239**
e-mail and, 53, 239
AT&T Mail, Internet addresses on, 20
attaching files to e-mail, **65–67**
MIME attachments, 65, **246**
receiving other kinds of files, 67
receiving uuencoded files, 65–67, 233, 252
sending uuencoded files, 65–66, 233, 252
automating ftp logins with .netrc files, 143, 149
autoselecting articles in newsreaders
in nn newsreader, 117–118
overview of, 101, 239
in tin newsreader, 113–114, *114*
in trn newsreader, 108

B

Backspace key, 11
bar symbol. *See* pipe symbol (|)
BBSs. *See* bulletin board systems
Big Dummy's Guide to the Internet, 14, 239, 241
.bin files, 142
binary files
defined, **128**, **134**, **239**
downloading, 134–136, 234–235
protocols for, 134
uploading, 136–137, 234–235
BinHex files, 66–67, **239**
bitnet
defined, **81**, **239**
listserv program and, 74
biz Usenet hierarchy, 81
bookmarks
defined, **240**
to gopher servers, 174
in lynx Web browser, 189
for veronica searches, 178

bozo filters, **101**, **240**
"Bringing It All Back Home Page," 199
browsers. *See* WorldWide Web browsers
browsing. *See* reading
bulletin board systems (BBSs)
connecting to Internet via, 202
defined, **240**
Fidonet BBSs
defined, **242**
Internet addresses on, 20
business domains (.com), 19
bye command, 8

C

canceling
deletion of articles in trn newsreader, 107
messages in elm e-mail program, 19, 24
processes, 10
stopped processes, 11
Usenet articles, 82, **240**
case sensitivity
in directory names, 126
in file names, 129
cat command, 129, 138
cd command, 126–127, 233
CERFnet Archives, 166
changing
to child directories, 126
default editor for e-mail programs, 58, 233
default home page in lynx Web browser, 190
directories, 126–127, 234
irc nick (names), 54
passwords, 6
to working directory, 126
your "real name" on Usenet, 233
chatting, **52–54**, **233**
defined, **240**
versus e-mail, 53
ending conversations, 54
with irc command, 53–54, 233
joining conversations, 54
listing existing conversations, 54
overview of, 52–53
synchronous communications and, 53
with talk command, 53, 233
telnetting to chat programs, 53
chfn command, 233

child directories. *See also* directories
  changing to, 126
  defined, **125**
chmod command, 234
client-access accounts, 202
collecting, e-mail addresses, 46
.com domain, 19
comics, 200
commands. *See* UNIX commands
communications software, connecting to Internet with, 4–5, 204–205
comp.answers newsgroup, 11
comp.unix.shell newsgroup, 11
comp Usenet hierarchy, 80
composing e-mail, **56–59**. *See also* text editors
  with text editors, 56, 233
  with word processors, 56–58
compressed files
  defined, **240**
  file extensions for, 142
CompuServe
  connecting to Internet via, 3, 202–204, 212, 216
  e-mail on, 38, *39*
  Internet addresses on, 20
  public data networks (PDNs) and, 206, 212
  reading Usenet newsgroups on, 120
connecting to Internet, **2–5, 201–230**. *See also* accessing; PPP accounts; SLIP accounts
  via bulletin board systems (BBSs), 202, 240
  client-access accounts, 202
  cost of, **205–206**
  dialing service providers, 4–5
  direct connections, **202**
  finding service providers, **205–207**, 229–230
  Freenets, 206, 242
  hardware requirements, **203–204**
  via Macintosh or IBM-compatible environments, 4
  modem connections, **202–203**
  modems for, 203–204
  online information about service providers, **229–230**
  via online services, 3, 202–204
  public data networks (PDNs), 206, 212
  service providers listed alphabetically, **213–228**
  service providers listed by area code, **207–212**
  software requirements, **204–205**
  SprintNet, 206, 212
  types of connections, 2–3, 202–203
  university accounts, 206
  via UNIX environments, 2–3
conversations. *See* chatting
converting
  DOS text files to UNIX text files, 134, 235
  UNIX text files to DOS text files, 235
copying. *See also* downloading
  documents
    with lynx Web browser, 189
    with www Web browser, 192
  files, 131, 234
copying and pasting, UNIX commands, 12
core dump files, 10
cost of connecting to Internet, **205–206**
cp command, 131, 234
creating
  address books in pine e-mail program, 34–35
  aliases in elm e-mail program, 27–28, *28*
  directories, 127, 234
  files, 129
  killfiles
    in nn newsreader, 117–118
    overview of, 101, 245
    in tin newsreader, 113–114, *114*
    in trn newsreader, 108
  .newsrc files, 233
  text files with word processors, 137
  vacation messages, 41–42, *41*, 232
crossposting to multiple newsgroups. *See also* posting
  in nn newsreader, 117
  overview of, 100–101, 241
  in tin newsreader, 113
  in trn newsreader, 107
Ctrl key combinations
  Ctrl-C (canceling processes), 10
  Ctrl-R (repeating command line), 11–12
  Ctrl-U (deleting commands), 11
  Ctrl-Z (stopping processes), 10
  Ctrl-\ (canceling processes), 10
culture, Internet, 200
customizing lynx Web browser, 190

cutting-and-pasting
  with pico text editor, 65
  text from terminal window to a file, 138
  UNIX commands, 12
  with vi text editor, 62

D

death of Internet, imminent, predicted—*film at 11*, 89, 244
Delete key
  canceling processes, 10
  deleting commands, 11
deleting
  commands, 11
  core dump files, 10
  directories, 127, 234
  e-mail
    in elm program, 26
    in pine program, 34
  files, 130, 234
  overview of, 11
Delphi
  connecting to Internet via, 3, 202–204, 212, 217
  Internet addresses on, 20
  reading Usenet newsgroups on, 120
dialing service providers, 4–5
direct connections to Internet, 202
directing results of UNIX commands to files, 129, 234
directories, 123–128. *See also* files
  changing, 126–127, 234
  child directories
    changing to, 126
    defined, 125
  creating, 127, 234
  deleting, 127, 234
  directory trees, 124, *124*
  versus DOS directories, 125
  listing files in, 127–128, 234
  versus Macintosh folders, 125
  naming, 126
  networks and, 124
  overview of, 124–125, *124*
  parent directories
    defined, 125, 247
    double period (..) for, 126–127, 233

paths
  defined, 124, 125
  double period (..) in pathnames, 126–127
  renaming, 131
  subdirectories, 125, 250
  working directory
    changing to, 126
    defined, 125, 252
    displaying, 126, *126*
displaying working directory, 126, *126*
documents. *See* articles; files; home pages
domains
  .com, 19
  defined, 241
  .edu, 19, 241
  .gov, 19, 243
  .mil, 19
  .org, 19, 247
  types of, 19
dos2unix command, 134, 235
DOS
  converting DOS text files to UNIX text files, 134, 235
  converting UNIX text files to DOS text files, 235
  DOS directories versus UNIX directories, 125
dot. *See* period (.)
downloading files, 130, 133–138, 234–235. *See also* copying; ftp; uploading
  binary files, 134–136, 234–235
  defined, 133
  doing it, 135–136
  from gopher servers, 135, 172–173, *172*
  PPP and SLIP accounts and, 134
  and printing, 130
  protocols for, 134–136, 234–235
  text files, 134–136, 234–235
  text transfers across modems, 137–138, 251
  from WorldWide Web, 135
Dylan, Bob, home page, 199

E

800 numbers. *See also* telephone numbers
  for service providers, 205–206, 212
editing
  .newsrc files, 95, 100

editing—e-mail gateways

in pico text editor, 64–65
in vi text editor, 61–62
editors. *See* text editors
.edu domain, 19, 241
Electronic Frontier Foundation (EFF)
  Guide to the Internet, 14, 173, 196, 241
  WorldWide Web address, 200
elm e-mail program, 17–29. *See also* e-mail
  canceling messages, 19, 24
  creating aliases in, 27–28, *28*
  deleting e-mail, 26
  exiting, 26–27
  FAQs, 17
  forwarding e-mail, 25–26
  manual pages, 17
  reading e-mail, 22–24, *22–23*
  replying to e-mail, 18, 24–25, *25*
  saving e-mail, 24
  sending e-mail, 18–22, *21*
  signature files in, 28–29
  spell checking in, 62
  starting, 18, *18*, 232
  tagging messages in, 29
  uploading messages composed offline, 19
  Usenet newsgroup, 17
e-mail, 15–54. *See also* mailing lists; text editors
  accessing
    archie searches via, 158
    ftp via, 149–150, 158
    InterNIC via, 14
    Usenet newsgroups via, 92
  asynchronous communications and, 53, 239
  attaching files to, 65–67
    MIME attachments, 65, 246
    receiving other kinds of files, 67
    receiving uuencoded files, 65–67, 233, 252
    sending uuencoded files, 65–66, 233, 252
  changing default text editor for e-mail programs, 58, 233
  versus chatting, 53
  collecting addresses, 46
  composing, 56–59. *See also* text editors
    with text editors, 56, 233
    with word processors, 56–58
  etiquette (netiquette), 29, 43–44
  finding addresses, 46–52
    with finger command, 47–49, 232, 242
    with the Knowbot, 52, *52*, 245
    with Netfind program, 49–52, *51*
    with postmaster@ addresses, 46–47
    real names associated with addresses, 47
    with whois command, 48–49, 232
  flaming, 44, 242
  forwarding your e-mail to another account, 42–43
  going on vacation, 40–42
    after returning from vacation, 42
    creating vacation messages, 41–42, *41*, 232
    unsubscribing to mailing lists, 40, 75
  mail program, 35–36
  newsreaders versus e-mail programs, 92
  online services and, 20, 38, *39*
  overview of, 15–17
  pine program, 29–35. *See also* pico text editor
    creating address books, 34–35
    deleting e-mail, 34
    exiting, 34
    forwarding e-mail, 33
    reading e-mail, 31–32, *32*
    replying to e-mail, 33
    saving e-mail, 32–33
    sending e-mail, 30–31, *31*
    signature files in, 35
    starting, 29, *30*, 232
  .plan files and, 47–48, 232, 248
  posting to Usenet newsgroups via, 93
  PPP accounts and, 16, 37
  recovering lost messages, 40
  replying to Usenet articles via
    in nn newsreader, 116
    overview of, 83, 98
    in tin newsreader, 112
    in trn newsreader, 106
  security, 67–68
    anonymous remailing services, 68, 238
    encrypting e-mail, 67–68, 242
    Usenet newsgroups and, 67–68
  sending
    to other networks, 20
    to Web page owners, 189
  SLIP accounts and, 16, 37
  UNIX shell accounts and, 16
  windowed mail programs, 16, 36–37
    Eudora program, 37, *38*, 242
    offline mail readers, 37, 205, 247
e-mail gateways
  defined, 2

sending e-mail to other networks via, 20
Empty.tv.com parody of MeTaVerse home page, 199
encrypting e-mail, 67–68, 242
entering
   search text in veronica, 179
   UNIX commands, 7
Enterzone hypermedia magazine, 199
error messages, 12
etiquette
   for e-mail, 29, 43–44
   in mailing lists, 76
   in Usenet newsgroups, 79, 83–87
Eudora e-mail program, *37*, *38*, 242
exact time, 166
exit command, 8
exiting
   elm e-mail program, 26–27
   gopher servers, 175
   lynx Web browser, 190
   newsreaders
      nn newsreader, 117
      overview of, 100
      tin newsreader, 112
      trn newsreader, 107
   pico text editor, 63
   pine e-mail program, 34
   vi text editor, 60
   www Web browser, 192
external modems, 204

F

faq command, 12
FAQs (frequently asked questions)
   defined, **242**
   for elm e-mail program, 17
   finding, **242**
   for ftp, 140
   for Internet legends, 200
   on mailing lists, 75
   overview of, 11, 14
   on Usenet newsgroups, 85
   for WorldWide Web, 195
fax numbers, for InterNIC, 14
fax/modems, 204
Fidonet BBSs
   defined, **242**
   Internet addresses on, 20

file extensions
   for compressed files, 142
   .html, 186, 189, 198, **244**
file transfers. *See* ftp
files, **128–131**. *See also* articles; directories; home pages
   appending results of UNIX commands to, 129, 234
   attaching to e-mail, **65–67**
      MIME attachments, 65, **246**
      receiving other kinds of files, 67
      receiving uuencoded files, 65–67, 233, 252
      sending uuencoded files, 65–66, 233, 252
   binary files
      defined, **128**, **134**, **239**
      downloading, 134–136, 234–235
      protocols for, 134
      uploading, 136–137, 234–235
   copying, 131, 234
   creating, 129
   deleting, 130, 234
   downloading, 130, **133–138**, 234–235. *See also* ftp; uploading
      binary files, 134–136, 234–235
      defined, **133**
      doing it, **135–136**
      from gopher servers, 135, 172–173, *172*
      PPP and SLIP accounts and, 134
      and printing, **130**
      protocols for, 134–135, **136**
      text files, 134–136, 234–235
      text transfers across modems, **137–138**, 251
      from WorldWide Web, 135
   listing files in directories, **127–128**, 234
   making files readable by others, 234
   moving, 131, 234
   naming, **129**, 131
   networks and, 124
   opening
      in pico text editor, 64
      in vi text editor, 60
   overview of, 123, 128
   pdial file, 229
   printing, 129–130
   printing man pages to files, 13
   renaming, 131, 234
   text files
      converting DOS files to UNIX files, 134, 235

converting UNIX files to DOS files, 235
creating with word processors, 137
defined, 128, 134, 251
downloading, 134–136
sending text via modem, 137–138
transferring, 57–58, *57*
uploading, 136–137
transferring. *See* ftp
types of, 128
uploading
  defined, 133, 251
  doing it, 136–137, 234–235
uuencoded files, 65–67, 233, 252
viewing contents of, 129, *130*, 234
film at 11, 89, 242
filtering services, reading Usenet newsgroups via, 93
finding
  EFF's Guide to the Internet, 14, 173, 196
  e-mail addresses, 46–52, 232
    with finger command, 47–48, 49, 232, 242
    with Knowbot, 52, *52*, 245
    with Netfind program, 49–52, *51*
    with postmaster@ addresses, 46–47
    real names associated with addresses, 47
    with whois command, 48–49, 232
  FAQs, 242
  ftp sites, 140–141
  gopher servers, 173
  mailing lists, 71–72
    general lists of lists, 71
    specific lists of lists, 72, *72*
  Mosaic program, 192
  PGP program, 68
  service providers, 205–207, 229–230
  Usenet FAQs, 85
  Usenet newsgroups, 82
finger command
  finding e-mail addresses with, 47–48, 232, 242
  for soft drink machines, 49
flamebait, 76, 83, 242
flamewars, 82–84, 242
flaming, 44, 242
following hypertext links
  in lynx, 187, *187*
  in www, 191
Forgotten Site List (FSLIST), 229

forward slash (/)
  in irc commands, 54
  for root directory, 124
forwarding e-mail
  with elm program, 25–26
  with pine program, 33
  your e-mail to another account, 42–43
Freenets, 206, 242
freezes. *See* troubleshooting
frequently asked questions. *See* FAQs
FSLIST (Forgotten Site List), 229
ftp, 139–150, 235–236
  anonymous ftp, 140, 238
  automating logins with .netrc files, 143, 149
  command summary, 235–236
  defined, 140, 242
  via e-mail, 149–150, 158
  FAQs, 140
  file transfers, 141–148
    binary files, 144, 235
    command overview, 146, 235–236
    defined, 242
    identifying compressed files, 142
    if your modem hangs, 146
    listing files, 143–144, *145*
    logging in, 142–143, *144*
    Macintoshes and, 146–148, *147–148*
    overview of, 141
    PCs and, 146
    text files, 141, 144
    transferring files, 141, 144, *145*
    transferring multiple files, 144, 235
    turning off prompting, 144, 235
  finding
    EFF's Guide to the Internet, 14
    ftp sites, 140–141
    Mosaic, 192
    PGP program, 68
    Usenet FAQs, 85
  ftpmail, 149–150, 158, 242
  gopher servers and, 167, 175–176, *175*
  Help, 146
  mirror sites, 141
  ncftp, 148–149, 235
  passwords and, 140, 141
  RFCs (Request for Comments), 14
  starting, 235

G

gateways
  defined, **243**
  e-mail gateways
    defined, **2**
    sending e-mail to other networks via, 20
  listserv/usenet gateways, 92–93
  between Usenet newsgroups and mailing lists, 78, **92–93**
GEnie, Internet addresses on, 20
geography facts, 166
gnu Usenet hierarchy, 81, 243
gopher servers, **167–180**
  accessing other gopher servers, 173
  bookmarks, 174, 178
  defined, **243**
  downloading files, 135, 172–173, *172*
  exiting, 175
  finding, 173
  finding *EFF's Guide to the Internet*, 14, 173
  ftp and, 167, 175–176, *175*
  general procedures, **168–169**
  Help, 175
  for InterNIC, 14
  jughead, 169, **180**, 244
  navigating gopherspace, 170–171, *171*
  NetCruiser for Windows, **176–177**, *177*
  overview of, 167–168
  reading documents, 171–173
  starting gopher clients, 169, *169*, 236
  telnetting to, 170, 236
  TurboGopher program, 176
  veronica, 169, **178–180**
    accessing, 178, *179*
    asterisk (*) in searches, 179
    bookmarks for, 178
    defined, **252**
    entering search text, 179
    limiting the number of matches, 180
    selecting search types, 178–179
    viewing search results, 180
  viewing Internet addresses, 174
  versus WorldWide Web, 183
gossip
  music industry gossip, 199
  Usenet newsgroups, 78
government documents, 166
government domains (.gov), 19, **243**

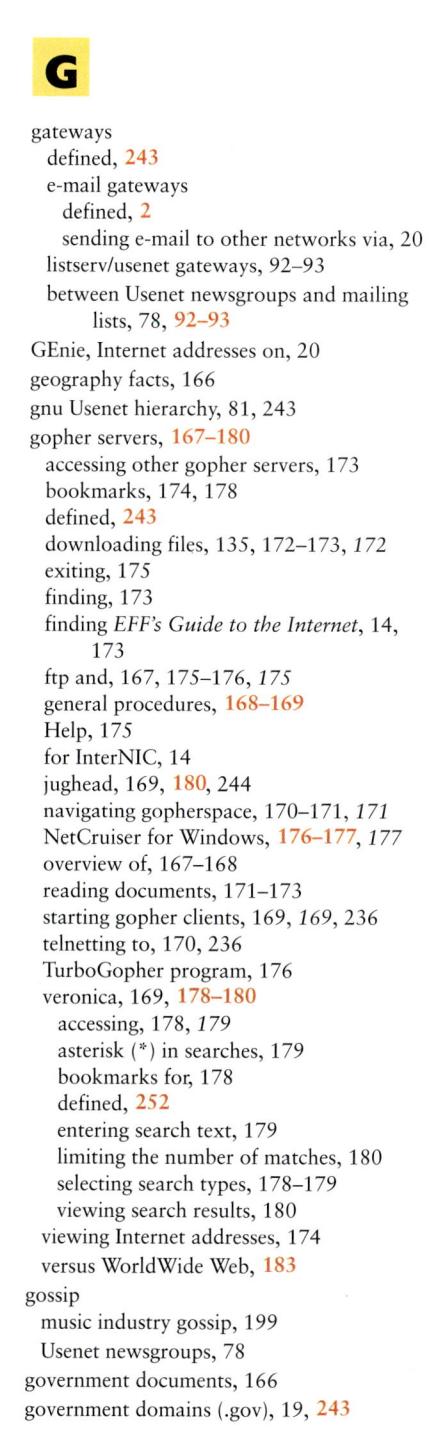

Grateful Dead home page, 199
groups. *See* Usenet newsgroups
Guide to the Internet (Electronic Frontier Foundation), 14, 173, 196, 241
.gz files, 142
gzip and gunzip programs, 142, 243

H

h command, 12
hanging up, 8, 11
hangs. *See* troubleshooting
hardware requirements for connecting to Internet, **203–204**
Help, **12–14**. *See also* FAQs; troubleshooting
  for ftp, 146
  for gopher servers, 175
  help commands, 12
  InterNIC, 13–14
  man command, 12–13, *13*
  in newsreaders
    nn newsreader, 117
    overview of, 100
    tin newsreader, 113
    trn newsreader, 107
  for pico text editor, 63
  RFCs (Request for Comments), 14
  for telnet, 164
  for Usenet newsgroups, 90
  for vi text editor, 60
  for WorldWide Web, **195–196**
hiding menu options in tin newsreader, 111
hierarchies, of Usenet newsgroups, 79–82, **243**
home directory. *See* working directory
home pages. *See also* articles; files; hypertext; WorldWide Web
  changing default in lynx, 190
  defined, **244**
  overview of, 184
  returning to in lynx, 189
  starting browsers at, 185, 190
.hqx files, 142
Hypernews, 200
hypertext. *See also* home pages; WorldWide Web
  defined, **244**
  following links
    in lynx, 187, *187*

in www, 191
in signature files, 102
WorldWide Web and, 182
HyperText Markup Language (HTML), 186, 189, 198, 244
HyperText Transport Protocol (HTTP), 186
Hytelnet program, 164–165, *165*, 236, 244

I

IBM-compatible environments. *See* PC environments
indexes. *See* jughead; veronica
internal modems, 203–204
Internet
  connecting to, 2–5, 201–230. *See also* accessing; PPP accounts; SLIP accounts
    bulletin board systems (BBSs), 202, 240
    client-access accounts, 202
    cost of, 205–206
    dialing service providers, 4–5
    direct connections, 202
    finding a service provider, 205–207, 229–230
    Freenets, 206
    hardware requirements, 203–204
    via Macintosh or IBM-compatible environments, 4
    modem connections, 202–203
    modems for, 203–204
    online information about service providers, 229–230
    via online services, 3, 202–204
    public data networks (PDNs), 206, 212
    service providers listed alphabetically, 213–228
    service providers listed by area code, 207–212
    software requirements, 204–205
    SprintNet, 206, 212
    types of connections, 2–3, 202–203
    university accounts, 206
    via UNIX environments, 2–3
  death of, 89, 244
  defined, 244
  EFF's Guide to the Internet, 14, 173, 196, 241
  hanging up, 8, 11
  logging in, 5–6

logging out, 8
personalities and culture, 200
InterNIC
  defined, 244
  overview of, 13–14
  service provider lists, 229
  telnet site information, 166
interrupting. *See* stopping
irc command, 53–54, 233, 244
irc nick (name), changing, 54

J

jobs. *See* processes
jughead, 169, 180, 244. *See also* gopher servers
junking. *See* deleting

K

Kaminski, Peter, 229
kermit protocol, 135–136, 234, 244
Kerouac, Jack, home page, 199
Kibo WorldWide Web address, 200, 245
kill command, 11
killfiles
  defined, 245
  in nn newsreader, 117–118
  overview of, 101
  in tin newsreader, 113–114, *114*
  in trn newsreader, 108
killing. *See* canceling
Knowbot, finding e-mail addresses with, 52, *52*, 245

L

.lhz files, 142
Library of Congress, 166
line length, in newsreaders, 98
links. *See* hypertext; WorldWide Web
listing
  chat conversations, 54
  files in directories, 127–128, 234
lists. *See* mailing lists
listserv program, 74

listserv/usenet gateways, 92–93
logging in
  defined, **245**
  to Internet, **5–6**
  remote login programs. *See* telnet
  rlogin command, 164, 236, 249
  to telnet, 162–164, *163*, 236
logging out
  defined, **245**
  of Internet
    by hanging up, 11
    overview of, 8
  of telnet, 163
lp or lpr command, 130
ls command, 127–128, 234
lurking
  defined, **245**
  on mailing lists, 75–76
  on Usenet newsgroups, 85
lynx Web browser, **184–190**. *See also* WorldWide Web browsers
  bookmarks, 189
  changing default home page, 190
  copying documents, 189
  customizing, 190
  exiting, 190
  following links, 187, *187*
  going directly to URLs, 188, 236
  navigating in, 186–188, *188*
  reading documents, 185–187
  returning to home page, 189
  sending e-mail to page owners, 189
  starting, 185, *185*, 236
  telnetting to, 185
  viewing URLs and HTML text, 189

M

Macintosh environments. *See also* PC environments; PPP accounts; SLIP accounts
  Anarchie program, **158–160**, *159–160*
  BinHex files, 66–67, **239**
  connecting to Internet via, 4
  Eudora e-mail program, **37**, *38*, 242
  folders versus UNIX directories, **125**
  ftp file transfers with, 146–148, *147–148*
  Mosaic Web browser, 184, **192–193**, *193–194*

TurboGopher program, 176
mail program, **35–36**. *See also* e-mail
mail readers, 37, 205
mailing address, for InterNIC, 14
mailing lists, **69–76**. *See also* e-mail
  defined, **245**
  ctiquette, 76
  FAQs, 75
  finding, **71–72**
    general lists of lists, 71
    specific lists of lists, 72, *72*
  gateways between Usenet newsgroups and, **78**, **92–93**
  guidelines for participating on, **75–76**
  lurking on, 75–76, 245
  overview of, 69–71
  posting to
    defined, **70**
    doing it, 75
  reading newsgroups via, **92–93**
  subscribing to, **72–74**
    defined, **250**
    overview of, 72–73
    people-administered lists, 73
    robot-administered lists, 74
  unsubscribing to, 40, **74–75**
    defined, **251**
    people-administered lists, 74
    robot-administered lists, 74
    when going on vacation, 40, 75
  versus Usenet newsgroups, **70**, 78
making. *See* creating
man command, 12–13, *13*
man pages
  defined, **12**
  for elm e-mail program, 17
  for Knowbot manual, 52
  for man command, 13
  for ncftp, 148
  printing, 13
marking articles as unread
  in tin newsreader, 111
  in trn newsreader, 106
MCI Mail, Internet addresses on, 20
menu options, hiding in tin newsreader, 111
messages. *See* e-mail
MeTaVerse home page, 199
military domains (.mil), 19
MIME attachments, 65, **246**
mirror ftp sites, **141**

misc Usenet hierarchy, 80
mkdir command, 127, 234
modems
   for connecting to Internet, 203–204
   defined, **246**
   modem connections to Internet, **202–203**
   text transfers across, **137–138**, **251**
moderated Usenet newsgroups, 88, **246**
more command, 138, 234
Mosaic Web browser, 184, **192–193**, *193–194*
moving
   files, 131, 234
   newsgroups to top of list
     in tin newsreader, 109
     in trn newsreader, 104
moving around in. *See* navigating
Multipurpose Internet Mail Extensions (MIME) attachments, 65, **246**
music and arts Web pages, 199
music industry gossip, 199
mv command, 131, 234

N

names
   changing irc nick (name), 54
   real names
     changing on Usenet, 233
     defined, **248**
     finding real names associated with addresses, 47
   of Usenet newsgroups, **81–82**
naming. *See also* renaming
   directories, 126, 131
   files, 129, 131
navigating
   in gopherspace, 170–171, *171*
   in lynx Web browser, 186–188, *188*
   in pico text editor, 64
   in vi text editor, 61
ncftp, **148–149**, 235
NCSA What's New Page, WorldWide Web, 196
NetCruiser for Windows, **176–177**, *177*, **194**, *195*
Netfind program
   defined, **247**

   finding e-mail addresses with, 49–52, *51*
netiquette. *See* etiquette
netizen, **247**
.netrc files, automating ftp logins with, 143, 149
networks, directory and file management and, 124
news filtering services, 93
news Usenet hierarchy, 80
.newsrc files
   creating, 233
   defined, **247**
   overview of, 95, 100
   in tin newsreader, 109
   in trn newsreader, 103
newsreaders, **91–121**. *See also* Usenet newsgroups
   autoselecting articles
     in nn newsreader, 117–118
     overview of, 101, 239
     in tin newsreader, 113–114, *114*
     in trn newsreader, 108
   bozo filters, 101, 240
   creating killfiles
     in nn newsreader, 117–118
     overview of, 101, 245
     in tin newsreader, 113–114, *114*
     in trn newsreader, 108
   crossposting to multiple newsgroups
     in nn newsreader, 117
     overview of, 100–101, 241
     in tin newsreader, 113
     in trn newsreader, 107
   defined, **84**, **247**
   versus e-mail programs, **92**
   exiting
     nn newsreader, 117
     overview of, 100
     tin newsreader, 112
     trn newsreader, 107
   Help
     in nn newsreader, 117
     overview of, 100
     in tin newsreader, 113
     in trn newsreader, 107
   hierarchies and, 80
   identifying yourself on Usenet, **99**
   line length in, 98
   marking articles as unread
     in tin newsreader, 111
     in trn newsreader, 106

newsreaders—newsreaders

moving newsgroups to top of list
  in tin newsreader, 109
  in trn newsreader, 104
Newswatcher for the Macintosh,
  119–121, *121*
nn newsreader, **114–118**
  autoselecting articles, 117–118
  creating killfiles, 117–118
  crossposting to multiple newsgroups, 117
  exiting, 117
  Help, 117
  posting responses, 116
  reading articles, 114–115
  replying to articles via e-mail, 116
  saving articles, 116
  selecting articles, 115
  selecting newsgroups, 115
  starting, 114, 233
  starting threads, 116
online versus offline newsreaders,
  101–102, 205, 247
overview of, 91–94
posting responses. *See also* crossposting
  with nn newsreader, 116
  overview of, 98–99
  threads and, 98–99
  with tin newsreader, 112
  with trn newsreader, 106
reading articles
  from filtering services, **93**
  from mailing lists, 78, **92–93**
  with nn newsreader, 114–115
  from online services, **120**
  overview of, 96–97, 97
  with tin newsreader, 111
  with trn newsreader, 97, 102, 105
replying to articles via e-mail
  in nn newsreader, 116
  overview of, 83, 98
  in tin newsreader, 112
  in trn newsreader, 106
rn newsreader, **118–119**, 233
saving articles
  with nn newsreader, 116
  overview of, 97
  with tin newsreader, 111
  with trn newsreader, 106
selecting articles
  with nn newsreader, 115
  overview of, 96
  with tin newsreader, 110–111, *110*
  with trn newsreader, 104–105, *104*

selecting newsgroups
  with nn newsreader, 115
  overview of, 96
  with tin newsreader, 109–110
  with trn newsreader, 103–104
selecting threads with tin newsreader, 110
setting up, **94–95**
signature files and, 92, 99
starting
  nn newsreader, 114, 233
  overview of, 96
  tin newsreader, 109, *109*, 233
  trn newsreader, 102–103, *103*, 233
starting threads
  in nn newsreader, 116
  overview of, 99
  in tin newsreader, 112
  in trn newsreader, 107
subscribing and unsubscribing to
  newsgroups, **94–95**
threaded versus unthreaded newsreaders,
  101, **251**
tin newsreader, **108–114**
  asterisk (*) in, 111
  autoselecting articles, 113–114, *114*
  creating killfiles, 113–114, *114*
  crossposting to multiple newsgroups, 113
  exiting, 112
  Help, 113
  hiding menu options, 111
  marking articles as unread, 111
  moving newsgroups to top of list, 109
  .newsrc files, 109
  plus sign (+) in, 110
  posting responses, 112
  reading articles, 111
  replying to articles via e-mail, 112
  saving articles, 111
  selecting articles, 110–111, *110*
  selecting newsgroups, 109–110
  selecting threads, 110
  starting, 109, *109*, 233
  starting threads, 112
trn newsreader, **102–108**
  autoselecting articles, 108
  canceling deletion of articles, 107
  creating killfiles, 108
  crossposting to multiple newsgroups, 107
  exiting, 107
  following threads, 105, 106
  Help, 107
  marking articles as unread, 106

moving newsgroups to top of list, 104
.newsrc files, 103
posting responses, 106
reading articles, 97, 102, 105
replying to articles via e-mail, 106
saving articles, 106
selecting articles, 104–105, *104*
selecting newsgroups, 103–104
starting, 102–103, *103*, 233
starting threads, 107
types of, 101–102
windowed newsreaders, 101, 119–121, *121*
WorldWide Web as a newsreader, 102
nixpub public-access providers, 230
nn newsreader. *See* newsreaders
non-profit domains (.org), 19, 247
number sign (#), in irc conversation names, 54
numbers, in threads, 110

O

"ob" (obligatory) comments, in newsgroups, 98, 247
offline mail readers, 37, 205, 247
online information about service providers, 229–230
online versus offline newsreaders, 101–102, 205, 247
online services
  connecting to Internet via, 3, 202–204
  e-mail and, 38, *39*
  Internet addresses for, 20
opening files
  in pico text editor, 64
  in vi text editor, 60
.org domain, 19, 247

P

Packet Network PSINet, 206, 212
pages. *See* home pages; hypertext; WorldWide Web
parent directories. *See also* directories
  defined, 125, 247
  double period (..) for, 126–127, 233
passwords, changing, 6

paths. *See also* directories
  defined, 124, 125
  double period (..) in pathnames, 126–127
PC environments. *See also* Macintosh environments; PPP accounts; SLIP accounts
  connecting to Internet via, 4
  converting DOS text files to UNIX text files, 134, 235
  converting UNIX text files to DOS text files, 235
  ftp file transfers in, 146
  NetCruiser for Windows, 176–177, *177*, 194, *195*
pdial file, 229
PDNs (public data networks), 206, 212
people-administered mailing lists
  subscribing to, 73
  unsubscribing to, 74
percent sign (%), restarting and canceling stopped processes with, 11
period (.)
  double period (..) for parent directory, 126–127, 233
  listing files beginning with, 127
personalities, Internet, 200
PGP (Pretty Good Privacy) encryption program, 67–68
phone numbers. *See* telephone numbers
pico text editor, 63–65. *See also* text editors
  editing in, 64–65
  exiting, 63
  Help, 63
  navigating in, 64
  opening files in, 64
  saving in, 63
  spell checking, 65
  starting, 63
  typing in, 63
pine e-mail program, 29–35. *See also* e-mail; pico text editor
  creating address books, 34–35
  deleting e-mail, 34
  exiting, 34
  forwarding e-mail, 33
  reading e-mail, 31–32, *32*
  replying to e-mail, 33
  saving e-mail, 32–33
  sending e-mail, 30–31, *31*
  signature files in, 35

starting, 29, *30*, 232
pipe symbol (|), in ls command, 127–128, 234
.plan files, 47–48, 232, **248**
plus sign (+), in tin newsreader, 110
Point-to-Point protocol. *See* PPP accounts
posting. *See also* cross-posting
  to mailing lists
    defined, **70**
    doing it, 75
  to newsgroups via e-mail, **93**
  responses to newsgroups
    with nn newsreader, 116
    overview of, 98–99
    threads and, 98–99
    with tin newsreader, 112
    with trn newsreader, 106
postmaster@ addresses, 46–47
posts. *See* articles (Usenet)
pound sign (#), in irc conversation names, 54
PPP accounts. *See also* Macintosh environments; PC environments
  archie searches on, 152
  defined, **202**, **248**
  downloading and, 134
  e-mail and, 16, 37
  gopher access, 176
  Mosaic browser, 192
  Web browsers on, 184
  windowed newsreaders and, 119
Pretty Good Privacy (PGP) encryption program, 67–68
printing
  files, 129–130
  man pages to files, 13
private keys, 67, **248**
problems. *See* troubleshooting
processes
  canceling, 10
  stopped processes
    canceling, 11
    restarting, 11
  stopping, 10–11
Prodigy
  connecting to Internet via, 3, 202–204
  Internet addresses on, 20
prompt
  turning off ftp prompt, 144, 235
  UNIX prompt, **6–7**

propagation of Usenet articles, 101, 248, 251
protocols
  defined, **248**
  for downloading files, 134–135, **136**, **234–235**
PSINet, 206, 212
public data networks (PDNs), 206, 212
public keys, 67, **248**
public-access providers, 206, 230
pwd command, 126, *126*, 233

Q

question mark (?)
  ? command, 12
  as wildcard in UNIX commands, **128**, 130
quick reference, for UNIX commands, 231–236
quitting. *See* exiting

R

R.E.M. home page, 199
reading. *See also* newsreaders
  articles
    from filtering services, **93**
    from mailing lists, 78, **92–93**
    with nn newsreader, 114–115
    from online services, **120**
    overview of, 96–97, *97*
    with tin newsreader, 111
    with trn newsreader, 97, 102, 105
    on WorldWide Web, 102
  documents
    in gopher servers, 171–173
    in lynx Web browser, 185–187
    in www Web browser, 191
  e-mail
    with elm program, 22–24, *22–23*
    with pine program, 31–32, *32*
  newsgroups via mailing lists, 92
real names
  changing on Usenet, 233
  defined, **248**
  finding real names associated with addresses, 47
real time conversations. *See* chatting
rec Usenet hierarchy, 80

receiving
   text transfers via modem, 138, 251
   uuencoded files, 65–67, 233, 252
recovering e-mail messages, 40
redirecting results of UNIX commands to files, 129, 234
redirection symbol (>), in UNIX commands, 129
remote login programs. *See* telnet
removing. *See* deleting
renaming. *See also* naming
   directories, 131
   files, 131, 234
repeating UNIX commands, 11–12
replying
   defined, **249**
   to e-mail with elm program, 18, 24–25, *25*
   to Usenet articles via e-mail
     with nn newsreader, 116
     overview of, 83, 98
     with tin newsreader, 112
     with trn newsreader, 106
Request for Comments (RFCs), **14**
restarting stopped processes, 11
retyping UNIX commands, 11–12
RFCs (Request for Comments), **14**
rlogin command, 164, 236, 249
rm command, 130–131, 234
rm core command, 10
rmdir command, 127, 234
rn newsreader, **118–119**, 233
robot-administered mailing lists
   subscribing to, 74
   unsubscribing to, 74
running. *See* starting

S

saving
   articles
     in nn newsreader, 116
     overview of, 97
     in tin newsreader, 111
     in trn newsreader, 106
   e-mail
     in elm program, 24
     with pine program, 32–33
   in pico text editor, 63

   in vi text editor, 60
sci Usenet hierarchy, 80
.sea files, 142
security
   anonymous remailing services, 68, 238
   encrypting e-mail, 67–68, 242
   Usenet newsgroups and, 67–68, 84
selecting
   articles
     in nn newsreader, 115
     overview of, 96
     in tin newsreader, 110–111, *110*
     in trn newsreader, 104–105, *104*
   newsgroups
     in nn newsreader, 115
     overview of, 96
     in tin newsreader, 109–110
     in trn newsreader, 103–104
   search types in veronica, 178–179
   threads in tin newsreader, 110
sending
   e-mail
     with elm program, 18–22, *21*
     to other networks, 20
     with pine program, 30–31, *31*
     to Web page owners, 189
   text transfers via modem, 137–138
   uuencoded files, 65–66, 233, 252
Serial Line Internet Protocol. *See* SLIP accounts
service providers, 4–5, **205–230**. *See also* connecting to Internet
   defined, **249**
   dialing, 4–5
   finding, 205–207
   listed alphabetically, **213–228**
   listed by area code, **207–212**
   online information about, 229–230
setenv command, 5
setting up newsreaders, 94–95
shell accounts
   defined, **249**
   e-mail and, 16
signal-to-noise ratios, on Usenet newsgroups, 88, **249**
signature files
   defined, **249–250**
   in elm e-mail program, 28–29
   hypertext codes in, 102
   newsreaders and, 92, 99

signature files—text editors

in pine e-mail program, 35
slash (/)
  in irc commands, 54
  for root directory, 124
SLIP accounts. *See also* Macintosh environments; PC environments
  archie searches on, 152
  defined, 202, 250
  downloading and, 134
  e-mail and, 16, 37
  gopher access, 176
  Mosaic browser, 192
  Web browsers on, 184
  windowed newsreaders and, 119
soc Usenet hierarchy, 80
soft drink machines, fingering, 49
software requirements for connecting to Internet, 204–205
spell checking
  in elm e-mail program, 62
  in pico text editor, 65
  in vi text editor, 62
SprintNet, 206, 212
Star Trek newsgroups, 88
starting
  archie clients, 152–154, 236
  elm e-mail program, 18, *18*, 232
  ftp, 235
  gopher clients, 169, *169*, 236
  lynx Web browser, 185, *185*, 236
  ncftp, 235
  newsreaders
    nn newsreader, 114, 233
    overview of, 96
    tin newsreader, 109, *109*, 233
    trn newsreader, 102–103, *103*, 233
  pico text editor, 63, 233
  pine e-mail program, 29, *30*, 232
  threads
    in nn newsreader, 116
    overview of, 99
    in tin newsreader, 112
    in trn newsreader, 107
  vi text editor, 59, 233
  www Web browser, 190–191, *191*, 236
startup files, starting elm e-mail program from, 18
stopped processes, canceling and restarting, 11
stopping processes, 10–11

subdirectories, 125, 250
subscribing
  defined, 250
  to mailing lists, 72–74, 92–93
    gated to Usenet newsgroups, 92–93
    overview of, 72–73
    people-administered lists, 73
    robot-administered lists, 74
  to news filtering services, 93
  to newsgroups, 94–95
switches in archie searches, 153
synchronous communications
  chatting and, 53
  defined, 250
system freezes. *See* troubleshooting

T

tab damage, 99
tagging messages, in elm e-mail program, 29
talk command, 53, 233
talk Usenet hierarchy, 80, 250
.tar files, 142
telephone numbers
  800 numbers for service providers, 205–206, 212
  for InterNIC, 14
telnet, 161–166
  accessing
    archie searches via, 154–158, *156–157*, 236
    chat programs via, 53
    gopher servers via, 170, 236
    lynx Web browser via, 185
    www Web browser via, 190
  defined, 162
  Help, 164
  Hytelnet program, 164–165, *165*, 236, 244
  InterNIC information on telnet sites, 166
  logging in, 162–164, *163*, 236
  logging out, 163
  overview of, 161–162
  rlogin command, 164, 236, 249
  telnet sites to check out, 165–166
terminals, indicating type of during login, 5
testing propagation of Usenet articles, 101, 248, 251
text editors, 55–68

changing default editor for e-mail
     programs, 58, 233
composing e-mail with, 56, 233
defined, **251**
overview of, 58–59
pico, **63–65**
  editing in, 64–65
  exiting, 63
  Help, 63
  navigating in, 64
  opening files in, 64
  saving in, 63
  spell checking, 65
  starting, 63, 233
  typing in, 63
text transfers and, **137–138**
vi, **59–62**
  common mistakes, 62
  creating .plan files, 47–48, 232
  editing in, 61–62
  exiting, 60
  Help, 60
  navigating in, 61
  opening files, 60
  overview of commands, 19–20
  saving, 60
  spell checking, 62
  starting, 59, 233
  tutorial, 60
  typing in, 59–60
text files
  converting DOS files to UNIX files, 134, 235
  converting UNIX files to DOS files, 235
  creating with word processors, 137
  defined, **128**, **134**, **251**
  downloading, 134–136, 234–235
  sending text via modem, 137–138
  transferring, 57–58, *57*
  uploading, **136–137**, 234–235
text transfers across modems, **137–138**, **251**
The Well, 200, 212
threaded newsreaders, **101**, **251**
threads
  defined, **82**, **251**
  following in trn newsreader, 105–106
  and posting responses to articles, 98–99
  selecting in tin newsreader, 110
  starting
    in nn newsreader, 116
    overview of, 99

  in tin newsreader, 112
  in trn newsreader, 107
time, exact, 166
tin newsreader, **108–114**. *See also*
     newsreaders
  asterisk (*) in, 111
  autoselecting articles, 113–114, *114*
  creating killfiles, 113–114, *114*
  crossposting to multiple newsgroups, 113
  exiting, 112
  Help, 113
  hiding menu options, 111
  marking articles as unread, 111
  moving newsgroups to top of list, 109
  .newsrc files, 109
  plus sign (+) in, 110
  posting responses, 112
  reading articles, 111
  replying to articles via e-mail, 112
  saving articles, 111
  selecting articles, 110–111, *110*
  selecting newsgroups, 109–110
  selecting threads, 110
  starting, 109, *109*, 233
  starting threads, 112
transferring files. *See* downloading; ftp;
     uploading
trn newsreader, **102–108**. *See also*
     newsreaders
  autoselecting articles, 108
  canceling deletion of articles, 107
  creating killfiles, 108
  crossposting to multiple newsgroups, 107
  exiting, 107
  following threads, 105, 106
  Help, 107
  marking articles as unread, 106
  moving newsgroups to top of list, 104
  .newsrc files, 103
  posting responses, 106
  reading articles, 97, 102, 105
  replying to articles via e-mail, 106
  saving articles, 106
  selecting articles, 104–105, *104*
  selecting newsgroups, 103–104
  starting, 102–103, *103*, 233
  starting threads, 107
trolling Usenet newsgroups, **83**, **251**
troubleshooting, **9–12**. *See also* Help
  canceling processes, 10
  canceling stopped processes, 11

troubleshooting—unsubscribing

deleting commands, 11
error messages, 12
logging out by hanging up, 11
restarting stopped processes, 11
retyping commands, 11–12
stopping processes, 10–11
TurboGopher program, 176
tutorial for vi text editor, 60
Tymnet, 206, 212
typing
  in pico text editor, 63
  in vi text editor, 59–60

U

uncompress program, 142
uniform resource locators. *See* URLs
U.S. government
  documents, 166
  domains (.gov), 19, 243
university accounts, 206
university domains (.edu), 19, 241
unix2dos command, 235
UNIX
  converting DOS text files to UNIX text files, 134, 235
  converting UNIX text files to DOS text files, 235
  defined, 6, 251
UNIX commands, 231–236
  ? command, 12
  for archie searches, 236
  bye, 8
  cat, 129, 138
  cd, 126–127, 233
  for chatting in real time, 233
  chfn, 233
  chmod, 234
  for composing e-mail, 233
  cp, 131, 234
  cutting and pasting, 12
  deleting, 11
  for directing results of to files, 129, 234
  dos2unix, 134, 235
  for downloading and uploading files, 234–235
  entering, 7
  error messages, 12
  exit, 8

faq, 12
finger, 47–48, 49, 232, 242
ftp commands, 235–236
  for gopher searches, 236
h, 12
help commands, 12
irc, 53–54, 233, 244
kill, 11
  for logging in to other computers, 236
logoff, 8
lp or lpr, 130
ls, 127–128, 234
man, 12–13, *13*
  for managing files and directories, 233–234
mkdir, 127, 234
more, 138, 234
mv, 131, 234
passwd, 6
prompt, 144, 235
pwd, 126, *126*, 233
quick reference, 231–236
  for reading Usenet newsgroups, 233
redirection symbol (>) in, 129
repeating, 11–12
retyping, 11–12
rlogin, 164, 236, 249
rm, 130, 131, 234
rm core, 10
rmdir, 127, 234
setenv, 5
  for starting mail programs, 232
talk, 53, 233
  for telnetting to other computers, 236
uudecode, 66, 233, 252
uuencode, 66, 233, 252
vacation, 41–42, 232, 252
  for Web browsers, 236
whatis, 157
whois, 48–49, 232
wildcards in, 128, 130
UNIX directories. *See* directories
UNIX environments, connecting via, 2–3
UNIX files. *See* files
UNIX prompt, 6–7
UNIX shell accounts
  defined, 249
  e-mail and, 16
unsubscribing
  defined, 251
  to mailing lists, 40, 74–75
    people-administered lists, 74

robot-administered lists, 74
    when going on vacation, 40, 75
  to newsgroups, 94–95
unthreaded newsreaders, 101
uploading
  defined, 251
  files, 136–137, 234–235
  messages with elm e-mail program, 19
urban legends, 200, 251, 251
URLs (uniform resource locators). *See also* WorldWide Web
  defined, 251
  going directly to, 188, 192, 236
  overview of, 184, 186
  starting browsers from, 184, 185
  URLs to check out, 199–200
  viewing, 184, 189, 192
Usenet, defined, 79, 252
Usenet newsgroups, 77–90. *See also* newsreaders
  accessing via e-mail and mailing lists, 92–93
  acronyms, 86–87
  alt.fan.warlord newsgroup, 99
  anonymity on, 67–68, 84
  articles
    canceling, 82, 240
    defined, 82
    replying to, 83
  changing your "real name," 233
  comp.answers, 11
  comp.unix questions, 11
  comp.unix.shell, 11
  defined, 80, 247
  for elm e-mail program, 17
  etiquette, 79, 83–87
  FAQs, 85
  finding, 82
  flamewars, 82, 83–84
  gossip, 78
  guidelines for participating, 79, 83–87
  Help, 90
  hierarchies, 79–81, 243
  identifying yourself on Usenet, 99
  lurking on, 85, 245
  versus mailing lists, 70, 78
  moderated newsgroups, 88, 246
  names of, 81–82
  "ob" (obligatory) comments, 98, 247
  overview of, 77–79
  posting to via e-mail, 93

quality of, 88–89
reading. *See also* newsreaders
  via filtering services, 93
  via mailing lists, 78, 92–93
  via online services, 120
  on WorldWide Web, 102
selecting
  in nn newsreader, 115
  overview of, 96
  in tin newsreader, 109–110
  in trn newsreader, 103–104
signal-to-noise ratios, 88, 249
Star Trek newsgroups, 88
for testing propagation of articles, 101, 248, 251
threads, 82
trolling, 83, 251
types of, 88
uudecode command, 66, 233, 252
uuencoded files, 65–67, 233, 252

V

vacation command, 41–42, 232, 252
veronica, 169, 178–180. *See also* gopher servers
  accessing, 178, *179*
  asterisk (*) in searches, 179
  bookmarks for, 178
  defined, 252
  entering search text, 179
  limiting the number of matches, 180
  selecting search types, 178–179
  viewing search results, 180
vertical bar symbol. *See* pipe symbol (|)
vi text editor, 59–62. *See also* text editors
  common mistakes, 62
  creating .plan files, 47–48, 232
  editing in, 61–62
  exiting, 60
  Help, 60
  navigating in, 61
  opening files, 60
  overview of commands, 19–20
  saving, 60
  spell checking, 62
  starting, 59, 233
  text transfers and, 137–138
  tutorial, 60
  typing in, 59–60

viewing
    contents of files, 129, *130*, 234
    HTML text, 189
    Internet addresses in gopherspace, 174
    URLs, 184, 189, 192
    veronica search results, 180

W

weather reports, 166
The Well, 200, 212
whatis command, 157
What's New Page, WorldWide Web, 196
whois command, 48–49, 232
Whole Internet Catalog's Top 50, 200
wildcards, in UNIX commands, **128**, 130
windowed mail programs, 16, **36–37**
    Eudora program, **37**, *38*, 242
    offline mail readers, 37, 205, 247
windowed newsreaders, 101, **119–121**, *121*
Wired Magazine, 200
word processors. *See also* text editors
    composing e-mail with, **56–58**, *57*
working directory. *See also* directories
    changing to, 126
    defined, **125**, 252
    displaying, 126, *126*
WorldWide Web, **181–200**
    accessing
        ftp via, 197
        gopher servers via, 196–197
        telnet via, 197–198
        Usenet newsgroups via, 102, 198
    addresses. *See* URLs (uniform resource locators)
    contents of, 183
    defined, **252**
    downloading files, 135
    FAQs, 195
    finding
        EFF's Guide to the Internet, 14, 173, 196
        PGP program, 68
    versus gopher servers, **183**
    Help and information, **195–196**
    home pages
        changing default in lynx, 190
        defined, **244**
        overview of, 184
        returning to in lynx, 189
        starting browsers at, 185, 190
    HTML (HyperText Markup Language), **186**, 189, 198, **244**
    HTTP (HyperText Transport Protocol), 186
    hypertext and, **182**
    NCSA What's New Page, 196
    overview of, 181–183
    subscribing to news filtering services from, 93
    URLs (uniform resource locators)
        defined, **251**
        going directly to, 188, 192, 236
        overview of, 184, 186
        starting browsers from, 184–185
        URLs to check out, **199–200**
        viewing, 184, 189, 192
WorldWide Web browsers
    defined, **240**, **252**
    general procedures, 184
    lynx, **184–190**
        changing default home page, 190
        copying documents, 189
        customizing, 190
        exiting, 190
        following links, 187, *187*
        going directly to URLs, 188, 236
        leaving bookmarks, 189
        navigating in, 186–188, *188*
        reading documents, 185–187
        returning to home page, 189
        sending e-mail to page owners, 189
        starting, 185, *185*, 236
        telnetting to, 185
        viewing URLs and HTML text, 189
    Mosaic, 184, **192–193**, *193–194*
    NetCruiser for Windows, **194**, *195*
    types of, 183–184
    www, **190–192**
        copying documents, 192
        exiting, 192
        following links, 191
        going directly to URLs, 192, 236
        reading documents, 191
        starting, 190–191, *191*, 236
        telnetting to, 190
        viewing URLs, 192

X

xmodem protocol, 134, 136, 234

Y

ymodem protocol, 134–136, 234–235

Z

.Z files, 142
.zip files, 142, 253
zmodem protocol, 134–136, 235

[1619] A Guided Tour of the Internet

GET A FREE CATALOG JUST FOR EXPRESSING YOUR OPINION.

Help us improve our books and get a ***FREE*** full-color catalog in the bargain. Please complete this form, pull out this page and send it in today. The address is on the reverse side.

Name _____ Company _____

Address _____ City _____ State ____ Zip _____

Phone (____) _____

1. **How would you rate the overall quality of this book?**
   - ❏ Excellent
   - ❏ Very Good
   - ❏ Good
   - ❏ Fair
   - ❏ Below Average
   - ❏ Poor

2. **What were the things you liked most about the book? (Check all that apply)**
   - ❏ Pace
   - ❏ Format
   - ❏ Writing Style
   - ❏ Examples
   - ❏ Table of Contents
   - ❏ Index
   - ❏ Price
   - ❏ Illustrations
   - ❏ Type Style
   - ❏ Cover
   - ❏ Depth of Coverage
   - ❏ Fast Track Notes

3. **What were the things you liked *least* about the book? (Check all that apply)**
   - ❏ Pace
   - ❏ Format
   - ❏ Writing Style
   - ❏ Examples
   - ❏ Table of Contents
   - ❏ Index
   - ❏ Price
   - ❏ Illustrations
   - ❏ Type Style
   - ❏ Cover
   - ❏ Depth of Coverage
   - ❏ Fast Track Notes

4. **Where did you buy this book?**
   - ❏ Bookstore chain
   - ❏ Small independent bookstore
   - ❏ Computer store
   - ❏ Wholesale club
   - ❏ College bookstore
   - ❏ Technical bookstore
   - ❏ Other _____

5. **How did you decide to buy this particular book?**
   - ❏ Recommended by friend
   - ❏ Recommended by store personnel
   - ❏ Author's reputation
   - ❏ Sybex's reputation
   - ❏ Read book review in _____
   - ❏ Other _____

6. **How did you pay for this book?**
   - ❏ Used own funds
   - ❏ Reimbursed by company
   - ❏ Received book as a gift

7. **What is your level of experience with the subject covered in this book?**
   - ❏ Beginner
   - ❏ Intermediate
   - ❏ Advanced

8. **How long have you been using a computer?**
   _____ years
   _____ months

9. **Where do you most often use your computer?**
   - ❏ Home
   - ❏ Work
   - ❏ Both
   - ❏ Other _____

10. **What kind of computer equipment do you have? (Check all that apply)**
    - ❏ PC Compatible Desktop Computer
    - ❏ PC Compatible Laptop Computer
    - ❏ Apple/Mac Computer
    - ❏ Apple/Mac Laptop Computer
    - ❏ CD ROM
    - ❏ Fax Modem
    - ❏ Data Modem
    - ❏ Scanner
    - ❏ Sound Card
    - ❏ Other _____

11. **What other kinds of software packages do you ordinarily use?**
    - ❏ Accounting
    - ❏ Databases
    - ❏ Networks
    - ❏ Apple/Mac
    - ❏ Desktop Publishing
    - ❏ Spreadsheets
    - ❏ CAD
    - ❏ Games
    - ❏ Word Processing
    - ❏ Communications
    - ❏ Money Management
    - ❏ Other _____

12. **What operating systems do you ordinarily use?**
    - ❏ DOS
    - ❏ OS/2
    - ❏ Windows
    - ❏ Apple/Mac
    - ❏ Windows NT
    - ❏ Other _____

13. On what computer-related subject(s) would you like to see more books?

_____
_____
_____
_____

14. Do you have any other comments about this book? (Please feel free to use a separate piece of paper if you need more room)

_____
_____
_____
_____

- - - - - - - - - - - - - PLEASE FOLD, SEAL, AND MAIL TO SYBEX - - - - - - - - - - - - -

SYBEX INC.
Department M
2021 Challenger Drive
Alameda, CA
94501

How to Send E-Mail to People on Other Online Services

Network	Username	Internet Address
America Online	Mang	mang@aol.com
Delphi	Mang	mang@delphi.com
CompuServe	75555,5555	75555.5555@compuserve.com
GEnie	Mang	mang@genie.com
MCI Mail	555-7777	555-7777@mcimail.com
Prodigy	Mang	mang@prodigy.com
AT&T Mail	Mang	mang@attmail.com
Fidonet BBSs	1:2/3	f3.n2.z1@fidonet.org

As you can see, the only real tricky ones are CompuServe, for which you have to change the comma in the CompuServe address to a dot in the Internet address; and Fidonet, for which you have to reverse the order of the three numbers and then put them after f, n, and z. (If you are given only two numbers, in the form a/b, then assume that they are the n and f numbers and that the z number is 1.)

Also, if you're not sure of an MCI Mail patron's number, you can send mail to *lastname*@mcimail.com, and you'll receive back a list of MCI Mail users with that last name and their correct e-mail addresses.

How to Get Connected

Here's an outline of the steps you need to take to get Internet access. Appendix A explains more of this in detail.

1 Consider the type of connection you want. There are direct connections and modem connections.

A direct connection is a computer attached to a network that itself is connected to the Internet. Many university accounts work this way, as do some work-related Internet connections. There are also direct connections to Internet gateways that allow the sending and receiving of Internet e-mail but not much more.